The Postcolonial African State in Transition

KILOMBO: INTERNATIONAL RELATIONS AND COLONIAL QUESTIONS

This is the first series to mark out a dedicated space for advanced critical inquiry into colonial questions across International Relations. The ethos of this book series is reflected by the bricolage constituency of Kilombos – settlements of African slaves, rebels and indigenous peoples in South America who became self-determining political communities that retrieved and renovated the social practices of its diverse constituencies while being confronted by colonial forces. The series embraces a multitude of methods and approaches, theoretical and empirical scholarship, alongside historical and contemporary concerns. Publishing innovative and top-quality peer-reviewed scholarship, Kilombo enquires into the shifting principles of colonial rule that inform global governance and investigates the contestation of these principles by diverse peoples across the globe. It critically re-interprets popular concepts, narratives and approaches in the field of IR by reference to the "colonial question" and, in doing so, the book series opens up new vistas from which to address the key political questions of our time

Series Editors: Mustapha K. Pasha, Aberystwyth University
Meera Sabaratnam, SOAS University of London
Robbie Shilliam, Queen Mary University of London

Titles in the Series
Meanings of Bandung: Postcolonial Orders and Decolonial Visions, edited by Quỳnh N. Phạm and Robbie Shilliam
Politics of the African Anticolonial Archive, edited by Shiera S. el-Malik and Isaac A. Kamola
Asylum after Empire: Colonial Legacies in the Politics of Asylum Seeking, Lucy Mayblin
Decolonizing Intervention: International Statebuilding in Mozambique, Meera Sabaratnam
Global Development and Colonial Power: German Development Policy at Home and Abroad, Daniel Bendix
The Postcolonial African State in Transition: Stateness and Modes of Sovereignty, Amy Niang

The Postcolonial African State in Transition

Stateness and Modes of Sovereignty

Amy Niang

ROWMAN & LITTLEFIELD INTERNATIONAL

New York • London

Published by Rowman & Littlefield International Ltd
6 Tinworth Street, London SE11 5AL, United Kingdom
www.rowmaninternational.com

Rowman & Littlefield International Ltd.is an affiliate of Rowman & Littlefield
4501 Forbes Boulevard, Suite 200, Lanham, Maryland 20706, USA
With additional offices in Boulder, New York, Toronto (Canada), and Plymouth (UK)
www.rowman.com

British Library Cataloguing in Publication Data

A catalogue record for this book is available from the British Library
ISBN: HB 978-1-7866-0652-5
         PB 978-1-7866-0653-2

Library of Congress Cataloging-in-Publication Data Is Available

ISBN 978-1-78660-652-5 (cloth: alk. paper)
ISBN 978-1-78660-653-2 (pbk: alk. paper)
ISBN 978-1-78660-654-9 (electronic)

♾™ The paper used in this publication meets the minimum requirements of American
National Standard for Information Sciences—Permanence of Paper for Printed Library
Materials, ANSI/NISO Z39.48-1992.

Printed in the United States of America

To Harald Kleinschmidt

Contents

Acknowledgements

I would like to express my sincere thanks to Robbie Shilliam and Meera Sabaratnam, who have been incredibly supportive editors on top of being inspiring scholars and colleagues. Their comments and those of the different reviewers have helped improve the manuscript. I'm most grateful for the assistance provided by Dhara Snowden, Rebecca Anastasi, Lisa Whittington and the Rowman & Littlefield team.

Meera Venkatachalam generously read and critiqued a full draft of the manuscript. She has been and remains a wonderful interlocutor on all things West African. The late Michel Izard was very kind to share some of his archival materials with me and to engage in extensive discussions about Voltaic societies. This book builds upon my PhD project and it greatly benefited from the supervision and guidance of Paul Nugent, Sara Dorman and Andrew Lawrence. I'm grateful to Siba Grovogui for his generous insights on the project. Jean Comaroff also provided feedback on the general orientation of the book.

A valuable encounter, many years ago, with the work of Joseph Ki-Zerbo inspired my curiosity for precolonial African history and forms of political rationality that informed governance traditions among the Bamana, the Mossi, the Bobo, the Wolof and many other societies.

My overall intellectual debt goes to Harald Kleinschmidt. Beyond a sustained and patient attention for my very early attempts at understanding the precolonial African state, he always provided detailed and considerate comments on my work, and he encouraged me to be persistent in seeing this project through.

I would like to thank my colleagues in the Department of International Relations at the University of the Witwatersrand. The steady support of friends Robtel Neajai Pailey, Holly Davis, Wendy Willems, Christian

Schonaers, Janis Rosheuvel, Toni Haastrup, Yacine Gaye, Safiatou Ndiaye Diop, Colette Gordon, Mopeli Moshoeshoe and also family, especially my parents, my sister Rokhaya, and the Ndiaye team, Mustafa, Momar and Abbi, has been particularly motivating.

Professor Ousmane Sene of the West African Research Center and his dedicated staff provided a welcoming home during my African Humanity Program (AHP) residency in Dakar during which parts of the manuscript were completed. The project benefited from generous funding from the American Council for the Learned Society through the AHP. Funding for previous fieldwork came from the West African Research Association. Many thanks also to Salah Hassan who facilitated a research fellowship at Cornell University, which enabled access to the resources of the Africana library.

The *Journal of Ritual Studies* gave permission for the reproduction of the article "Rituals as Political Reference" which corresponds to Chapter 5 of the book. Where it was not explicitly indicated, references for some of the historical accounts are mostly derived from conversations with Mossi and other interlocutors in Ouagadougou and Ouahigouya. I'm grateful for the hospitality and support of Zakaria Sorgho, Ibrahima (Ila) Ouedraogo and Mohamed Ouedraogo, Vieux Karim and Ousmane in Ouagadougou and Ouahigouya. My colleagues Maurice Bazemo and Ali Ouedraogo were of tremendous help during my different stays in Ouagadougou. Many other people, too many to list here, have guided my questions and provided many insights, patiently and with great generosity. Shortcomings are solely mine.

Chapter 1

Political History as State Ideology

INTRODUCTION

The present book contends that the state in African contexts—whether precolonial, colonial or postcolonial—was always a transient phenomenon that pushed against internal 'others'. From this perspective, postcolonial state failure is the result of the disarticulation of the mechanisms that gave constitutional and normative meaning to cultural values and practices and to political legitimation processes of both state and non-state fields of action. The book thus returns to a neglected question that, to this project, is crucial to understanding the difficulties of the postcolonial African state, namely: *What was the state internally built against,* or What social forms did the advent of the centralized state displace? Answers to this question can shed light on various dimensions of the current African state, including but not limited to the absence of sovereignty, the lack of legitimacy, the withdrawal of the citizenry from constitutional life, the collapse of state institutions and the difficult integration of 'traditional' and diverse modes of meaning-making in the modern state. In addressing the above question, this book also offers a perspective on a set of fundamental, related sub-questions about the state with salient contemporary resonance; for instance What is the nature of the state? How did it come about? Why does it continue to endure as the *most persistent form* of sociopolitical organization (Spruyt 1994)? These questions seem pertinent today in the context of the precariousness and failures of the postcolonial African state. In fact, if much has been said about the conditions of the African state, many more questions remain to be examined.

The aim of the book is twofold. First, it seeks to revisit a notion of state in which stateness and statehood appear to disregard the historicity of the centralized state that emerged in Europe after the 1648 treaties of Westphalia

1

and extended to the rest of the world through conquest and colonization. The lack of attention to the temporal and spatial specificities of the events leading up to, and the institutions emerging from, Westphalia also obscures the nature of state practices and their ideological predicates and justifications. I refer here specifically to the processes of institutional development that favour the sovereign hegemony of the state and the attending rights and privileges to define order, security and the parameters of the good life.

The second aim of this book, while also to historicize the African state, is to reexamine African concepts of authority, power, legitimacy, moral order and subjectivity in light of the difficulties of state and governance of the postcolonial state. Ultimately, this book seeks to bring into focus the internal material and symbolic dimensions and dynamics of the postcolonial African state as an avenue for understanding its struggle with sovereign control and legitimacy. My concern is therefore to problematize a notion of political authority and power on one hand and a notion of social order and cohabitation on the other and away from a strictly statist understanding. This entails juxtaposing relations between formal institutions and larger signifying practices within diverse societies with multiple cultural expressions that endow the desires and aspirations of historical agents with particular textures.

The purpose of this reexamination is to place the structural and functional flaws of the postcolonial state in the context of domestic institutional developments linked to state formation in Africa before, during and after colonialism. The various insights provided in the disciplines of comparative politics and international relations (IR) on postcolonial African politics will remain part of my investigation. However, this project is motivated by questions of when and why state-related processes made sense or didn't and to whom. This question, it seems, is an important one that begs for answers.

A leitmotif of this book is therefore a productive doubt about an established obsession, in political theory, with the Westphalian common sense of stateness and the relative disregard not only of other species of state but also of *what statehood means to the entities that must give it its legitimacy*. In the liberal narrative, there is a strong but unsupported presumption that the centralized state is better suited to provide order, justice and security. It has to be understood that the liberal state is an ideal and nothing more, therefore even the things it is meant to achieve, namely order, rule of law and the good life, are not necessarily obtained in Europe, its original formulator. There is also the equally unsupported presumption that the historical state has unlimited persuasive and disciplinary capacities to impose its rationality and logic on populations captured in the myth of sovereign democracy. In this light, the centralized state would be the most accomplished and necessary stage of institutional transformation.

This account is in contrast to the present project where the human capacity to imagine creative arrangements and the historical experiences of such arrangements in West Africa are proposed. This book shows that most if not all historical processes of centralization in Africa were to various degrees *attempts at centralization*, and as such they were incomplete, always in the making and therefore subject to reform. It would take the colonial system to realize centralization while dismantling the very basis of precolonial systems of authority.

I here propose an analysis of the state in a different ecological context than exists in Westphalian common sense, one marked by distinct moral dispositions, different belief systems, different regimes of social interaction and different material interests. These could eventuate in variations in political forms and strategic alliances under specific circumstances. In fact, environmental and ecological perspectives give great insight into the logic of settlement and social formation. There is nothing absolutely original in saying that institutions were always devised and adapted to specific environmental circumstances. Certainly in the Voltaic region, the centralized state form was not the most 'natural' response to physical and environmental constraints. A view of the state as institutional perfection fundamentally disregards the fact that it was often imposed through colonial rule rather than internally generated. Capitalism in turn created and reinforced the conditions for a kleptocratic rule that served private interests. However, while we continue to use the same language of prebendism, patrimonialism and 'corruption' to describe the nature of African politics, in reality the parameters of power drastically shift as we look closely at specific periods—so much so that our concepts are not necessarily capturing these adequately.

In reality, stateness in and of itself was never an intrinsic quality. Michael Mann has elaborated on this fact by convincingly demonstrating its cyclical, reversible and malleable nature (1993, 63–70). In contrast, statelessness is not just an alternative form to the state. It can be the result of many things. In one instance, it can be a manifestation of marginality produced by states as much as *what states were built against*. In another, it can be a different species of social organization that generates forms of authority, order and legitimacy that differ from the centralized state that emerged in Europe and was transported to Africa and the rest of the world through colonization and the spread of 'norms'. As I show later in the selected West African case, the state has always competed with other social forms. But in stark contrast to Hendrik Spruyt's thesis (1994), the competitors of the state in this case are not necessarily proto- or micro-states as was the case with the city states of Europe. The competing political entities are of different kinds. Indeed, in loosely stratified societies, the parameters of social interactions favour centralization-inhibiting traits in favour of social forms that require careful examination.

This book seeks to problematize the notion of state power in two directions. First, as intimated above, in a critique of the very historicity of stateness by showing that historically the state was never *the norm* in so far as political authority was concerned. Second, by arguing that it constitutes a departure from disciplinary common sense in IR that locates the rise of the sovereign state to prominence in costly struggles that confronted competing claims on particular territories. Yet the institutions and apparatuses of the European state were forged even as Europe was building empires through the acquisition of colonies.

The concurrency in state building and empire building in the context of rising capitalism has led to many lines of enquiry into the African state, some of which might be relevant to the current African condition, some of them less so. At any rate, the two processes of imperial expansion and state formation in Europe cannot be disassociated. If they required different strategies, they both mobilized similar scientific and military technologies in a political economy of violence that shaped the European nation-state while subjecting non-European societies to extensive forms of violence, exploitation and dehumanizing practices. An extrapolation of the account of the European state outside Europe therefore tends to be fraught with constitutive errors.

The triumph of the sovereign state over other forms of social organization serves to vindicate its primacy over other institutional forms.[1] The argument, however, that the sovereign state was an external construct that gained currency in Africa as an imposed model obscures internal institutional arrangements, particularly before contact with Europe. The singular focus on the current dysfunctional system in fact prevents explorations of past state processes as intellectual resources for thinking about the current crisis of the African state and ways in which to envisage possible solutions. These include the internal logic and structural constraints—in addition to the disabling effect of neoliberal empires—against which the state had to be developed.

STATE(NESS) AS HISTORICITY: A MISREADING

As a reflection of civilizational and imperial discourses, the myth of Westphalia (in theory) and European-initiated international orders (in practice) have consolidated the idea of the state and sovereign morality as centralized, unitary and necessary. The related narratives reduce history to an ingratiating account that casts a presumed superior identity (the Western state) over inferior domestic ones (for instance, Spruyt's Hanzas) or those of supposed barbarians and 'uncouth singletons' in Africa, the New World and elsewhere. As I show later, this latter tendency of depreciating the organizational capacity and legitimacy of alternative social and moral forms is not limited to Europe. The Mossi certainly painted indigenous Gurunsi in such a light; their emphasis on statehood and decorum was part of broader processes of othering, alienation and marginalization. Regardless of their lack of empirical validity, the related narratives rob alternative social forms, even those competing with the state for sovereign authority and legitimacy of agency; that is, the capacity to imagine forms of social living that befit specific circumstances.

In what follows, I intend to stress the limits of the Westphalia model in order to provide a direction to alternative understandings of the crisis of the postcolonial state. Taking my cue from the works of Charles Tilly, Hendrik Spruyt and Jens Bartelson on state formation in Europe as a comparative backdrop for my analysis, I wish to add a new inflection to the manners in which the historical European state may have shaped the forms, structures and modes of authority of the postcolonial state at a constitutional level. These texts are also important in highlighting the historicity of the European state and, therefore, the limits of any analysis seeking to examine other state forms as mere replicas.

In *Coercion, Capital and European States* (1990) and other writings, Charles Tilly offers a peculiar view of the state that differs from that frequently offered in Westphalian common sense. One of his key concepts is that of the European state as a predatory machine. This is to say, one central condition of the emergence of the centralized state was its inclination and ability to dispense with pre-existing rivals, social forms and modes of authority. He also describes the success of the nation-state as partly a result of the organic relationship between domestic and international politics that acted as both an opportunity and a constraint in the drive for capitalist and resources accumulation to support the state's military, material and war-making capacities. This perspective matters for understanding the nature of the postcolonial state in that the latter emerges not only as a result of the eradication of prior forms and norms of governance by the colonizing state but also as a result of the replacement of domestic structures with alien European ones. It is significant to my analysis that Europe's imperial powers simultaneously destroyed both anterior African structures and the ability of some of the surviving populations to engage in political experimentation in areas where this was permitted by the colonial authorities.

Spruyt also offers a compelling view of the advent of the historical centralized European state. He examines the institutional legacy of the feudal system in European state formation. Whereas the status claims of the centralized state form are taken for granted in most accounts, Spruyt shows that there was nothing deterministic, necessary or inevitable about the nation-state as we know it (1994). In fact, the fall of city-states, sovereign monarchies, urban leagues and independent communes—as various political forms that co-existed alongside the nation-state—was not always due to military defeat but rather to the capacity of the sovereign state to articulate strategically organizational hierarchies and systems of standardization, all of which made it more attractive than other forms. In Spruyt's analysis, the internal/external dynamic also becomes the framework that produces the conditions for the consolidation of sovereign states.

On the other hand, Bartelson, in *A Genealogy of Sovereignty* (1995) and *The Critique of the State* (2001), explores with great insight the roots of the success of the sovereignty claims of the state in the West. His critique of the apparent boundlessness of state sovereignty informs a view of the analytical difficulty of thinking beyond the state for the latter constitutes, even in the most critical discussions of the state model, the *condition* as well as the *object* of analysis.

If Spruyt validly critiques Westphalian common sense by providing texture and complexity to the tumultuous historical context that produced sovereign states, he does so within the very logic of Westphalia. However, he convincingly describes how the state emerged out of a diverse pool of possible models that included the German Hanseatic League, Italian city-states, and other crisscrossing jurisdictions by capitalizing on a greater efficiency with regard to trade and security. In the case of Africa, it bears noting that states and state-like organizations had competitors, and the competition between any state and its competitors greatly shaped its institutions and modes of operations. Hence, for instance, the Sokoto Caliphate, the Bamana city-states of Segu, the Theocracy of Masina, and the more pervasive stateless structures can be seen as alternative historical formations to their local competitors as well as the colonial state. As these came to disintegrate in the nineteenth century, the colonial state proved more efficient but more in the sense that Tilly would understand it than Spruyt would. From a Tillian viewpoint, the colonial centralized state had the technology and the means of a voraciousness that allowed it to prevail over pre-existing ones.

In what follows, I too have retained the use of 'states', states system and 'sovereignty' to describe indigenous West African political structures—ones that existed prior to colonial rule and continue to manifest themselves today—for lack of better terms. The purpose of this approach is to talk more productively about the social structures that sustained African political life before the colonial state and whose symbols and rituals continue to hold sway in the public imaginary of constitutional life.

The present study thus contrasts and complements historical and anthropological studies on African social and political structures and institutions. For instance, in the Africanist literature, anthropologists who have worked on the

Kusasi, Gurunsi, Lobi, Konkomba and other Voltaic groups are not immune to reflexes similar to those of political scientists; they utilize the term 'non-state' very broadly to describe acephalous groups. However, the same studies often provide enough material and insights to envisage social formation and political authority in non-centralized societies—in fact, to envisage these spaces in their own internal dynamics and on their own terms, and in the manner they might have therefore constituted alternative modes of governance vis-à-vis states and how they might have contained, interconnected with, instrumentalized or rejected them.[2]

These studies can be complemented by James Scott's thesis on the extent and effects of attempts at enclosure by the centralized state (2009). Historically, these attempts entailed not so much an effort to shift people from non-state zones to areas of state control but rather were an internal colonization of the periphery itself so that the latter could be transformed into a fully governed, fiscally useful zone (10). In the West African region, a similar movement of enclosure congealed at the intersection of late-colonial expansion and intensified trading activities between colonial stations and prominent centralized states (Ashanti, Waalo, etc.). In fact, in the late nineteenth and early twentieth centuries, a massive exodus of formerly indentured communities spurred great institutional transformations in the Middle Niger Valley (Roberts and Klein 1989).

While many so-called acephalous, stateless Voltaic groups exhibited a strong aversion to centralized rule, they constituted incredibly complex communities that endured. Some of these constituted into new 'ethnic' groups; some attempted to reproduce the political structure of centralized politics without their rigid hierarchy. The state/non-state dynamic becomes an important explanatory framework where the state's capacity to deploy its hegemony is politically contested or culturally arrested. The explanatory power of this dynamic is limited, however, in explaining the formation of 'hybrid' forms such as the Dagara who could engage at once in resistance against or in alliance with neighbouring states under different historical circumstances. The absence of a supreme ruler in acephalous societies was not an indication of anarchy; it often reflected an understanding of *the political* as a category of action that is intimately woven into other categories of social action such that its practice requires the mobilization of multiple linguistic, ritualistic and intellectual resources for its legitimation (Fortes 1940).

My central argument is therefore that political life occurred outside the state but not between the extreme poles of centralization and anarchy. But this can only be made obvious when we shift the focus of analysis to political authority rather than state practice *tout court*. I further argue that neither state/ stateness nor non-state/statelessness are historically unchanging concepts, nor might they be considered environmentally produced oppositional norms, particularly in historical contexts that bear a strong imprint of trading routes and networks as well as economic flows that operated locally, regionally and globally.

In fact, one of the main problems in the study of the state is that the concept has been taken to be absolute and immobile. Political confederations, clan alliances, loosely stratified formations and the variety of social organizations that dotted the Voltaic region did not evolve in complete isolation from broader regional and global trends. Like the states that surrounded them or sought to engulf them, these communities were very much caught up in the historical forces of globalization. There were for instance groups that operated across and outside states and that attached themselves to kings and political entrepreneurs for opportunistic purposes. Zamarina mercenaries were such a group that was active across the whole region; they did not have a care for the state and its ideological and political boundaries; they lent their services to kings and princes across the whole region, trading and raiding as the need arose.

Gradations of stateness indicated the existence of social experiments that were not necessarily propelled by a statist logic but which resulted from an impetus for many groups to redefine a position strategically in relation to emerging regional states, either in alliance, in opposition, in resistance or in indifference to them. The Mossi states system emerged in the sixteenth century in a context of regional effervescence that gave non-centralized societies a geopolitical frame within which to position themselves vis-à-vis centralized groups. The decline of the greatest empire around the Niger Bend, the Songhai Empire, inaugurated critical transformations made further complex by intensified commercial relations with Europeans, particularly Portuguese entrepreneurs. At the same time, the Fulbe expansion reorganized trading structures and networks in West Africa in a way that created opportunities for groups outside centralized zones to capitalize on economic relations with states and state actors. Rethinking statelessness under such circumstances therefore allows us to understand social change in non-Western modernities while enabling a critical rethinking of a global history where these trends can take centre stage.

There were many stateless groups on the fringes of the expanding Mamprugu-Dagbon-Mossi states system, at the borders of present-day Ghana, Burkina Faso, Niger and Mali. Some of them bore the brunt of slave raiding, particularly between the seventeenth and nineteenth centuries, and were later subjected to corvée labour and conscription under colonial rule. There is for instance a long tradition of migration of Burkinabe men to southern Ghana who set up numerous *zongo* villages (Schildkrout 1978).[3] Like other subjects of the French Empire, they sought to dodge head taxation, corvée, and conscription if they were not trying to find alternative means to meet tax payments for families back home. This history of escape from the state has partly been obscured by common abolitionist views, derived from European Enlightenment, that contend that Africans were incapable of generating an autonomous antislavery discourse and practice despite many instances of slaves and slave communities that strove to initiate new types of relationship and demarginalizing structures outside the restrictive master/slave model (for a useful discussion of this see Ismail Rashid [2000, 659]).

The Voltaic region presents an interesting context for populations opposed to incorporation into rigidly structured states. Examples abound of dissident groups that retreated from the stifling grip of Dagbon, Ouagadougou, Yatenga and similarly centralized states. In this part of West Africa, the so-called first settler societies had no hills, no deserts, no marshes, no forests, no mangroves in which to hide. Dissident populations therefore had to turn their aversion to centralized states into cultural, ritualized and coded forms of resistance. Outside political cores, many groups elevated the ritual and cultural aspects of public morality above a crude form of power politics. Within centralized polities, non-dynastic groups retained social agency, cultural knowledge and the constitutional right to legitimize, endorse or invalidate the action of officeholders. Among the Dagara and the Gurunsi, contingent alliances with neighbouring states and clans became the basis for rapidly shifting formations that interspersed long periods of withdrawal.

If there is a common difficulty in thinking outside the state form, there is an even greater difficulty in deploying appropriate tools to think theoretically about unfamiliar forms such as these. A view of institutional multiplicity or diversity from a synchronic, rather than diachronic, approach avoids the tendency to take too evolutionist a perspective on institutional development while integrating change and transformation as integral to the life of social institutions. In fact, even orthodox evolutionist scholars do not always see evolution in an incremental manner but more as a process of change informed by need rather than some innate disposition.

Now, how to move away from thinking that is steeped in the state framework and to move toward an understanding of politics in terms of multiple sources of power and multiple sources of authority. There is always the issue of size, scale, sophistication and accumulative know-how, and we could not entirely dismiss their importance as we map out political nodes. Examples of diverse social formations across the Mamprugu-Dagbon-Nanun-Mossi regions thus serve as useful illustrations in tackling the question of what institutional arrangements and organizations paved the way for the emergence of the state and its subsequent consolidation and how these came to be subsumed and even disappear in its wake.

STATE FAILURE AND OTHER DEBILITIES: A REVIEW

Analyses of the African state are inseparable from the production, in the humanities and the social sciences, of an idea of Africa (Mudimbe 1985, 1988, 1994). The predominant representation of the African state that is produced is one that is incompetent, illegitimate and predatory (Mbembe 2001, 9; Ferguson, 2006). From this broad representation arise a number of questions which have broadly framed three clusters of work that focus respectively on the capacities and the performance of the state, the extent of its representativeness and the degree of its legitimacy within African societies. These questions often engage the African state as a problem to be solved. I associate the questions above respectively with (1) political science literature on the African state, (2) neocolonial theories and (3) the interventionist literature.

Failed-State Literature

Theorists of state failure have made Africa a most fertile terrain of analysis. They generally operate on the basis of a set of assumptions, hypotheses and 'logical' expectations such that they can only see aberration and abnormality where one could otherwise see productive differences. Their questions are often framed in a normative, comparative outlook. The leading figures of this body of literature are mainly Joel Migdal (1988), Robert Jackson (1992; 2000), William Zartman (1995) Christopher Clapham (1998), Pierre Englebert (1997), Robert Rotberg (2004) and a few others.

The first aspect of their normative assessment is the use of the Westphalian order as the *fons et origo*, the ideological reservoir of sovereign morality. The second assumption is that the African state's systemic deviance is due to a lack of the kind of wherewithal associated with 'viable' states. The issue of capability—to deliver welfare, security, law and order and other political goods—becomes a mantra variously adapted from Migdal's thesis that a taxonomy of states could be established on the basis of their capacity 'to *penetrate* society, *regulate* social relationships, *extract* resources, and *appropriate* or use resources in determined ways.' Simply put then, 'strong states are those with high capabilities to complete these tasks, while weak states are on the low end of a spectrum of capabilities' (Migdal 1988, 4; Hill 2005; Rotberg 2004, 2).

If this thesis sounds quite convincing in its simplicity, it is also profoundly flawed. I want to point out two main problems. The first one is epistemological and it relates principally to the historicity and instrumentality of the European nation-state. It intimates that African states could never redeem themselves given an original defect: they were not like the European sovereign state, they could ever only aspire to become inadequate, flawed versions of it. There was an original dilemma for would-be independent states would either have to be fast-tracked into European state models in complete disregard for their historicity and instrumentality or ushered under duress at the risk of imposing alien and alienating bureaucratic machines (the latter tendency by and large characterizes postcolonial state formation processes in Africa). Yet the promises of liberal modernity (i.e., law and order and the good life) have never been entirely fulfilled, even in Europe, its birthplace.

The second problem resides in the very uses and goals of the failed-state literature; the chief aims of the failed- or collapsed-state literature are 'to investigate and explain why state failure occurs; to develop and outline ways of identifying failed states; to identify states that are failed or are in danger of failing; to describe processes of failure; and to consider how state failure can be either prevented or reversed' (Hill 2005, 145). The thrust of this literature is therefore an ideological endeavour—to issue certificates of good health and prescribe treatment plans. At the least, it strips African societies of any actual internal dynamics other than the ability to disintegrate. It is historically decontextualized, it is caricatural about African political culture and it is devoid of sensible engagement with African juridical traditions, cultures and imaginaries.

(Neo)patrimonialist Literature

An idea of Africa is also produced in variations of the patrimonialism/neopatrimonialism theories, often amalgamated in the predatory state theory. Analysts of the neopatrimonialist strand are concerned with the exercise of power and the instrumentalities of state institutions in postcolonial Africa. The patrimonialist perspective in reality is a version of the state-failure thesis that extrapolates the latter to explain just about every imaginable aspect of African social life. It inflates institutional instability into a pathology and a permanent crisis. Scholars of neopatrimonialism have their preferred themes (authoritarianism, corruption, nepotism, political rationality and underperformance), their objects of predilection (networks, economic structures, civil wars, class structures, political parties and coalitions) and a tendency to blame African political elites for state dysfunction on the specious motive of reclaiming African agency (Chabal 1992; Englebert 1997).

According to this literature, rent-seeking is the raison d'être of African political elites and by extension the overarching explanatory factor of the distorted trajectory of the African state: predatory, nebulous and caught in intricate, extended, interest-based networks that parasitize its structures and operations. However, the description of how these networks function in relation to state power, resource accumulation and the constitution of political parties is just that: a description that leaves out the constitutive ideas, the particular challenges and historical circumstances that mediated the independence era. In fact, the most glaring deficit of this and similar schools of thought is empirical; it is the disconnect between theory and reality and the fact therefore that they tell us 'surprisingly little about the state in Africa' (Nugent 2010, 35).

Scholars such as Jean Francois Bayart and Stephen Ellis (2000) argue that African political leaders deliberately maintain artificial dependency structures with external actors, particularly donor states and institutions, so as to capture resources and reproduce a corporate class of political cronies (Bayart 1993; Bayart et al. 1999). The neopatrimonialist school maintains therefore that the nature of the African state is at best understood as a progressive process of personalization, privatization and criminalization, and the discrete crystallizations of mechanisms of integrating and linking the state and different social constituencies around patron and client relationships.

While Bayart and others thus describe the operation of African states in terms of networks, their framework of analysis—that is, the criminalization thesis—fundamentally relies on problematic generalizations and methodological shortcuts which have been eloquently described by Zubairu Wai (2012). What the perspective describes is a set of symptoms of failure of governance. Africa of course is the place where these symptoms are strongest but state failure thus described can be applied to a variety of contexts including Greece in the context of financial and political crisis, the United States where government and policy operations are often high-jacked by partisan politics, Belgium with its disablingly polarized fractions, and even the European Union in the midst of an increasing threat of disintegration.

Patrimonialist scholars are certainly justified in contending that informal alliances have turned the state into an interest-based venture (Bayart 1993)[4] that brings together political elites and a limited portion of society as stakeholders of an entity that has deviated from its primary role as producer of public goods. What is typically missing in their analyses, however, is an examination of the ways in which the interpenetration of state and communal and ethnic entities—while rationalized by a rhetoric of proximity and inclusion—constitutes a perversion of the traditions and values they are purporting to reproduce.

Postcolonial state-society alliances are indeed informed by interests rather than values. One can go even further and contend that postcolonial structures, more than any previous forms, have produced states *against* societies—in other words, a form of statelessness within centralized states that pits the great majority of citizens against a state strictly speaking made of a political elite and co-opted allies. However, patrimonialist theories deal in caricatures;

they paper over the fact that the 'crisis' of the African state is fundamentally about *the fracture of accountability*; it is about the gap of language and of thought, about the fact that 'rulers have turned to brigandage for lack of a national past by which to judge and, in judging bind themselves' (Lonsdale 1986, 156). Modernity forced the construction of versions of the past and imaginations of the future that rendered subsequent realizations of subjective consciousness at best skewed.

Interventionist Literature

Recently, a third eclectic body of work has (re)constituted a stock of ideas productive of representations of Africa that are reminiscent of the colonial era. This literature can broadly be termed 'interventionist'. It pertains to a set of arguments that borrow heavily from both the state failure and collapse literature and humanitarian as well as development perspectives. It prescribes bills of health in the form of trusteeship, custodianship and guardianship (if not de-certification of UN membership)—in other words, the removal of those entitlements and rights for those states crippled by a disease of incapacity until such a time when they will be deemed fit for self-government.[5] Specifically, the interventionist literature makes a direct, causal link between state failure in the Global South, particularly in Africa, and insecurity in the Global North, for state failure is a sure path to anarchy. Its proponents therefore advocate *the restoration of the rule of law through the restoration of the state*.

In effect, in the revival of nineteenth-century discourses on the necessity to establish European-style instruments of power and governance in Africa under European guardianship, interventionist scholars deliberately silence the dislocating and alienating effects of colonial reason, episteme and policy on African societies. Interventionist scholars elevate to a normative category a pre-independence requirement that prospective states conform to European juridico-political instruments and jurisprudence as prerequisites for membership in the international community. This is quite troubling.

Quite fundamentally, the three bodies of work—despite a few worthy insights into African politics in so far as its institutional operationalization goes—are located in a problematic scholarship that has not quite figured how to understand African social formation outside an imperfect comparative, normative and prescriptive outlook. In my view, the difficulty in getting to grips with the African state must be seen not merely as a matter of assessing how well African countries have fared in comparison to the European nation-state—and even less as a matter of determining the types and stages of evolution at which they might be located—but precisely as an effort to move beyond modernist and postmodern, evolutionist and patrimonialist frames of reference and to engage the materialities, the instrumentalities and the intentionalities that underpin governance and subjecthood in diverse African contexts.

For all these reasons, rethinking the African state requires a rigorous analytical effort and historical engagement. Such a task requires first and foremost that we un-understand the state as we know it and start thinking more fruitfully about how different historical communities have gone about conceptualizing institutions that adequately embody different figures of authority, of order, of self and of interrelating and the crucial connections that underlie them.

⚔ UN-UNDERSTANDING THE STATE

The history of state formation that comes out of the bulk of the scholarship presented above is largely disfiguring. This book is an attempt to provide useful pointers toward overcoming its underlying postulates, its inbuilt biases, the formulation of its working questions and its problematic assumptions with regard to social formation.

The first troubling assumption has to do with the goal of the state in Europe and elsewhere. This goal was to create the conditions for (redistributive) social justice through juridical, parliamentary, bureaucratic and even military means (i.e., the principles of the liberal state). The second assumption, which is historically uninformed, was that the remnants of pre-existing African institutional and cultural forms (traditions and cultural practice) were at odds with the modernization project: (i.e., statization). The eradication of the latter was consequently a prerequisite for the transfer of a European-like state model that would create those conditions that were thought to be the markers of the success of the European state—something that postcolonial leaders barely questioned given the ease with which they adopted institutions bequeathed by colonialists. In fact some of them engaged in a de-traditionalization crusade that led to the dismantling of customary authority structures and other institutional implements seen as regressive and anti-revolutionary. In Burkina Faso, this trend took the form of a relentless witch-hunt mainly against the Mossi chieftaincy and their exclusion from public affairs under the presidency of Thomas Sankara. Like many others, Sankara believed that Africans had to shed lived experience and inherited memories, their identities and their traditions, if they were to become modern and mature citizens.

The failed and patrimonialist theses are not only a bad reading of African history (if any at all) but also a dangerous one. First, they obscure an understanding of past and present attempts to formulate sociopolitical forms that are at odds with or challenge a blanket deployment of centralized political states and empires. These experiments range from the constitution of runaway or freed slave villages in West and Central Africa and cultural forms of resistance abstracted in ritual and religious forms in the Congo, in the Voltaic region and elsewhere to *y'en a marre* movements spearheaded by disillusioned youths across the continent since the 1990s.

Second, this literature can never help us make sense of the sort of ideas of freedom and notions of self and subjectivity—in fact the inherited political memories that are being experimented with or invoked in these movements. Yet such an understanding is absolutely crucial if we are to make sense of uses of, subscriptions to and struggles against political leadership, political parties, sociopolitical networks, secularism and so forth in postcolonial Africa.

Finally, the instrumentalized dependency argument advanced by Bayart and others is a deliberately dehistoricized and partial account that leaves out the perverse effects of the 'basic structural determinants inherited from the colonial era, which set definite limits to the actions of the state and to a large extent pre-determined the trajectories of its formation' (Doornbos 1990, 181). The very assumption that the formal state *as* devolved by the European colonial regime to African elites—in essence an exploitative, predatory, authoritarian and parasitic mode of government—was an ideal conjunction of will, morality, capacity and aspiration is a historical fallacy. In fact, to many, independence amounted to a mere Africanization of the colonial power system in the nomination of African governors in place of European governors.[6]

In my view, the most unhelpful and damaging aspect of this literature is ultimately a lack of informed investigation into the *what* (What African state?) and the *why* (What moral and political project were African states made for?). In the absence of such rigorous work, an assessment of state failure solely in terms of levels of performance becomes a fairly easy exercise.

This is not to say that there has been no attempt at historicization of the functions and the instrumentalities of the state; of the juridical adjudication of political struggles over the meaning of institutions, power and governance as self-expression; of 'traditions' as a principle of diversity and of the modalities of the modernization project in determining the distribution of access, entitlement and privileges. I place my fellow travellers in three categories of scholars who have seriously addressed the idea of the normativity of the Westphalian state and the modalities of political authority as framed by specific historical, epistemic and cultural requirements.

Focusing on sovereignty as an anchor-problem in writings on the state, a number of political scientists have carried out a thorough critique of the Westphalian model of statehood as fundamentally problematic in the disciplines of politics and international relations. This first category includes R. B. J. Walker (1992), Charles Tilly (1975; 1990), Hendrik Spruyt (1994), Jens Bartelson (1995), and Benno Teschke (2003). These scholars show that in the context of Europe, the sovereign state, despite a constitutive propensity for predation, established institutions as containers that could be filled up with meaning and intent. The *republique* was that instrument of collective possibility; it built nations and turned an original imposition into a legitimate structure. Even Tilly recognizes these positive features. In France in particular, the decapitation of the king was only a first step; it was followed by the elaboration of the republic as an embodiment of collective will and aspiration, as something that belonged to everybody. In fact, the incorporation of social orders as a process of legitimation became an internal problem that inflected a direction to state formation in Europe.[7] The postcolonial African state, having adopted the sovereign state model, never achieved a similar transformation. In other words, the republic—as an imported innovation—never was the translation of indigenous conceptions of the public good nor did it come to embody them over time.

In the second category, Mahmood Mamdani (1996) and Siba Grovogui (1996) are two among the few scholars who have convincingly demonstrated how experiments in the transfer of European constitutional forms and juridical frameworks in Africa were underlined by teleological strategies meant to sustain a specific juridico-political order—in other words, continued government *over* African peoples, institutions and resources. Achille Mbembe (2001) for his part shows how colonial governmentality manufactured difference through the institution of alienating procedures of *commandment*. This book also seeks to provide historically informed accounts of institutional regimes that have produced numerous structures of dependency. These have inevitably had an enduring influence on the institutional development of the postcolonial African state, its political institutions, its economic development and its global positionality.

A third category of scholars whose work informs the orientation of my project includes political anthropologists and historians, specifically Jean and John Comaroff, Meyer Fortes, Edward Evans-Pritchard, Paul Nugent, Tom McCaskie and Michel Izard, who have usefully interrogated the ethics of governance in African settings in ways that take into account the multiple and multidimensional coordinates of power and governance in precolonial and postcolonial Africa (Fortes and Evans-Pritchard 1940; John L. Comaroff 1998; Jean Comaroff 1985; Comaroff and Comaroff 2006; Izard 1992; Nugent 2010). In the Burkinabe context in particular, Izard's pioneering work has encouraged a bolder interpretation of the signs and materialities, the vocabulary and codes, and the agents and objects of culture, power and governance in precolonial Moogo, the subject of this book. In his *States and Social Contracts in Africa*, Paul Nugent relies on a social contract framework to try and understand the sources of precariousness of the principles that bind state and society and the possibility for socio-institutional reform in the various articulations of the contract in different times and places using a comparative approach. Based on a different time period, McCaskie's careful and nuanced interpretation of power and authority in nineteenth-century Ashante provides a most useful template for how one can bring *different levels* and different practices of politics located in paraphernalia and décor, constitutions and compacts, and social codes and rituals into the conversation.

This book is therefore closely aligned with bodies of literature that both critique a notion of *stateness* as given, static and irreversible and contribute toward opening up new avenues for thinking across and 'outside the state'. Some of the most interesting works on state formation are indeed those that question the myth of Westphalia (Teschke 2003)—some of these are about the state proper, some of them ask the question *Why the state?* and others engage institutional experiences that require a novel political vocabulary. Among these inquiries, non-state-centred ideas and arguments are crucially important in political analysis. On one hand, they allow a sound critique of a ubiquitous Eurocentric understanding of state formation in both its historicity and adequacy. On the other hand, they provide glimpses into political processes outside Europe in their very functions and instrumentalities. In fact, thinking without the state forces us to exercise relative awareness about the very categories of *state* and *stateness* with which we typically work.

Historians and political anthropologists of the non-West have gone about looking for political formations, namely state-like forms, on their way to modernity and in historically progressive and instrumental terms. For these scholars, states are to be identified wherever existed a centralized apparatus that provided law and order and a recognizable and discrete class of professional rulers led by a sovereign figure who had the capacity to distribute and delegate power down a hierarchical structure.[8] Such an obviously simplistic model is easily put to test by the complex arrangements I discuss in this study and which show that there is nothing linear and straightforward about such a model and its premises.

In relation to the above, James Scott's examination of forms of non-state experiences and experimentations in South East Asia seems quite important to me even though I suspect that his strong predilection for 'statelessness' has relatively limited import for my critique of the state. Scott frames historical attempts to escape the state in terms of resistance and anarchy, thus dispelling many myths of primitivism and un-civilization postulated against groups that have evolved outside centralized state systems. He contends that societies living outside the confines of statehood made a conscious and deliberate choice to evade the oppressive dictates of administrators, from Ming China to colonial India to the postcolonial nation-states, and that each of these in turn sought to subdue and subordinate 'hill peoples' and make them 'fiscally legible' while modernizing them. In the expanse of what he and

Willem van Schendel have termed 'Zomia' and which straddles Southeast Asia (Vietnam, Thailand, Siam, Burma, southern China and even portions of India and Afghanistan), various uphill populations have managed to construct life forms that have resisted state assault.

Where I disagree with Scott relates to the question of governance. For Scott, it would seem that the only possibility of governance outside the state (political governance) is non-governance, rebellion and anarchy; in other words, non-centralization equals non-government. In addition, despite the fact that he problematizes the presumption of the primacy of the centralized state, Scott seems to take for granted 'state' and 'non-state' as conceptual spaces that only need to be filled up with specific historical content. In saying this, however, I'm not suggesting that alternative analyses successfully escape the sort of *statist determinism* that makes us think with or from the state—statelessness exists because states do. My point is that awareness of such a limitation should attenuate the difficulty in thinking about order, authority and meaning as if they could only be produced by state institutions. In addition, I demonstrate in the following chapters that various registers of governance play out outside state settings in intergroup alliances, in structures of production (Comaroff and Comaroff 1991, 128), in ritualized enactions of cosmogonic beliefs and in physical anatomies among other terrains.

This book proposes to examine constitutional processes that governed political life in a precolonial African society. One of the main arguments I advance, developed below, is that centralization was always a transient, uncertain, even dangerous endeavour for states could be undone as easily as they arose. In fact, full centralization was to be realized only under the colonial regime. However, in dismantling precolonial structures, the colonial state's aim was never to replace them with an African sovereign state, or in other words, to institute a European-style government that made provisions for civic rights and entitlement and popular participation. On the contrary, the colonial powers' ultimate aim was to establish a hierarchy for *differentiated government* (Mamdani 1996). In essence, the colonial endeavour was this. Grovogui (1996) demonstrates with great insight that all the ideologies that were introduced under colonial rule, from the conquest to colonial administration and systems of trusteeship, were in effect put in place to dismantle pre-existing structures. In this process, international law became the instrument of an ideology of occupation, alienation, expropriation and marginalization. The result was a hierarchization and classification of Africans between categories of citizens and categories of subjects, a theme thoroughly analyzed by Mamdani (1996) who elucidates the working of two concurrent but unequal modes of government devised to serve the different categories.

Given the insights of the scholars mentioned above and others who have ploughed through the complex and uneven histories of precolonial and colonial political authority structures, the state failure and patrimonial strands of thinking—despite their different interest and emphases—share a self-indicting, common problem. They strip African political systems of any real internal dynamic, whether historical, constitutional, juridical or other. Furthermore, *they lack a complexified space/time dimension of institutional analysis.* The reason for all this is actually a simple story. It is the result of the projection of the myth of Westphalia—a singular path to sovereignty—onto African terrain and an obsession with the sovereign state as a unit of analysis. A deviant, dysfunctional state is therefore what these scholars have found in lieu of a close imitation of the Westphalian nation-state.

Un-understanding the state thus means that we suspend prevailing justificatory, normative accounts of the state in the form of rigid categories that inevitably create 'proper' states as opposed to underperforming, incongruent, inchoate and inadequate ones. In this vein, commonly established accounts of the role of the state as the provider of law and order must be revised. Theories of state failure make no analytical distinction between the ontological basis of the state and its reasoned objectives. For them, the very existence of something called the state—in their understanding a Westphalian prototype— necessarily produces order, abundance and the good life for all. The African state might well be on its way to Westphalia but if so, there are multiple trajectories and social experiments that have prevailed at particular historical junctures and about which we can gain understanding by examining different systems of signs and symbols, different social codes and relationships. I propose to do just that with reference to political formations that developed across the Voltaic region between the sixteenth and the nineteenth centuries, with particular emphasis on the trajectory of the Mossi states.

THE STATE IN TRANSITION: A PROPOSAL

My thesis is that the organization and function of states differ in time and space and that in the lands of the Mossi, there emerged one that very closely aligned the sphere of politics with that of ritual enaction of social experience. This alignment not only textured the experience of politics, it allowed for unique relations not only with different factions of government but also between state and populations. On one hand, these relations are understood in the context of the articulation of the modalities of a juridical compact between diverse communities locked in a common questioning of the nature of their world. On the other hand, these predispose political rule as the articulation of the translatability of the compact and the desire of pre-state groups to constitute themselves in a dialectical interaction with the state, weaving strategic or limited relations—from collaboration, integration, indifference, avoidance or rejection—in order that they can pursue their interests regardless of the sort of design the state might have for them.

For those subjected to the state imperative, the moral cause of political rule was indistinguishable from the virtue and the purpose of rule. Political power was seen as a central component of structures of relation that cohered to achieve social order without any underlying assumption that the latter was the preserve of a distinct 'state'. In effect, the distinction between different spheres of social action amalgamates authority *to a state's capacity to organize social life* beyond and despite the ordering effects of overlapping rapports and relationships conceived at the intersection of locality and descent, the realm of ancestors and the realm of nature, kinship and territoriality.

Even if we take Mossi accounts at face value—despite a marked state-centrism and a tendency for triumphalism—there was an underlying impermanence that characterized state formation as an uneven process of adjustments and reformations of a flexible moral order. States waxed and waned according to political fortunes, struggles over succession, dynastic wars that resembled civil wars, the exclusion of political rivals, the resistance state entrepreneurs encountered in their movement of expansion and so on.

The history of the *Naam*, the principle of political authority among the Mossi, is in fact a formidable account of fission as constitutively inbuilt in its framework: the proliferation of *naam* polities constructed according to the same principles as the parent polity was both a mechanism of survival and of reproduction of the state form. Between the fifteenth and the nineteenth centuries, seats of power multiplied, political centres flourished and royal residences and cities dotted the Voltaic region. The state was constantly recreated, displaced and reformed. What kept this constant movement together was a conceptual model, an ideological project that had to be adapted to pre-existing forms. Group migration, strife, epidemics, drought, demographic haemorrhages and other phenomena were often responsible for state dislocation, amalgamation and reconstitution; small states often got absorbed into imperial structures while small *naam* orders emerged alongside non-centralized politics.

What this dynamic process was indicative of can be read in many ways but I will focus on two. First, there is the continuity thesis—the preferred version of Mossi political entrepreneurs—that contends that the state needed to replicate and reproduce itself while expanding; the disparate *naam* units were informed and brought together under the same logic of state formation. The end result was going to be consolidated *naam* orders that would integrate all 'ungoverned' communities in their wake. A second reading sees in the fluidity and the constant dissolution and reconstitution of the *Naam* a pragmatic mechanism of survival in the midst of contingency and precariousness. In this sense, the state was never just a 'model' to be developed in a linear fashion;

it was instead a transient form constantly challenged by rejection, resistance and the limits imposed upon its rhetorical and institutional legitimation by pre-existing temporal and spatial modes of structuring. In places where the *Naam* model was relatively firmly implanted emerged innovative forms of cohabitation where the logic of the state was subjected to the requirements of these pre-existing modes of legitimation.

I use 'state in transition' essentially to mean two things. On one hand, as illustrated by the Mossi and similar experiences in the Voltaic region, the state was never the sole location or sole guardian of political authority and moral order; the institutionalization of state power was always bound to integrate, negate, mediate or be subjected to pre-existing understandings and practices of authority. A dynamic history of frequent upheavals, interregna, reconstructions, collapse and reconstitution and so forth—in fact structural transience—precisely attests to the impermanence of the state while underlying authority structures endured and mutated. On the other hand, I use the notion of 'state in transition' to try and get to grips with a historical puzzle that has yet to find adequate explanation; that is, the seemingly endless reproduction of a constitutive political structure—in my area of interest the *Naam* model or more loosely *Naam* ideology—across the Voltaic river systems, but also similar configurations in parts of West and Central Africa and also in Southern Africa.

The closest attempt in my view to resolve this puzzle has been Ivor Kopytoff's frontier theory that postulates a 'frontier-conditioned ideology' as a movement that impels the reproduction of pre-existing social formations through migration and the movement of ideas. For Kopytoff, the 'frontier' consists of politically open areas nested between organized societies but 'internal' or 'interstitial' to the larger regions in which there are found. As attractive as the frontier framework might be, however, *intentionality* and *agency* are notoriously difficult categories to work with and it is not clear that either Kopytoff or other historians of the African state have properly integrated these elements. The development of Mossi ideology was a mixture of intentionality and propagation through the interpenetration of different groups. If the Mossi sought to clone the Mamprusi-Dagomba-Mossi basic model (see chapter 2) while expanding the state system partly as a way of resolving succession disputes, non-Mossi groups had a less systematic, less consistent attitude toward this model. In fact, they commonly rejected or subverted the *Naam* model while some of them kept the basic *Naam/Tenga* dichotomy (see the following arguments).

The state-in-transition perspective here tempers a functionalist tendency to take the state as a given rather than as a process of formation to be understood and explained in all its complexity. Furthermore, in showing variations and gradations of institutionalization on the basis of a common source of political ideas and principles across present-day Ghana, Niger, Burkina Faso, and Mali, I wish to suggest that it might be more fruitful to think of state formation within the broader Voltaic region rather than of Mamprugu, Dagbon, Nanun, Ouagadougou, Yatenga, and other formations in isolation. I further develop the state-in-transition thesis below in five related arguments.

First, I argue throughout the book that the *Naam* provided a unified symbol of the body politic among the Mossi. Moreover, the state was built around political ideas introduced by 'naturalized' migrants who transformed pre-existing mental constructs, cultural constellations and moral orders in line with temporal developments and the requirements of public life and the political economy.

The original catalyst for the elevation of the *Naam* as the source of philosophical and jurisprudential orientation for political authority, society making and the constitution of subjectivities was a particular context of experimentation with different political forms. In the absence of a fixed and irreversible institutionalization of ideas of authority, the latter could occupy multiple sites of action that were not strictly defined by the perspective of the state or statehood per se. The *Naam* as model and ideology therefore had to be elaborated, developed and adjusted to take into account pre-existing ideas of authority, morality, order and subjectivity. In thinking about multiple centres of authority, my argument is not that these competed for prominence or that their action was defined by a logic of competition against the *Naam*. My argument is rather that synchronic alternates to the structures patterned along the *Naam* were strongly expressed in ideas, values, norms and practices rather than in institutional forms designed to compete explicitly with the state. *In that very sense, the state was never the prime mover of social action.*

Second, state bearers put forth a strategic if not convenient distinction between 'the political' and the 'non-political' as discrete fields of action. But such a distinction obscures two undercurrents that marked the Mossi political experience, and this calls for a critique of state ideology in relation to accounts of historical experience. The distinction illuminates an attempt, by state builders, to redefine social life by recalibrating pre-existing, multiple temporalities that enabled order and authority *without the centralized state*. The Mossi ideological project was essentially an attempt to become the single author of the historical experience, in other words to be the sole *hermeneus*.[9] However, this attempt was decisively countered by pre-existing forces contained in the sphere of *Tenga* (earth-divinity; ritual sphere). As a result, centralization was always a transient and precarious phenomenon. It was necessarily contested, malleable and a work in progress in its very provisionality.

A reading of authority and morality through and in the 'non-political' spheres of social intervention, therefore, does two things for me. It allows me on one hand to break a common boundary between epistemology and ontology. On the other hand, it allows me to question another common distinction between a mighty 'subject' and an infinitely pliable 'object' that is central to Western political theory. More specifically, it allows me to show that the ideology of the *Naam* was a potent model around which the condition for the institutions of political chief and ritual chief could be construed *within a common symbolic field.*

The following chapters are an attempt to reconstruct aspects of that history but also to abstract key ideas of political theory that animate our understanding of political formation; namely—but not limited to—authority, order, legitimacy and power. In putting this together, I want to rethink a notion of sovereignty that is not inherently linked to and determined by the state, the church and similar centralized structures because centralization of power does not always correspond to popular modes of life, modes of recognition, memory, conceptions of the real and so on.

Third, there was a degree of congruence, in the African precolonial experience, between the iterative nature of the persistent negotiation of the modalities of cohabitation and the related articulation of the appropriate political forms. This congruence was manifested either in binary structures of political ruler and ritual ruler where governing and governed communities engaged in a mutual imagination of, or an active separation between, a sphere of power and a sphere of rituals where there were moral, material and ideological constraints to common aspirations and to the possibility of building a single community of purpose. The institutions of slavery, coercive labour-system and the institutionalization of social experience as state reason led to an active production of marginality. Yet what this book shows is that the state-building ideas allegedly introduced by an enlightened few confronted a range of possibilities from indifference to assimilation. The life of these ideas becomes an account of the modalities of translation, articulation and *mise en forme* of a field of convergences and contradictions marked by a common quest for order and morality *in difference.*

Fourth, the notion of *encounter* has therefore to be recognized as central to the elaboration of a political model that confronted differently endowed groups invested in their distinct perceptions of order with different wills and sets of aspirations. State rhetoric found its limits as a language of stigmatization productive of negativities where state control came up against multiple temporalities. The state's inflated discourse of its own goodness and necessity, of its vision as the magnetic centre from which radiated the rays of civilization and so forth, is couched in unidirectionality. In reality, modes of engagement with stateness or statist forms varied between outright avoidance, collaboration, intermittent participation and open dissidence and rejection. Commonly for state builders, however, assimilation became the preferred mode of engagement, one that required a capacity to integrate diversity in a way they were not always able to do. Chapters 2 and 4 further expand upon these ideas.

Fifth, in the cohabitation of different registers of morality, the legitimation of power became a process that confronted different values and common sense through their ritualized adjudication. The ritual framework—characterized by its languages, its cyclical performances, its rites of initiation, renewal, sanction, legitimation and restoration captured, more persuasively than any other idiom, the fundaments of political common sense and the subjectivities, the values and the imaginaries that informed the dispositions of Africans as historical agents and which state builders sought to respond to or exploit in many ways. The enactment of constitutions as social charters through rituals mediated particular understandings of self-rule as much as they mediated social conflict. My argument is that these rituals created regimes of order, of selfhood (being) and of morality that necessarily shaped political action both explicitly and implicitly.

This book thus advances four related propositions. I first wish to make a distinction between the state as experience and the state as institution. The former mobilizes the twin processes of institutionalization and abstraction of a set of ideas, values, identities and imaginaries; the latter is an account of the constitution of state power. In the following chapters, I show that there were a multiplicity of political structures in the Voltaic region, different degrees and gradations of stateness so to speak, that drew from the same fund of ideas of governing principles.

Second, the awkward notion of the economy of affect, the politics of the belly, the mechanics of power accumulation and similar theses translate an uneasy, problematic, yet inexorable, fragmentary interpenetration of and mis-appropriation of memories, cosmologies and past constitutional possibilities under constrained present conditions. An argument this book makes time and again is that the African state will always be seen as problematic as long as the twin question of *root* (rooting) and *correspondence* (between collective understanding and memory of historical experience and the nature of present institutions) is not resolved. To be sure, there are significant constitutional lessons from Voltaic political trajectories that bear noting. For instance, permutations of the demarcation between different spheres of social action generated different values and institutions that fostered political consultation and accountability. Further, the formulation of historical statements by the state—for its own aggrandizement and benefit—were successfully countered by cultural practices and commentaries that enabled contestation, dissent and disengagement. This much is suggested by processes of legitimation of state power which solely depended on non-state agents, processes and institutions. It would not be wise for anyone to try to reconstruct or reinvent these but the recognition of pragmatic limits should not preclude the possibility of extracting, abstracting and adapting their key components.

Third, the formulaic distinction between a 'zone of political rule' versus a 'zone of the ungoverned', between a 'sphere of power' versus a 'sphere of rituals' or by extension a distinction between *the political* and *the non-political* as discrete and as antagonistic realms is as simplistic a reading as it is productive of a longstanding concern about the nature of the political and power. In so far as political rule predates the state as institution, non-state forms of governance did not require the state to govern them; political entrepreneurs merely revived what had been there in a latent, submerged, differently articulated form on which they superimposed state discourse. I propose therefore that one can investigate the constitutive dimension of African political experience, in fact one should endeavour to do so, outside apparent centres of political action such as ritual spaces and artisans' workshops.

Fourth, as a constitutional, ethical and functional project, the modern African state has proved to be most inadequate. The postcolonial state is essentially a construct whose identity (adapted European constitutional orders), logic (transfer of colonial authority to African elites) and purpose (the actualization of private wills) among other things have no bearing on the political imaginaries of its constituencies. The state, for many subjected to its rule, is an alienating machine that dominates society and has achieved neither hegemony nor legitimacy nor consensus over its status. The malaise of the African state is very much a manifestation of a quest for meaning spurred by inhibited and constrained political imaginaries and imaginations discordant with past political experience and cultural knowledge.

I agree with Raymond Williams and Eric Cheyfitz that in entertaining certain pastoral visions of an ideal past, there is often untold historical violence upon history in the reconstruction of foundational and explanatory myths (Williams 1973, 35–39, 50; Cheyfitz 1997, 55). It is therefore not my intention here to invoke a quaint, idyllically untroubled Africa but to show how particular idioms of authority, values and entitlements, social relations and status carried the imaginaries and the imaginings of historical agents into organic arrangements that endured and were sustained by these.

These arrangements were certainly not devoid of tension, contradictions and arbitrary violence: captives for instance bore the brunt of physically demanding chores while being subjected to the violence of estrangement. However, what I'm trying to get at is that in places where the state sought to bridge the violence of power through ideology, people could draw on resources to enable modes of remedy and restoration in mediating conflict, the abuse of power, the violation of moral order and so forth.

These were registers of ideas, values and institutions that have a strong bearing on the subjective consciousness of postcolonial African actors and therefore on the African condition particularly where present arrangements are a far cry from recollections of past conventions. While being subjective and fragmentary, these recollections nonetheless conjure up a strong desire for different modes of self-rule and meaning-making and as such provide a political language as well as resources for the assessment of the legitimacy of political power. The confrontation of mental constructs and their ambiguous absorption into essentially dislocated postcolonial structures have provided a backdrop to a permanent malaise.

My study does not purport to provide a solution to the malaise of the post-colonial state. What it does do on one hand is to give pointers on the sort of resources, material and non-material, that sustained precolonial formations despite a great internal diversity. On the other hand, in showing that the history of social formation in the West African region was a very multi-linear, unstraightforward process whereby the centralized state was one model among others and not even the most common one, it opens up a discussion about the relevance of thinking about sovereignty not as a discrete phenomenon (that has to be imposed on people) but in terms of *mutuality* and *cooperation*. The postcolonial centralized state not only took sovereignty away from people, it negated the possibility for people to bring to bear their mental construct, their values and interests in the institutions that govern them. In doing so, it took away the humane dimension from institutional possibilities.

THE *NAAM* AND *TENGA*: A NORMATIVE ORDER AND ITS LEGITIMATION

The precolonial Mossi state—like its Mamprugu, Dagbon and Nanun counterparts—was constructed around an original idea of political authority: the *Naam*. The *Naam* encompasses the body of representations of knowledge and imaginaries of the state. It embodied the Mossi state in its twofold project of establishing a political order and of shaping the contours of social experience as a whole. This book shows that, despite its all-encompassing reach, the *Naam* was essentially a model fabulated by its precursors as the *fons et origo* of all life forms, and as such it justified the imposition of state structures over pre-existing social arrangements. The *Naam* was always a receding idea, longed-for and yet demanding for it required perfection in aspiration.

Two centuries after its formulation in the fifteenth and sixteenth centuries, the *Naam* became the model par excellence that governed most if not all attempts at state formation in the Voltaic region. However, there was nothing deterministic about its development. The *Naam* was not always carved out of the harmonious coevolution of a society and a state over a long period of interactions. In reality, the *Naam* model had to contend with the capacity for resistance of pre-existing social structures. Its founders sought to subdue the putative representatives or earthpriests of 'first settlers'. Earthpriests and other first-settler figures and populations operated under the moral authority of *Tenga* as a specialized realm and the body of representations and knowledge of the 'non-political'. The many locations of *Tenga* (ritual sites, private spaces, fields, trees and untamed nature) bear the traces of struggles over and contradictions that traverse the formulations of structures of cohabitation and collective identity. These struggles were less salient among stateless groups given that both political and ritual rule were often located in the same figures.

The Mossi envisaged the parameters of social action as determined by both the realms of the political and that of the ritual. The model is fairly widespread across the African continent and it points to a conception of power that has not been properly integrated in analyses of state formation and political legitimacy in Africa.[10] I wish to demonstrate how the binary construct of the *Naam* versus *Tenga*—in other words the 'zone of the governed' versus the 'zone of the ungoverned'—constitutes analogized articulations of imaginaries of authority (an ethics of legitimation), of cultural ethos (beliefs, values, artistic expression) and positionalities (social statuses and relations, entitlements) which in reality were brought together by a juridical compact whose terms were to be regularly revisited through ritualized procedures. The finality of the legal order was not a problem-solving, pragmatic response to contingent social contraventions. Rather, legal ideas and norms, like rituals, were deeply ontological. They were woven into mutually bounding relationships, the legibility of which was both internal and experiential.[11] In this particular sense, ancestors and spaces of dwelling were construed as agential locations singularly endowed with a disposition to restore broken morality. In so far as the moral order was a collectively authored possibility, the sources of public authority were diverse and multiple. They were invested in reclaiming, for the community's own recovery and healing, the presence of ancestors alongside those living and those yet to be born; ritual performers thus elevated a community's ills and resolve to a universal order to speak to all ills and wills.

Tenga (*Tengan*) is a concept that designates neither a geographical location nor an ethnic grouping of 'society' at large. It consists of distinct social practices, a framework of interdependent relationships, a certain ecological homogeneity and a particular disposition against rigid hierarchy. It refers to an ecocultural field of identities, values and subjectivities invested in social equilibrium. Ultimately, at the heart of definitions of collective identity is a battle of representations: the state projects itself as a site of integration and institutional coherence. The boundaries of *Tenga* (or lack thereof) are articulated around a notion of moral stability.

The success of the centralized state model resulted from a double process whereby internal dissent against the state model in the form of open rebellion or silent defiance was often framed in the language of the state so much so that alternative reconstructions of the state seemed to remain within the dominant order. However, the *Naam* provided the most potent incentive in shaping political institutions. It provided original institutional answers to the question of the management of social diversity through the apparently contradictory but innovative twin processes of *homogenization* and *hierarchization*. The claims of legitimacy of Mossi rulers were thus underpinned by a desire to become and to provide a prototype of state over the geographical reach of Moogo.

As a counter-discourse to the Mossi formulation of state, *Tenga* had a unique characteristic to it. It thwarted state claims for the monopoly of sociopolitical legitimacy while its tenants adhered, gave the impression of adhering to, the dominant order. Agency, within the realm of *Tenga* was not just a matter of reaction to a threat of extinction but rather the means of preservation of pre-existing forms and structures, therefore denoting a constant tension between invention and convention, cooperation and destabilization. Faced with the challenge of a rising state, the agents of *Tenga* invested meaning and intent in their practice of resistance through a series of rituals and cultural practices that had to be constantly reworked in order to respond to anxieties generated by state power. This study seeks to liberate these rituals from their fossilized categorizations and to extract key analytical formulations from them.

The tensions between political rulers (Mossi royals) and spiritual representatives (earthpriests) over overlapping prerogatives shaped as much as they constrained the state project. The interconnected dynamics of these tensions with generational and kinship tensions give a complex picture of the imperatives and the challenges of state-making in a precolonial society. I argue that these tensions were sublimated and were only partly resolved in the promotion of the Mossi state. I also argue that the Mossi exercised a form of *rational control* over the state's historical discourse and this provided relevance to their continued legitimacy as rulers. This rational control was achieved through linguistic and ideological reproduction of institutional structures of the *Naam* across Mossi society.

Just as McCaskie has indicated in a different context, I try to examine ideology, in the Mossi context, in the manner in which it enables both a reproduction of the state and a transcendence of the gap between power and legitimacy. In so doing, I try to avoid the temptation to view ideology in its crude, instrumentalist function. Because of the various tensions discussed previously, ultimately, this book is arguing that ideology does not rest with anyone in particular but that it is reproduced in the very interaction of discourse with historical processes.

The book is organized as follows. Chapter 2 revisits the origins of the distinctions between 'states' and 'stateless societies' in the Mamprugu-Dagbon-Nanun-Moogo area. It assumes that the region constitutes a united politico-cultural area that draws on a common stock of intellectual ideas and resources that were utilized and organized differently in a way that produced gradations of stateness across the region. The chapter argues that statelessness was *at once what the state was built against as much as what it emanated from*. It therefore focuses on political authority rather than the state as organizing principle of the diversity of forms that have existed in the region.

Chapter 3 identifies Tenga as an active zone of political action; it makes visible its strategies of political action and the *political implications* of its most ordinary interventions in both the formally divided sociopolitical and socio-ritual spheres. This chapter also seeks to bring into the conversation the productive distinction between *politics* and *the political* variously framed by Carl Schmitt, Jean-Luc Nancy, and Philippe Lacoue-Labarthe. It points out two problems with the liberal concept of politics: that the fixation of power, in the hands of a sovereign, is a prerequisite of the possibility of order; in other words, that power is something that exists and circulates in fragmentary forms, and without its monopolistic organization, there can only be danger, uncertainty, hostility and ultimately disorder. The second problem is what the distinction suggests, that there is something of a special *quality* to the political that can be isolated and opposed to the social and a whole range of 'non-political' purviews.

Chapter 3 argues that the distinction between the political and the non-political, the product of a dynastic discourse, was crucial to the statization process that swept the Voltaic region starting in the sixteenth and consolidating toward the end of the nineteenth century. The elevation of the *Naam* as the highest embodiment of the political was a statement on the value of the latter, as endowed with the greatest normative quality. An implication of this was the exclusion of 'non-political' from the sphere of politics.

Chapter 4 looks into the relationship between the constitution of the notion of the political as framed in the *Naam* and the production of *mossiness* and identity in Moogo. From the perspective of the *Naam*, *gurunsi* and other *nyonyonse* (indigenous) groups were shorthand for uncivilized, uncouth and backward. There was a strong element of a fixed, static and crucially essentialist understanding of identity and cultural difference. This was, however, at odds with a history of intense interactions among groups which was articulated around the *pogsiure*, or delayed exchange of women, practiced among Voltaic groups. Both Ouagadougou and Yatenga adopted an assimilationist policy in their homogenization project. The Mossi state became most competent in ascribing identity even where statuses were relationally *particulate*; it was particularly effective with regard to captive populations that made up the majority of its subjects.

Chapter 5 examines the modalities of cohabitation and the operationalization of legitimacy using the examples of the centralized states of Ouagadougou and Yatenga. The chapter argues that there is an *ethics of togetherness* that is enacted in the performance of rituals, particularly the enthronement voyage of *ringu* without which a Mossi king cannot become a sovereign. Unless one understands how rituals are used, in the attempt to conciliate two seemingly discrete spheres of social authority, the formulation of the possibility of sovereignty as something that is contingent and transferable makes little sense. This chapter uses the enthronement ritual of *ringu* to contextualize and conceptualize belief as central to state formation and political legitimacy in Moogo.

While ideology can be seen as a tension to be negotiated between indigenousness and otherness, rituals expressed the Mossi theory of kingship as well as its changing character over time. During the *ringu*, a king is 'made', kingship is established and social components reunited with the past (ancestors) and the future (those yet to be born). In the absence of these types of legitimation processes—either because of ideological repression or the relegation of past constitutional and juridical forms and social and cultural practices to mere folklore—the concluding chapter suggests that both the colonial project of modernization and the postcolonial imperative of decolonization amounted to interventions with dislocating effects for African societies disempowered and effectively unable to mobilize, in their rapport with the state, a whole register of ideas, values and beliefs that shaped and continue to shape their subjective consciousness.

Postcolonial states approached customary rule either through accommodation or marginalization. In Ghana and Uganda for instance, after an initial neglect, the postcolonial state has eventually come to recognize the epistemological relevance of past institutions represented by the chieftaincy. However, within this recognition, the chieftaincy was always to be subjected to the control of the state for the latter, despite an apparent desire to accommodate, had no real place for parallel moral authorities. Consequently, chiefs have for the most part been co-opted to do the dirty job of the state, in South Africa and Mozambique crudely so but also elsewhere. In Senegal for instance, the state has confronted the possibility of a parallel, religious order that could potentially challenge its authority by co-opting religious leaders in the national project.

At any rate, across Africa, the recognition of customary, traditional and other non-state forms of authority has translated to mere 'devolution' of state power in decentralization schemes. Added to this is the fact that chiefs since the colonial times have seen their authority discredited and emptied of its previous legitimacy. In Burkina Faso, a state narrative of modernization, under Thomas Sankara, was framed against 'tradition', represented by the Mossi chieftaincy. Sankara's revolutionary liberation project sought to eliminate domestic symbols of legitimacy and thwart attempts to resurrect alternative modes of governance; everything from the past was conveniently labelled backward, regressive and counterrevolutionary. Under the revolutionary government and subsequent experiments, political practice further drifted from previous historical experience while the state ceased to make sense as an organic institutional arrangement that reflects broad signifying referents.

As a consequence, neither capable of constituting themselves as fully fledged citizens under the postcolonial constitutional regime shaped by European juridical tradition and political experience nor able to engage in political experimentation through a deployment of African referential possibilities, postcolonial African agents are continuously caught in aborted revolutions that leave little institutional memory to build upon. These specific themes are the focus of chapter 6.

Something needs to be said about methodology. Two methodological traditions broadly inform my analysis, namely, structuralist and hermeneutical readings of historical processes, social action and its various representations. First, for a political scientist, a structuralist perspective yields many possibilities for theorizing on institutional formation at the intersection of cultural practice, social order and public morality. Michel Izard for instance adopted aspects of structuralist analysis in his examination of elements of power in the Mossi institutional history. Even though he sticks to a Mossi-centred reading of institutional formation through the constitutive distinction between the sphere of power and the sphere of rituals, his scrutiny of the operations of Mossi state power within a symbolic economy constituted of signs, codes and values and enacted in rites points to analytical possibilities in the elements of history and culture that govern people's preferences.

Despite its shortcomings, structuralism can help uncover a mental world, the subterranean undercurrents of ideas associated with the *Naam*; these then need to be retrieved through a work of deconstruction and of decoding of signs, moral codes, symbols and symbolic relations, metaphors and connections as they shape and are produced by structures and processes.

Second, a hermeneutical analysis of the formation of power and authority allows a good understanding of the operations of structures in relation to the operations of culture. It further allows the deconstruction of social symbols on the basis of *agents* (who elaborates them?), *intent* (for what purpose?) and *effects* (with what implications?). For instance, in investigating the bases of political legitimacy in Moogo, the idea of 'belief', through its various enactions, was a flexible container that could be undone and (re)filled with the interwoven imaginings of migrants, autochthons and a range of liminal figures of all aspects of human experience including politics, morality, and economic, normative dimensions of ideology and cultural practice.

But to read Africa's past in hermeneutical terms means to move away from a core concern in Western thought, and a strong tendency in empirical scientific methodology, to seek to establish generic universalistic criteria and universal laws based on entrenched presumptions that epistemological concerns and objects of human meditation are the same across historical and cultural experiences (McCaskie 1995, 21). McCaskie for instance draws on an *adapted* hermeneutical reading of cultural practice in precolonial Ashanti to show how ideas and values preside over things through transactions.[12] I find his and Izard's insights, procedures of enquiry and particularly their strategies for abstracting ideas from historical process quite useful. In using Mossi oral history as a main primary source for my research, I try to avoid a reading of traditional practices as static cultural text and rather to show how they are dynamic processes that respond to and accommodate change.

NOTES

1. 'Sovereign statehood' is a Pandora's box that is best left unopened for questioning its primacy risks destabilizing a number of disciplinary certainties, chief among which is the idea that politics is only possible within the state framework.

2. I owe an intellectual debt to Michel Izard not only for his brilliant and inspiring study of the Mossi states but also for generously sharing his archival and field material with me.

3. Colonial oversight of domestic life, in particular its processes of 'enumeration, serialisation, individuation and identification', were part of a design to displace the cost of governance onto African populations. The head and hut taxes were experienced by the latter as particularly oppressive (see J. L. Comaroff [1998, 330]).

4. Patrimonialism thus conceives of political governance as a particular mode that allows political elites to extend their tenure in power while accumulating private gains, whereas allied constituencies looked to gain entry into the state and share in its privileges.

5. See for instance Helman and Ratner (1993, 3–20) and Herbst (2012, 120–44). For a critique, see Martin Doornbos (2002, 805).

6. I'm aware of the different iterations of the 'postcolonial', whether historical, ideological, literary or political. The 'post' in postcolonial Africa does in no way translate in, or enforce discontinuity with, previous institutional and normative imperatives.

7. Critics of the French Republic like to say that if the king has been decapitated, the church has not entirely disappeared but some of its structuring logics, its rigidly

centralized and hierarchized operations and values, have been rather integrated into the republic.

8. MacGaffey (2013, 2–5) provides a useful critique of Africanist approaches to state formation from functionalists to structuralists and politically minded historians.

9. Building on McCaskie's study of state ideology in Ashante, I will show that the state sought to realize this goal by investing fields of knowledge and belief and through an appropriation of the intellectual and spiritual bases of selfhood, social order and collective realization.

10. My example cannot obviously be extrapolated to the whole of Africa. The binary construct—differently rendered in French as *chef de terre* or *chef de village*— is however a widespread model across West, Central and Southern Africa. See for instance Robert Harms (1987) for Central African examples.

11. I show in chapter 5 how rituals constitute a language of signs, symbols, gestures and practices and verbal and non-verbal utterances that abstract common understandings of norms and laws. Their intelligibility is inherently linked to wider cultural conceptualizations that transcend practical reason and material interests. In African political experiences and elsewhere in Europe or Asia, the language of rituals translated the language of legitimacy in so far as members of ritual communities were cognizant of the multiple references of cultural codes. See for instance, for medieval Europe, Michael Saltman (1987, 514–32).

12. Also useful are critiques of structuralist approaches to historical analysis.

Chapter 2

The Trail of the Horse

Stateness, Statelessness and the Ethics of State Inhibition

INTRODUCTION

In the domain of state-building, the originality of West and Central African political trajectories points, historically, to the openness of the political landscape. This particularity is signified by an ethics of hospitality that requires further analysis. This ethics and its likenesses necessarily emerged as a historical mechanism for managing the movements of culturally and ethnically diverse populations. Political openness and the attendant ethics of hospitality were thus constitutive of institutionalized political experimentation that paved the way for subsequent waves of state centralization in the nineteenth century. It is the manifestation of this experimentation that this chapter attempts to grapple with. To do so, I will examine key foundational accounts, legends and myths on state-making and state-building across West and Central Africa. I will focus particularly on the manner in which 'rulers' or 'governors' came to exercise power.

Several dimensions of foundational myths can be extrapolated analogically to mirror European trajectories in some manner: for instance, whether rulers ascended by invitation or imposed themselves by conquest or through superior networks often extending beyond the existing political society. For my purpose, it matters less whether state-builders were foreign or not to the places they came to govern. I am not impressed for instance that the legend of Sundiata may be likened to *I Song of Roland*, a heroic poem based on the Battle of Roncevaux in 778, during the reign of Charlemagne. Nor am I by the accounts that much of Europe too had been under dynasties and dynastic regimes of which the rulers belonged to particular families but were not necessarily natives of the lands that they ruled.

In addition to conflating phenomena, analogies also discourage the otherwise useful task of abstracting from African experiences in elaborating political theories. As Mamdani and others have shown, the analogic approach often strips Africa and things African of their originality. Beyond the fact of the traits found in the European experience, my focus here rests on the manner in which West African societies sought to address specific questions of sovereignty, identity, cohabitation and social change through innovative ways.

This chapter examines the political experiments of the Mamprusi-Dagomba-Mossi states. Mamprusi-Dagomba-Mossi states have several characteristics as well as political trajectories that impose their own questions on state-building, statehood and authority. One aim of this chapter is to underscore what distinguishes these states, including but not limited to the norms and practices that flow from the state as a result of the historically specific expectations of constituents. It is also the aim of this chapter to link the organization and function of state institutions to these specific historical demands and needs. Again, the pertinent questions necessarily have to be framed away from and outside the European and Western political experimentation and experiences generally filed under the rubric of 'Westphalia' as a historical model.

It is my contention that instead of prompting questions like 'Where are the rulers from?' and 'What is the nature of state institutions?' any proper inquiry into African cases should compel different lines of inquiry bearing on the envisaged role of the ruler and the nature of his rule. I am not only interested in the metaphysical representations of such questions but in their contingencies and the circumstances under which they are content *and* signification as political instruments. Contingently, and without irony, I will also consider *why there is no ascendant or paramount ruler in some circumstance and the reasons why that would be entirely ordinary and unproblematic.*

The reasons for the reorientation of the lines of inquiry into the African state is to move away from a problematic taxonomy of the African state (i.e., whether precolonial, 'inchoate', 'early' or another 'developing' form) that postulates cultural inherency and historical immutability or the permanency of the presumed conditions of the African state. The preferred lines of inquiry also reveal the violence of the colonial endeavour to accompany 'the natural course of evolution' of stateless societies by fostering the consolidation of powerful groups organized into 'native states' to support the *logical* acceleration of a process that was to fuse families into lineages and clans and 'tribes' into nations (Lentz 1994, 469).[1]

Colonial obsession with centralized polities as instances of 'civilized' and advanced social structures informed the treatment of different groups. In this view, the Lobi of the Voltaic region present a most baffling case of 'primitivism' and the quintessential example of how pre-state Africa was imagined:

> From an anthropological standpoint the Lobi are very interesting and important, as they represent the most primitive stage in the evolution found among the whole of the tribes falling into what I have termed the Mole (Mossi) group … a stage moreover through which all the other tribes have probably passed (Rattray 1932, 2:425).

They thus proceeded to extract from history justificatory accounts for the need to merge or separate groups and societies. Such an evolutionary view of social formation that leaves untreated the question of authority, order and morality in non-centralized settings tells us only *what these societies were not* (state-like) but little about what they were or what principles underpinned their organization. Hence the need to move toward understandings of social formation that do not presume a priori and without demonstration hierarchically framed and vertically ranked structures among and between social orders. Consequently, the use of the terms 'state', 'state-like' and 'stateless' in this text are only provisional and for conceptual clarity but they are not used analogically to hold any formations as models to be emulated. Indeed, I am not particularly wedded to a state-versus-stateless dichotomy but rather seek articulations of power along a continuum, from a highly centralized to a relatively decentralized structuration within complex horizontal and vertical hierarchy structures.

One key contention of this book is that state and stateless forms emerge from historical necessities and the modes of life and organizations preferred by the political society that establishes order for itself. These necessities are themselves functions of values, morality and ethics but also of their corresponding institutions at the time of inception of order. In this regard, one of my contributions is to examine what state and sovereignty are and how sovereignty manifests itself in various settings.

Among the Mossi, sovereignty as knowledge is indissociable from the representations and performances of a diffuse body of customs and intellectual heritage subsumed in the notion of *rog-n-miki*, which stipulates that social action is necessarily performed in the context of binding forms of interdependency between members of collective units.[2] According to Maurice Bazémo, *rog-n-miki* is 'that force that perpetuates the past. It enacts history. Through [*rog-n-miki*], the past and the future are lived in the present. It is a force that creates durability in favour of a socio-political order the biggest beneficiary of which was the ruling [society]' (1993, 199–200).

Viewed from this perspective, the absence of centralized or state-like institutions does not always convey institutional failure or lack of imagination. It may well be, as has been argued by others, that some societies developed *functional inhibitions* against centralization or that their ways of life and life-forms did not require high concentrations of power. The interesting question thus becomes not why such societies lacked state-like institutions but why, for what purpose and to what end did they develop inhibitions against centralization and the concentration of power.

Consequently, and if and when we take this axiom for granted, why are the resultant provisional hypotheses and assumptions important? The attendant questions might gravitate around the organization of political spheres or spaces; the role of authority; the conditions of legitimacy; the mechanisms of adjudication of justice; and the constitutionality of power.

From a different angle, the Hobbesian truism about centralized sovereign power as an antidote to anarchy must be revisited. It may well be that the absence of centralization opens up spaces as well as creates conditions for historic forms of violence. Yet for the purpose of analytical rigor, we may also wonder if there are forms of violence that flow from the Westphalian state such as it has developed and which would vindicate historical inhibitions to centralization. Whereas in Westphalian common sense, centralized state sovereignty has been opposed to anarchy, my questions are oriented toward the nature of the acceptable forms of violence and the ethics of the attendant expectations. I am also interested in the nature—or more properly the morality—of the dispositions subtending either centralized sovereign power or other forms encountered historically in Africa.

From the above perspectives, it may be said that under the Westphalian model, particular forms of violence, reflected in law, politics and ethics, emerged as indispensable political-economic imperatives. Even so, it is not my claim that the violence of the centralized state remains uniform over time. For instance, upon the advent of capitalism, the desire of merchants, bankers, industrialists and the like to control space for the purpose of access to resources and the production and distribution of goods for private ends led to laws that both assigned ownership and sanctioned property in terms that favoured historic forms of accumulation and concentration of wealth and resources.

To sharpen my questions, I wish to call attention to the fact that 'statelessness' prevented the sort of violence that attended the particular forms of social differentiation under a capitalist sovereign-state order. I recognize that the European model and the circumstances of its rise may not have been present in some of my chosen African examples. This difference does not nullify questions about the rationales and rationalities of alternative models of social organization; for instance, *What was the state built against? Why and under what circumstances did resistance to it emerge?* Some of the relevant questions have been posed by James Scott, but I am interested in a reading of the nature (in terms of social morality and symbolic order), form (aesthetic) and purpose (ethics) of social governance in African contexts of overlapping spatialities and temporalities.

The taxonomic frame state/stateless does not correspond neatly with the *structure*, *process* and *history* of social organizations in the region under consideration. Nor does this taxonomy align with the mechanisms that produced diverse streams of independent communities forced to fashion for themselves new communities or attach themselves to pre-existing ones. In precolonial Moogo, junior segments hived off as lineages expanded; individuals and groups were expelled for misconduct; individuals and groups fled social (in) justice or accusations of witchcraft; competitors for political office and disgruntled kinsmen walked away from their disappointment.

Moreover, given their frequency, interregna modulated the transfer of power, dynastical change and fissionary processes more firmly than regna. Structural transience meant an oscillation between boom and bust and the emergence of new social structures. The Dagara, Kasena, Gurunsi and other 'stateless' groups had nowhere to hide from conquerors. They had no mountain redoubts, no marshes or forests, no caves in which to retreat from state assaults.[3] Their resistance from then on could only be cultural and diffuse rather than open, defiant and institutional.

The conceptual division state/stateless is further undermined by the movement between kingship and chiefship, between regional polities and autonomous ritual units, which forces us to rethink the relationship between authority, knowledge and historical progress whether this relationship is framed within 'evolutionary, functionalist, materialist or Marxist' terms (McIntosh 1999, 3).

Ultimately, the absence of likenesses of the centralized state, or what is called 'statelessness', has to be assessed from a plurality of angles, not least the thrust and logic of related institutions. Two of these institutions are crucial in the present analysis, viz. the *Naam* and *Tenga*, because they help specify the spheres of social action afforded by social formations and organizations. I will spell these out more specifically with reference to the distinctions established in social practice under the two rubrics—which are symbolic realms within which the imperative of power and the social morality underpinning it are specified. The end is not just to point to the diversity of institutional experimentations in this region. It is also to specify the effects of historical attempts at centralization by various agents of states and associated forces of political hegemony. This illustration of social experimentation in this sense helps to highlight practices of power and government as well as the corresponding forms of authority and normative outlook that once characterized political life in the Voltaic region.

For political rulers, the *Naam* provides a form of territoriality defined by ancestral history and migration. The connections that link the *Naam*'s peripheral boundaries do not define the centre of a polity as its political core. Rather, ancestral references to lineage and origin define kingship (not kingdom) and

kinship. Ancestral history and conventions—whether specific episodes referring to pacts concluded with first-comer communities or the consecration
of regalia—give spatial meaning to the territoriality of the *Naam*: 'territory
as related to the *Naam* is the spatial support of words, gestures and acts
performed in contexts of the historical project of [state] creation' (Izard 1992,
515). On the other hand, the necessary preservation of spiritual boundaries
distinguishes territoriality as defined by the *Naam* from its conceptualization
according to the logic of *Tenga*. The latter is the realm of moral control of
social behaviour, sacrifices and 'magic wars [meant] to capture the souls of
the millet' (Izard 1992, 133).

Tenga is an area of spiritual contemplation removed from concerns over
territorial expansion or politics and devoted rather to the preservation of its
own condition. At least this is the view commonly held by promoters of the
Naam. And so the realm of the *Naam* rests on cultural references different
from those of *Tenga*. In reality, the realm of rituals imposes an ideological
limit that inevitably translates into a territorial limit to the expansion of the
Naam order (Izard 1973, 140).

Given the above, statelessness as 'produced' by centralized states was primarily a reformulation of social order on the basis of a rejection of a concentration of power. Centralized formations did not have to create their opposites
but rather structures that could pragmatically be brought under sway, often in
practical readjustment of spiritual boundaries. Further, the type of statelessness we are dealing with in this particular region can be understood in terms
of the production of 'peripheries of the *Naam*'.

If for state bearers this meant that centralized polities could be opposed
to non-centralized groups on the basis of political competency versus super-
stitiously minded groups, the core difference in effect resided in the way in
which different political systems sought to craft and refine a practice of the
Naam as a shared principle.

More crucially, the inhibition against centralization denotes a mechanism of
restraint against political rule that is confined to the domain of 'the political'.
Individual and public morality among decentralized societies were regulated
by a multiplicity of taboos, codes of conduct and various superstitions that
informed spatial occupation and symbolically charged moments of historical enactments that made and remade social meaning and (re)constituted
notions of personhood. These notwithstanding, stateless societies resorted to
governance practices typically found in centralized systems whenever a need
arose—for example, during wars, famines and other disasters—as a way of
stemming contingencies using modes of centralized government.

The ideas above are further developed in chapter 3 in which the notion of
statelessness is examined in relation to a notion of 'the political' where the
latter hinges upon a variable distinction that locates the production of 'the

political' in specific roles, figures and centres. The present chapter is more immediately concerned with demonstrating the diversity of social and political systems in the Voltaic region.

This diversity would tend to point—beyond the dialectics of state/stateless, political sphere/non–political sphere—to a variety of governance structures that underpinned the possibility of debate, divergence and conflict. These mechanisms become most salient when one does away with what Harald Kleinschmidt terms a *residentialist* bias in state-centred history writing. This bias overlooks the importance of migration in the creation and transformation of institutional structures for 'the circulation of objects, especially across the edges of societies, civilizations, and trading regions, is not merely a physical process but is also a movement and displacement of competing conceptions of things, a jostle of transaction forms' (Thomas 1991, 123). This is precisely what the operations of the *Naam*, as a 'traveling' idea across the Voltaic region, illustrate with great insight.

According to common views, state-like societies were characterized by a centralized authority, a bureaucratic machinery and judicial institutions—in short by the existence of a recognizable government. In contrast, stateless societies, often organized around lineage systems, stood out in their conspicuous absence of hierarchy and authority (Fortes and Evans-Pritchard 1940, 5–6). Robin Horton for one sought to problematize this simplistic view by proposing a reformed model. He identified three types of 'statelessness': (1) pure segmentary lineage systems such as the Nuer of Sudan and the Tiv and Igbo of Nigeria; (2) dispersed, territorially defined communities such as the Dagara, the Konkomba and the Nankanese (these tend to constitute federations of diverse lineage groups integrated through cult alliances); and (3) large, compact villages whereby juridical and ritual authority cut across cult societies, age groups and various other organizations (1976, 78).

Horton further articulated a definition of statelessness on the basis of four characteristics, namely (1) low concentration of authority—no particular individual or group that plays the ruler; (2) a rather limited effect of authority roles (when articulated) on most aspects of the life of subjects; (3) authority as derived from, and exercised as, expert knowledge and full profession virtually unknown; and (4) limited space of mandatory resort in the resolution of conflict.

A key point of interest here is the proliferation of political forms. The reasons for decline, collapse and reconfiguration can be located in both the geopolitical context and the internal flexibility of political structures. For these reasons, if there is more to 'segmentation, common descent, secret societies, earth priest, land-owning/landlessness' (Yelpaala 1983, 353) than the absence of centralized authority figures, this has to do with the operationalization of power as culture-specific and the need to manage diversity in a context of disjunctive migration trajectories.

In a regional context marked by the emergence of strong and highly centralized polities, a considerable number of non-centralized formations prevailed, which sought to preserve governance as a collective endeavour. It would seem that the relative flexibility that characterized stateless societies was a result of 'a collective imagination that envisioned society as an ever-changing interplay of statuses and roles'.[4] Such thinking permeated the outlook of the Ninisi, Fulsi, Tallensi, Kipirsi, Kasena, Nunuma, Kusasi, Konkomba, Birifor, Walla, Dagara, Nankanese and other indigenous Voltaic groups.

The groups above shared linguistic and historical links as part of the Gur/ Voltaic linguistic family.[5] For stateless societies, a narrative model puts forward territorial dispersion as the product of the 'disjunctive migration' of lineage segments (Horton 1976, 102–6). Where the Tallensi for instance retrace the central place of the earthpriest (*tengsob* or *tengsoba*; also *chef de terre*, ritual ruler, earth custodian) in imaginings of their earth-begotten ancestors (Fortes 1945, 21–27), the Konkomba recall the emotion of exodus, the forced removal from Dagbon as constitutive of their collective self (Tait 1961, 4).

In the precolonial Volta region, the figure of the earthpriest becomes central to a critical understanding of a different kind of mediation performed at the intersection of the political and all other dimensions of social action and ancestral intervention. The relative importance of the earthpriest was historically a function of their treatment within the polities that formed around and over their ritual rule.[6] In Dagbon, there was limited recognition of the significance of their political role; in Mamprugu the use of ideological constructs by state bearers kept their rule conspicuously distinct from the political order even when the foundation-marriage between a migrant-ruler and the daughter of a cult-priest tied political rule to ritual action.

In Moogo generally, the state actively sought to keep the earthpriests' rule at bay while marginalizing them; the two dimensions of social intervention (the *Naam/Tenga*) were at once made very distinct and reunited in the symbolic marriage of their respective divinities (sky and earth). Institutional variations thus generally affected the position and role of earthpriests across the region. In Gurma (Eastern Burkina), relatively rigid centralization meant that the figure of the ritual ruler was reduced to an honorary function (Ali Ouedraogo, interview, Ouagadougou, 11–30 April 2010).[7] But there are many gaps in the conquest and migration stories and in dynastic succession and also many discrepancies in matrices that sketch how clans and families were related.

These gaps have not been satisfactorily complemented by stories from the sphere of *Tenga* even when these provide plausible alternative accounts—no less coherent than dynastic stories—that render the centralized states' triumphant accounts partial truths that have nonetheless achieved the status of mnemonic, abstract and enduring ideological referents. The material for a work of historical reconstruction exists in abundance for the *most state-like* formations such as Dagbon and Moogo, less so for the least state-like formations. What is needed is a fresh look at this material but also an effort to retrieve meaning from 'silent' sources such as ritual practices.

The constitutive diversity to which I refer above operates in three related arguments that broadly structure the discussion below. First, the distinction between different spheres of social action, namely the realm of the *Naam* as opposed to the realm of *Tenga*, was foundational in the history of social formation in the Voltaic region. The reconciliation of the imperative of power (the *Naam*) and the imperative of social morality (*Tenga*) in institutional experimentations led to a variety of governance forms on a broad decentralized-centralized continuum; the modalities of cohabitation made the many attempts at centralization (Dagbon, Mamprugu, Ouagadougou, Yatenga) particularly difficult. For those who achieved a certain degree of centralization, the very condition of power was this.

To become hegemon required that one succumbed to that which one was able to possess and subdue. Second, the mechanisms, processes and trajectories of political experimentation are a means of illustrating the full range of institutional possibilities between 'stateness' (centralized sovereignty) and 'statelessness' (decentralized governance). To this end, one has to engage social experimentation as the structuration of cultural practice at different historical periods; the formalization of authority necessarily had to be determined by need and circumstance. In fact, the examples provided below show that this concern was a normative outlook common to all Voltaic societies.

Third, the dilemma posed by diversity, plurality and fragmentation—and the manner in which societies elected to resolve these—produced conflictual actualizations of principles of order, authority and interdependence. Ultimately, these were never resolved but rather sublimated, at least in proto-centralized forms, specifically in the elevation of political rule in infinitely elaborate codes and institutions designed to imprint its uniqueness. Before proceeding to these various arguments, I will present the general ecology of social organization of the Mamprugu-Dagbon-Mossi state-system.

THE ECOLOGY OF SOCIAL ORGANIZATION

The people indigenous to Moogo were the Lobi-Dagari, Gurunsi, Samo (Ninise), Nyonyose, Kibsi (Dogon), Kasena, Kusasi and so forth. They spoke languages that mostly belong to the Gur-family.[8] They were loosely gathered into large assemblages through symbolic alliances which could be effectively mobilized in times of stress for mutual protection and defence. Gomkoudougou Kaboré for instance describes the state of 'insecurity' that prevailed among the Ninissi and which led them to request protection from the Mossi against 'barbarian' Gurunsi and Kibsi in the sixteenth century.[9]

During what Kaboré calls 'the first century of the Empire', the Ninissi of Guillougou, unable to cope with the frequent raids of Gurunsi and Kibsi, would have asked Naaba Ouedraogo, Mossi founder, to help them get rid of their turbulent neighbours (Kaboré 1962, 612). Junzo Kawada, who relates Ouagadougou legends on the origin of Mossi domination, discusses similar themes. According to these, indigenous Yoyoose (*nyonyonse*) formulated the wish to be ruled by *nakombsé* migrants. This specific kind of account specifically focuses on the terms of accommodation and integration, of statelessness into state forms as the basis for protection.

In colonial times, the view was widespread that statelessness emerged as a form of escape from the oppressive grip of centralization. S. D. Nash, a district commissioner of northern Ghana during the early period of colonization, explained Tallensi resistance to colonial efforts to 'bring them in' as a result of the neighbouring centralized states' rapacity. He suggested that 'the whole of the Grunshi towns formed, in former times, the happy hunting ground for the Moshi, Mamprusi and Dagomba when in search of slaves … and so fresh is this in the memory of the people … that they run away on the approach of strangers' (Nash 1911 in Allman and Parker 2005, 32).[10] This account, while confirming a trend in West and Central Africa, also obscures the diversity of migration models and the diversity of political forms they generated.

Early French and British administrators expressed exasperation at the *elusive* history and character of the Dagara, Lobi, Kusasi, Gurunsi and other acephalous/stateless populations, in stark contrast with the polished, homogenous, familiar accounts of the centralized states of Ashanti, Dagomba and others.

Read was deeply dissatisfied with his Dagaba informants, who probably kept quiet or else told him stories … that were much less akin to a British officer's notion of history than were the legends and genealogies which the rulers of neighbouring kingdoms put forward. Moreover, the Dagara were not only lacking in historical consciousness, they were not even a united 'tribe', for, in Read's disgruntled words, they had no 'tribal organization' and knew 'no ceremonies of initiation to the tribe'. Just like their French counterparts west of the Black Volta, who complained about the 'anarchie complete' of the 'Dagari', British officers noted repeatedly that in much of the north-west, 'each compound is *practically a law unto itself*'.[11]

British anthropologists thus found the Lobi to be characterized by 'extreme independence' and a 'quick tempered disposition'.[12] Rattray was wrong to label the Lobi 'primitive' for elsewhere autonomy and quick-temperedness are signs of a capacity for self-government, a refusal of any form of sub-ordination and a statement of freedom even when one has to fight for it. Nonetheless, Rattray's observations are useful, not least in showing the ways in which cultural blinkers can distort colonial observers' capacity to discern modes of governance outside the Westphalian model as well as the essentializing and evolutionist outlook that produces a systematic hierarchical value. The British also remarked that the Dagarti-Lobi were prone to 'looting their more peaceful neighbours with impunity.'[13]

The observations above illustrate a long-standing debate on the African state, partly vitiated by a taxonomic battle between evolution scholars and others on the nature of state forms found in precolonial Africa—whether these were kingdoms, chiefdoms, inchoate states, mature states or proto-state systems. The key concern was fundamentally how to write about the state rather than what founding ideas, forms of interactions and mechanisms of social order constituted the bedrock of juridical and ethical sources of African social formations. A bigger issue behind all this was the fact that (1) there remains an overwhelming bias toward a history of states, and (2) consequently there can never be a history of African peoples and societies independent of a history of Europe precisely framed by a history of the state.

The history of Africa as we know it is Eurocentric, state-centred and appended to processes and institutions that developed elsewhere. One common argument for this has been that Europeans developed a propensity to write about those social forms they were familiar with. Consequently, the sort of history they were going to produce would heavily be determined by ideas they carried with themselves.

However, our knowledge of the history of stateless societies has gained in complexity beyond idealized portrayals of 'communalism' or 'tribal democracy' and the distorting view, prominent in conventional history, of their integration into the global political economy of the slave trade as outlying, slave-hunting grounds for centralized societies. Until the 1960s, little historical research was conducted on the Black Volta region compared to the relative attention that was being devoted to the Voltaic states of Mamprugu, Wa, Dagbon, Gonja and Moogo.[14]

From the beginning, the historiography of acephalous societies was very much coloured by accounts of centralized polities. Colonial accounts thus tapped into the foundational myths, legends and tropes of centralized polities; in these, stateless societies were merely a *residue*, an aborted attempt at state building.

A simplistic understanding of statelessness was that it was characterized by (1) conspicuous absence of a head (this absence makes a society susceptible to 'primitivism'), (2) no apparent hierarchy, (3) coercive power not apparently concentrated in one institution or person or group and (4) punishment of crimes not apparently the responsibility of a single judicial institution. There is also a related question of hierarchy in the admission of evidence. Dynastic accounts, genealogies and court chronicles depict a calculated, careful recording of the life of kings and princes.

The sort of artefacts (skins, cowries, bones, amulets and so on) one finds in shrines and other ritual spaces are hardly ever considered. However, precolonial stateless societies were 'characterized by mobility, overlapping networks, multiple group membership and flexible, context-dependent boundaries' (Lentz 1994, 459). They were also characterized by a multiplicity of locations and agents that participated in the production of political goods. These locations encompassed earth cults, clans, descent groups, lineage segments, technician and artisan guilds, age groups, secret societies and so forth. Social action in these various spheres interacted with state power and ideology in different ways: they resisted it, problematized it and interfered with its design (McIntosh 1999, 4).

This view was not uncommon among early anthropologists confronted with the unfamiliar patterns of social organization among stateless societies. In the absence of the expected Western-type jurisprudence and 'a system of rules emanating from an authoritative source in a hierarchically organized political system with government', they found stateless ways to be informed by 'lawlessness, anarchy, and notions of justice and remedy based upon the principle of self-help or the law of the claw and the fang' (Yelpaala 1983, 349).

To define a group as 'stateless' was to lay emphasis on their particular position in a hierarchy of values. The opposite view, such as that adopted by Scott and which consists in saying that statelessness is best understood as a deliberate political strategy, also has its limits. At the least, a number of stateless societies had little interest in or concern for centralized states. The dichotomized opposition between 'state' and 'stateless' thus becomes fairly limited:

1. Stateless societies predate the state.
2. Stateless societies do not always aspire to centralized stateness.
3. Stateless populations not only have to accommodate the state, they have to make sense of statehood for themselves.

In Moogo, what motivated individuals and groups to seek innovative forms of community-life outside the restrictive state model was at once simple and compelling: *subsistence* and *a capacity to construct meaning autonomously*. However, there were also chance movements of population as the multidirectional and multi-linear migration trajectories across Moogo suggest. As intimated in the introduction, social forms outside the state were never entirely isolated, nor were they definitive breaks from the latter; these experiments were often deployed in a dialectical relation to the state. Some even attempted to reproduce communities that were institutionally close to the state form. The Dagara are a good example of this tendency. The allure of the state was its prestige and the traits of civilization attached to it. However, a methodological difficulty of this diversity has been, for historians and anthropologists, to resolve the issue of *intentionality*.

What the gradations of stateness suggest is that we cannot rely on a single explanatory factor for a complex set of social formations. When everybody seeks to build social structures, it seems quite normal to find different degrees and qualities of stateness. This is certainly not to suggest that we need an alternative taxonomy of statehood based on the degree of stateness associated with different institutional arrangements. The idea is rather to show how different operations of authority could produce temporary institutions underpinned by both contingent and ontological factors in collective aspirations.

An important question that comes to mind is whether and *how* statehood was possible under circumstances of statelessness. The institutional development trajectories put forward by Spruyt and Bartelson among others are interesting models to use as comparative frames for a meditation on state formation outside Europe. In taking for instance Spruyt's train of thought with regard to the triumph of the sovereign state over other forms, we can see a similar pattern as partly characteristic of African institutional history: pre-existing, centralized states were consolidated by colonial authorities, and their rulers were made the main interlocutors and mediators of European colonization.

As a consequence of external intervention, the internal dynamics that previously countered and rendered centralization and the accumulation of power uncertain were effectively made inoperative. So even where the multiple and overlapping precolonial authority system had not disappeared, a more efficient system was mobilized by the colonial state in levying taxes, enforcing the conscription of foot soldiers and muscle for forced labour and deploying the coercive potential of its administrative and military power.

In colonial and postcolonial Burkina Faso, some of the characteristics of statelessness described by Scott—namely, resistance to the repressive policies of the centralized state such as forced labour, head taxes and conscription—were responsible for mass migration toward the Ivory Coast and the Gold Coast, and mass flight into *aires-refuges*, outlying areas outside the control and the exactions of the Mossi kingdoms and later the colonial administration and national governments (Breusers 1999, 447–67; Echenberg 1975).

Asiwaju notes that flight from colonial oppression was merely 'a continuation of the tradition of politically motivated migrations of the preceding epochs' (Asiwaju 1976, 579) through which ordinary people expressed dissatisfaction with oppressive authorities.

In fact, engineered sedentarization was a very uncertain and unstable endeavour for centralized states given the permanent threat of individual and collective exodus.

Stateless societies were characterized by intense intermingling of cultures, languages (Dagara/Lobi) and intermarriages.[15] In contrast to centralized states, the potential for coercion was relatively contained in part because of the difficulty in isolating and expanding political mechanisms outside the bounds of the multi-layered authority structures in which they were inbuilt without upsetting balanced, horizontal hierarchy arrangements or causing fission. In contrast, the proliferation of taboos, totems and prohibitions was a compensatory strategy for the absence of institutions of coercion.

Given the above, the categories of collaboration, alliance, resistance and rejection are not necessarily and always appropriate when attempting to understand non-state forms *in relation* to the state. For instance, the anti-state dynamic becomes crucially important when we try to make sense of the formation of the Tallensi, the Kasena (Kusasi), the Lobi and the Gurunsi—in other words, places where states have always struggled to extend hegemonic rights.

The state/stateless dichotomy becomes even more limited when one tries to make sense of the cultural dimensions of the political dynamics internal to so-called stateless societies. It is even less convincing an explanatory frame when one engages with modes of interaction that govern first-comer societies among each other. If elsewhere hills, mountains, deserts, mangrove marshes and forests were the catchment areas of stateless, non-state and extra-state societies, in Moogo the physical morphology did not allow for the constitution of 'natural enclaves' that could evolve in isolation from state forces.

My inclination for an exploration of the operations of authority, rather than power strictly speaking, is partly informed by the fact that historically, the level of concentration of power was contingent upon circumstances that were constantly in flux but did not always exhaust the basis of authority.

Whereas power could be vertical or horizontal and its exercise deliberative, consultative or exclusive, what inspired and enabled its recognition was the possibility of a permeation of social thought in the normalization process of authority. If the exercise of legitimate authority is to be governed by substantive values and norms, then it '[cannot] be defined by reference to the procedure by which authority is exercised but *only by reference to its legitimizing norms*' (Yelpaala 1983, 367; emphasis added), hence the need, ultimately, to transcend a dualistic view of two categories of intervention made at once antagonistic and complementary: one that protects, heals and restores and one that appropriates and destroys.

SOCIAL FORMATION AT THE INTERSECTION OF MOBILITY AND ENCOUNTER

For the Voltaic states, a political history of *encounter* necessarily meant that the organization, distribution and circulation of authority was subject to the fact of mobility as a defining feature. However, a residentialist bias in the analysis of social formation has meant that political history has shown little interest in addressing the movement of people as a subject for study in its own right. 'On the contrary, there has been an almost perverse refusal … to consider the social technological and logistical mechanics of human movement' (Adams, Van Gerven, and Levy 1978, 523).

Migration was not just central to social formation in the Voltaic region; it was the very condition for the possibility of *governance* as a mediation of difference between wandering individuals and groups on one hand, and their diverse indigenous hosts on the other. This suggests that we need to pay more attention not only to the relationship between state formation and migration but also to the movement of people and ideas as generative of change.

The dynamics between memory of events that might have, or might never have, taken place and historicity, subjectivity and the possibility for different life-forms requires further reflection and analysis. Strangers are at once central and marginal to social formation in West Africa. Migrants, refugees, wives, slaves, captives and bondsmen, traders, craftsmen, potters, blacksmiths, bards, warriors, scholars and pilgrims, political dissidents and others were at times subjects and at times conditions; they were structurally woven into sociopolitical transformations throughout history.

In fact, the West African past is largely defined by ceaseless movement and a subsequent mixing of peoples of various origin, capacity, and condition:

> The circulation of objects, especially across the edges of societies, civilizations, and trading regions, is not merely a physical process but is also a movement and displacement of competing conceptions of things, a jostle of transaction forms (Thomas 1991, 123 in Haour 2013, 11).

This is precisely what the Mossi example illustrates with great insight. Migration inflects an ambiguous yet useful measure of time, a reckoning of overlapping temporalities that mark past and present experiences. It is therefore best understood as a trope made to signify many things for 'past events are made comprehensible through the framework of movement, and migration used as a metaphor for the creation of new centres of settlement' (Haour 2013, 3). For this very reason, 'whether … traditions of origin are factually correct seems less interesting than the message they convey about understanding the past' (3).

In a recent archaeological engagement with liminality, Haour explores the ways in which 'communities create order' particularly with regard to the treatment of *those who are of, but not in society*. One could equally turn the question around and ask how outsiders shape the societies they encounter.

The migrationist angle shows that although there might have been eco-logical, economic, social or territorial motives to population movements in the Voltaic region, the ideological imperative, more specifically memories of migration, played a far more important role in shaping the political and social structures of Voltaic societies.

Even in places where the encounter migrant/first-comer binary did not lead to centralized organizations, the ideology of the *Naam* still served to concep-tualize and demarcate areas of competence and intervention in ways similar to those that prevailed in centralized structures.

The fact that migrations were conceptualized—in the subjective conscious-ness of the *Naam* holders—as the ideological reasoning and a justification for their right, their vocation for political rule made the economic imperative in particular less important. In this sense, migration memories do not necessarily have to derive from a migration that actually took place. Where migration and the condition of *stranger* could have constituted a disadvantage, in the Mossi case for instance, such an origin and its attending memories constituted the ideological foundation of their social organization.

There is a common, recurrent reference to an 'eastern' origin of Mamprugu-Dagbon-Nanun-Mossi states which is symptomatic of a certain attachment, within communities with a centralized rule, to the idea of an outside, alien origin (Moogo Naaba assistant, interview, 15 March 2006; Goungha Naaba, interview, Ouagadougou, 12 March 2006).[16] In reality, there was no single motivation and no single route for migration trajectories. The Dagara for instance generally contend they left a vague and metaphorical *tengkor* (old country) for a northwest direction or the opposite direction or from one des-tination back to a point of departure (Lentz 1994, 464–65). Similar stories of multidirectional migration patterns prevail across the region and they point to a key feature that has to do with the cognate dimension of mobility and migration.

The latter aspect is salient in the distinction of migration as a process of thought patterns generated by a 'nomadic mindset'. A useful conceptual tool in apprehending the explanatory links between migrations, perceptions, mem-ories and historical change could be what Kleinschmidt terms 'migrationisms … [as a set of] perceptions belonging to the cognitive environment of groups that transmit memories or migrations. They necessarily belong to the space of communication, of retrospectively commemorating groups, and have nothing in common with the attitudes and perceptions of migrants' (2003, 26–27).

The migrationist perspective takes on the question of change through an exploration of memories of migrations in the subjective consciousness of migrants. It reveals the central significance of the conceptual field of migration in political and social theory. As a predominantly archaeological mode of enquiry, it has a pragmatic quality far removed from the heroic generalizations of nineteenth-century ethnology and offers valuable insights into our interpretation of ethnographic data beyond the barren battle between evolutionism and diffusionism that raged in the early twentieth century (Adams, Van Gerven, and Levy, 1978, 487).

The migrationist perspective is based on the premise that migration memories do not necessarily have to derive from a migration that actually took place. In other words, perceptions of migration associated with the memories or experiences of previous generations are, for later generations, a valid source of historical knowledge even in places where corroborating dates and facts are lacking.

Alongside instances of migration memories historically and empirically supported by existing records, migration memories become rooted in the collective imagination. Migration memories are also often the object of deliberate and informed deletions within a collective pursuit of given identities (Kleinschmidt 2003, 23–24). The transaction of memories and the imprint of identity in the collective psyche appeal to exploratory research into the cognitive make-up of a group and society. Migration stories, settlement histories, stories of origin and so forth, therefore, form the basis for a critical understanding of the subjective consciousness of migrants and descendant communities.

THE VOLTAIC REGION: A COMMON CULTURE-AREA

As intimated above, the settlement history of West and Central Africa is replete with binary constructs of autochthony and foreignness that pertain to a long-standing history of migrations which have defined the cultural, social and institutional make-up of societies throughout the region.

The rise of what was to become the Mamprusi-Dagomba-Mossi states system took place in a context of mounting sociopolitical effervescence partly due to the decline of the greatest empire around the Niger Bend, the Songhai Empire on the one hand, and European, particularly Portuguese, commercial expansion on the other. At the same time, the Fulbe movement reorganized trading structures and networks in West Africa, with consequences for emerging Voltaic states from the middle of the eighteenth century onward with the growing importance of trade centres such as Ouagadougou, Bobo-Dioulasso and Ouroukoÿ and later other sociopolitical transformations (Mauny 1961, 447–48, 514; Lydon 2009; Lovejoy, 1980). Toward the middle of the sixteenth century, the emergence of the Gonja kingdom was the result of similar dynamics that brought a Malian cavalry force into the interstitial zone lying between the emerging Mossi states and the Akan kingdoms.[17]

The Mamprusi-Dagomba-Mossi states system comprises a southern group which includes Mamprugu (Mamprusi), Dagbon (Dagomba) and Nanun (Nanunmba, Nandom) and a northern group which includes Ouagadougou, Yatenga, Tenkodogo (Tãnküdgo) and a number of smaller formations such as Bulsa, Busu, Boussouma, Fada N'gourma, Ratênga, Tatênga, Zitênga and Yako.[18] Related to these are a number of non-centralized formations that share broad cultural, linguistic, sociological, physiological and ecological traits. It is a cultural area connected by thick strands of interactions. In fact, it could be termed a *community of the* Naam united by a common ancestor: Na Gbewa. It is a region broadly defined by a 'common fund of political ideas' through the movement of ideas and through a mechanism of *saturation* (Curtin et al. 1978).

If the common link is undeniable—as the Mamprusi see it: '*Ti zaa nyela yimu* [We are all one]' (Davis 1987), the intricate web of connections, at the linguistic, cultural and ritual levels is blurred by different mediation strategies of the first-comer/late-comer dichotomy. Drucker-Brown describes this process as a continuous link 'fashioned on the model of a filial tie, replicated in multiple courts, which is characteristic of the Mamprusi polity' (Drucker-Brown 1989, 485–501). However, her analysis of the replication and transmission of the *Naam* as a convection model that effects a circulatory movement within the polity is too narrow to capture the process of expansion of the *Naam* beyond the confines of Mamprugu. In fact, when local chieftaincies stop returning the *Naam* back to the centre, the circle is, so to speak, broken.

In the cluster of societies culturally united by the philosophy of the *Naam*, Mamprugu was the substrate, the source of a common fund of ideas. However, in the absence of archaeological research to fill existing gaps, some of the linkages between a Mamprugu core and satellite states across the Voltaic region remain conjectural (Drucker-Brown 1989, 485–501).

For one thing, there were variations in the form, content and importance of rituals performed in the installation, the legitimation and preservation of office. There were also linguistic variations (*Naam/Tenga* in Moogo and *Nam/Tengan* in Mamprugu-Dagbon). There were further variations in the sequence of events that led to the creation of key states, the actors involved and the places of action. However, the historical junctions, the corresponding patterns of political settlement and the structural consistence in models of integration are rather overwhelming and can only point to a common origin as well as a replication process achieved through migration, conquest, alliances and other frameworks of exchange.

In Mamprugu, Dagbon, Nanun, Tenkodogo, Ouagadougou and Yatenga, recognized as the most centralized, therefore most known Voltaic states, the making of a chief follows a very similar trajectory: it is a journey that turns an aspirant (ruler), 'captured' by earthpriests, into a sovereign after he has gone through multiple humiliation trials and through a transformative process of purification, disintegration and reconstitution. A crucial aspect of enthronement/enskinment is *the transfer of sovereignty* from 'the sphere of rituals' to that of politics, but this transfer is subject to numerous conditions for one does not *just* emerge as a chief, one is *made* a chief. In Dagbon, the established expression is *n'legi na* (to make someone a chief) or *nam le bu* (making *naam*; of enskinment).

In all the different kingdoms and in the decentralized polities, political incumbency is mediated by earthpriests. To equate this transfer to a secularization of power would however be misleading for it would be a retrospective reading of a precolonial practice. The constitutive ritual bond was never broken. In fact, a cruel or unjust Naaba could be discredited and stripped of his legitimacy. The point of the above is a common concern, in the complex transfer of sovereignty, to reiterate the principle of interdependency that underpins state/society, *Naam/Tenga*, the political and the non-political.

Archaeologists and historians have used the term 'interaction areas' to describe interconnections among different cultural regions, particularly regions that exhibit varying levels of internal resemblances. They contend that 'the side diffusion of similar tools, architectural forms and art styles within these areas are probable indicators of contact hence interdependence' (Wolf 1982, 58). The same could be said of sociopolitical forms that extend and develop beyond the confines of a given region, encompassing political structures and incorporating groups linked by ceremonial allegiance and kinship ties: 'Populations impinged upon other populations through permeable social boundaries, creating intergrading, interwoven cultural and social boundaries' (Wolf 1982, 71). The 'discovery' of unknown and isolated societies, a consequence of European exploration of parts of the Old World in Africa and Asia, occludes the history of these interconnections that are a testimony to the extended networks of interaction and the continued flow of exchange that characterizes world history. Wolf for one bemoans academia's failure to adequately acknowledge this phenomenon.

> Thus, the social scientist model of distinct and separate systems, and of a timeless precontact ethnographic present, does not adequately depict the

situation before European expansion; much less can it comprehend the world-wide system of links that would be created by that expansion (1982, 71).

The conditions that enabled these linkages are best captured through an account that stresses the centrality of migration in the history of social formation. In the Voltaic region, if the most predictable direction was from political centres to peripheries, and usually intersecting trading routes, migration also took the opposite direction and many tangents. This cultural area was not necessarily a homogenous, compact zone of contiguous territorial units but rather one interspersed by non-state zones such as Lobi, Dagaaba (Dagara), Gurunsi and Kusasi territories.

In fact, if centralization is to be used as a criterion for assessing institutional dispositions and preferences, there were zones of intense stateness (Dagbon, Moogho); zones of attenuated stateness so to speak (Mamprugo, Nanun); zones of transition and trading centres or junctions (Saalaga, Bobo Dioulaso) where salt, gold, slaves and other commodities were exchanged; and stateless zones or territories where states never managed to thrive. This translated into a very wide range of possible sovereignties, articulated by the need to entrust specific functions to specific individuals and institutions and the related necessity to preserve the interdependency of the multiple domains of social action. I expand below on this diversity and related institutional imaginaries.

An important point I also develop is the possibility of reading fission through migration the other way around—in other words, to see the expanse of the *Naam* model across northern Ghana and Burkina Faso as indicating a constitutive unity that was socially heterogeneous but which provided texture to the possibility of cohabitation through ritualized alliance, intermarriage, incorporation and assimilation as in Ouagadougou and in other polities (MacGaffey 2013, 9, 12–23).[19]

To think of state formation within a region rather than in its fragmented manifestation thus removes the imperative of classification of state/stateless and displaces focus onto the form and content of internal authority and modes of governance. In a context whereby the defining characteristics of foundational rule were mobility and fragmentation, a diversity of political systems emerged as migrant-rulers attempted to monopolize the production, the interpretation and the circulation of normative ideas. This desire came up against the production of norms and order, the capacity for corporate indigenous groups to interfere with the interpretation of power and authority. The tendency therefore to isolate the practice of 'politics' as separate from other spheres of action becomes analytically and historically flawed. I expand on this point in chapter 3. Fission also operated as antidote against excessive concentration of power in the hands of a specific individual or groups:

Fission is symptomatic of conflict, dominance, attempted dominance, and rejection of suppression or oppression and is an attempt to contain the stresses and antagonism within the social and political system and maintain the internal consistency and totality with the greatest amount of freedom possible. It is precisely to save the non-centralized state from the abuses of power and anarchy that fission provides an important option since in these systems the sources and objects of conflict are often corporately based (Yelpaala 1983, 356).

As the Mossi say, 'The *Naam* has to split so that it can survive'. Mobility thus produced various challenges for states' capacity to retain subjects but it was also symptomatic of productive fragmentation processes that gave rise to a variety of social structures. At the same time, multiple factors—local, regional, global and economic as well as political—converged in the creation of a world of opportunities for economic and political entrepreneurs alike.

Specifically, prominent formations such as Ashanti, Gonja and Songhai arose and waned but their fate was seldom determined by the development of the state as a specific institutional model.[20] Equally, founding histories provided multiple motivations for collective exodus. People moved around for political and non-political reasons alike such as flight from conquest or subordination or in a search for game, land, more clement climes, a just community and so forth. Tauxier for instance contends that the Dagari on both sides of the Black Volta came together as a group following persistent Mossi conquest campaigns (1912, 360–61). Delafosse (1912) attributes a similar formation process to many stateless Voltaic societies.

GENERIC CONSTRUCT: OF STRANGER-KINGS AND ACCOMODATING NATIVES

From a ruler's viewpoint, the political history of the Voltaic region is reduced to a single revolutionary idea, the *Naam*. Consequently, a common overarching feature is the fundamental contraposition between the *Naam* and *Tenga*—in other words, between the substance/source of political authority and *tengsobondo*, or ritual control over land and space.

The basic, generic model of social formation in Mamprugu-Dagbon-Moogo, in its centralized and less centralized forms, was articulated by a common narrative; its great variations translated exigent anxieties spawned by specific ecological, economic and structural configurations. The story typically begins with a wandering hunter or migrant coming from 'somewhere east' who decides to settle at a particular place inhabited by indigenous groups, generally agriculturalist but also hunters.

In Mamprugu, Dagbon and Nanun, the migrant typically marries the daughter of the moral leader of the putative autochthons, the earthpriest. The trope of the civilizing outsider or the adventurous hunter looking for game is filled with symbolic references, not least the ethics of hospitality that enabled the ritual incorporation of a range of others.

In Moogo, ritual alliance also occurred at a more abstract level in the union between the Mossi divinity *Wende* and the earth divinity *Tenga*, which gave birth to *Wennam*. This original encounter was productive of countless binaries, namely a distinction between migrant/autochthon, first-comer/late-comer, political rule/ritual governance, patrilinearity/matrilinearity and eventually citizen/subject. Model variations tend to follow ecological specificities; different permutations of the basic juxtaposition are found among the Zande, the Luba, the Kuba, the Bamana, the Alur, and other African societies. In these different examples, earth custodians are the backbone of an original (com)pact that legitimizes a political arrangement in which the position of earthpriests remains a sacred link to the ancestors (personal communication with Joseph Ki-Zerbo, March 2006).[21]

If in the context of limited resources foundational stories become valuable currency needed to shore up claims of primacy with respect to land, roles, entitlements and rights, they primarily served as mnemonic subterfuges to lock in ideas of self, subjectivity and direction—in relation to *where* one comes from—with wider processes of displacement and interactions. Under such circumstances, it is hardly surprising that migrant communities spoke in many tongues for stories of encounter and exodus and negotiated settlement with stories of rebellion juxtaposed in the same narratives—a trope similar to Bakhtin's heteroglossia, it often thrives in feedback processes between written and oral accounts (Bakhtin 1981).

Migrants invested these stories with a charter-like dimension as much as a flexible template capable of integrating everyday change, whether a crisis or innovation. Founding charters in particular style sociopolitical roles to promote or justify specific models, from vague references to pre-existing, 'ritualized', pre-state orders to discourses of revolution and innovation. Fortes for instance describes a typical amalgamation narrative:

> On the one side are those that claim to be descendants of immigrants from parts of the country other than their present habitats. On the other side are communities that claim to be autochthonous inhabitants. The two groups are found in every tribe, including the Mossi, Mamprusi and Dagomba, living side by side and indistinguishable from one another by broad cultural or linguistic criteria. Many of the immigrant communities claim descent from forbears of the Mamprugu ruling stock. Though now wholly amalgamated with the alleged aboriginal inhabitants, they have certain ritual observances and a system of

chieftainship similar to those of the Mamprusi ... the institution distinctive of the indigenous communities is the office of 'earth custodian.' This ritual office, involving priestly functions in connection with the cult of the Earth, is found among many West African peoples from the Senegal to the mouth of the Niger. In the Voltaic region it is the exclusive prerogative of autochthonous communities (1945, 6–7).

Fortes in turn conceptualized this trend as 'the dynamics of constant movement' (Fortes 1967). The Voltaic pattern, in other words the constitutive opposition between the *Naam* and *Tenga*,

was built into Mossi-Dagomba social structure and that its raison-d'être at the political level was to drive away from the seat of government certain sections of the population, e.g., supporters of possible competitors, or rejected candidates for chiefship. The immediate result of these expulsions was the reduction of tension and therefore the maintenance of political stability in the state (Illiasu 1971, 105).

The process of fission, spread and replication of political systems was neither new nor unique to the history of West Africa. Central polities would fragment and chiefly domains would break up and reform in a continuing process of fission and reconstitution. Thus Dagomba traditions have something to say about the creation of Nanunmba (Nanun) and in turn Mamprusi traditions about the foundation of its closest Mossi offshoot, namely, Tenkodogo. According to Dagomba traditions, Nmantambo, one of the brothers of Sitobu, ruler of Dagbon, went 'away from his anger' to establish Nanun (Tamakloe 1931, 14).

A similar explanatory frame is associated with the formation of the cluster of northern Mossi states, namely, Yako, Ratênga, Tatênga, Zitênga, Busu and other satellite polities that broke off from the Yatenga core. Fundamentally, in the regional aetiological stock, political schism provoked by disputes between brothers and male agnates, that is, candidates contending for position, served as a recognizable narrative metaphor. Dispute and delegation become the conceptual rupture that instituted difference in alliances, affiliation, cultural practice, rules of succession and inheritance, and hierarchical arrangements, among other things. As one informant explained,

There was a hierarchy of status between Mossi rulers: first came the Yatenga *naaba* (*rima* or 'sovereign'), then came the *nabisi* (princes), then *kombere* (provincial chiefs) and then the *tansobnanamse*, etc. In the authenticity of things, the chiefs of Ratênga, Tatênga, Busu, etc., are *kombere* who depended on the Yatenga Naaba. They could be his sons or brothers of men he trusted which he appointed at the various frontiers and corners. Nowadays, they are more or less independent. They can come to pay respect to the *naaba* or can also choose not to come and greet. But if they do come to pay respect, then they have to doff their hat. Even if these states were independent, if there arose an issue which they felt was too complex, they would still come and consult the *naaba* for a solution. In this way, there were still certain relations (Ila Ouedraogo, interview, Ouahigouya, 14 April 2010).

This is a narrative line designed to validate the premises of hierarchy while explicating the normative basis of fission:

It is axiomatic in this system; as Mamprusi say, that 'two chiefs cannot reside in a single place. If they do, one must be stronger'. Thus, the king who embodies *naam* directly received from Na Gbewa is stronger. But if he is to bring forth other chiefs, these must exercise *naam* at a distance. In order for *naam* to be effective it must be spatially distributed (Drucker-Brown 1981, 118).

It would then seem that the principle of fission was built into the very structure of the *Naam*; it ensured the preservation of the original model while providing particular *naams* for the many contenders. However, triumphant state-centric accounts can be read in reverse in a way that shows the particular difficulty that processes of fission, amalgamation and replication denoted even within the internal logic of the master-narrative.

First, it can be read to explain the fact that many state projects never actually came to fruition. Second, conceptually speaking, the state-centric account is singularly ill-equipped to account for a high level of institutional fluidity and transformation for it causes a need to conceptualize stability as an end result of social disintegration even when there are multiple ways to read instability differently. There are two possible ways to read fluidity here. On one hand, a continuity thesis—favoured in dynastic accounts—contends that institutional instability is the marker of a state that expands while reproducing itself: the disparate units are linked up by similarities in structure and in logic of formation. A second possibility makes of mutation a necessary mechanism of survival in the midst of contingency, precariousness, conflict, external influences and so forth. Even the strongest confederation could in fact be undone when the *naam* alliances ceased to be a reliable framework for survival.

Even as it travelled across regions and mutated into complex forms, the *Naam* model remained an ideological force that informed the cultural transformation of the societies it encountered. If interactions were limited between metropole and peripheries of the *Naam*—ritual relations between Mamprusi and Moogo were discontinued in the nineteenth century—the continuous reproduction of the *Naam* model embedded and validated a broad regional cultural experience. Its characteristics became, over time, part of the conservative force that defined and organized the political landscape of the region. However, the Mamprusi reference has to be seen as conceptual rather than historical for narrative divergences abound with regard to processes of formation of satellite states, in particular their fissionary sequence.

At any rate, the precedence of Mamprugu as core-polity has the greatest credence in most accounts.[22] Its immediate offshoots were Dagomba (Dagbon) and Tenkodogo (Tenkdugu) from which sprang Ouagadougou, Yatenga and Fada N'gourma.

Mossi conquerors operated as non-pastoral nomads who held the technological advantage of the horse, ease of mobility, a novel conception of social organization (the *Naam*) and a new god (*Wende*). More importantly, the waves of disparate horse-riding groups that entered Moogo from the Mamprugu-Dagbon states could be brought together on the basis of the common genealogical charter of the *Naam* and the appeal of a particular sense of mission to lead.

The account above comes down to this: state-making was a craft, an imported technology introduced on horseback by political entrepreneurs (Echenberg 1971, 241–43; Wilks 1985, 470).[23] What is implied is that the contrast between the relatively peaceful expansion of the Mossi and the relatively limited and at times violent expansion of the Mamprugu-Dagbon states is the result of different settlement histories as far as stranger-autochthon dynamics go. In any case, the particular circumstances that oversaw the encounter between migrants-frontiermen and indigenous groups, in particular the terms of violence and negotiation, cooperation and flight, are still not well known (Kohler 1971, 25; Pageard 1963, 45–46).

THE POLITICAL ECONOMY OF A STATE FORMATION

The context of state formation in the Voltaic region was one of limited economic resources given the nature of the climate and soil fertility with limited possibility of exploiting natural resources outside a few exceptions such as iron ore in Yatenga. Trade provided a valuable resource for centralized polities. Political rulers allied with mobile and transnational Hausa and Mande traders and literate Muslim traders who provided legal, financial and other services (MacGaffey 2013, 8).

Although the establishment of European trading posts on the Gold Coast did not at first have direct major consequences, the intensification of trade and trade-related activities (slave-hunting, raiding) between forest and savannah gave a boost to junction-cities such as Kumasi and Djenne and later Salaga, hence on the development of the Mamprusi-Dagomba-Mossi states. In particular, Yarse (Mande) and Hausa traders became key allies of state builders (Levtzion 1968, 8; Ferguson 1973; Izard 1969; Duperray 1985, 179–212).

Were the Mossi, as contends Tauxier, 'propelled by a powerful drive of expanding conquest' northward (1912, 459)? Were they driven by the desire to control the kola nut trade? According to Fage (1964) and Skinner (1964, 9), the restoration of imperial power in the Niger valley removed an important source of profit for the slave-raiding Mossi while putting effective limits on their expansion northward.[24]

By 1300, the Dyula were already settled in Begho southeast of Kong at Bono-Mansu seventy miles away (Fage and Tordoff 2001, 91; Grey 1975). It is not however clear when trade began although Delafosse (1912) links the introduction of Islam in Ghana in the eleventh century to that of the kola nut trade in northern Ghana long before that (Boahen 1961, 8–14). The development of trade in the kola nut presumably impacted the sociopolitical as well as religious dynamics of the region.

A common story goes that the Mossi thus needed new sources of slave supplies farther south. The pursuit of raiding outlets is however a limited explanatory framework given Illiasu's detailed exposition of the Mossi-Dagomba migratory patterns. Illiasu contends that these migrations were overwhelmingly informed by factional conflicts among power contenders. Thus Gbewa migrated from Grumah to Pusiga, leading a considerable following to Sana (Sanga), south of Fada N'gourma and then effectively conquered the Busansi and Kusasi. Gbewa's sons expanded the political core in subsequent struggles. Tohugu moved from Pusiga to Mamprugu and Sitobu from Pusiga to Yendi Dabari while Nmantambo moved from Bagale to Bimbila. These relocations all resulted in political formations, either as extensions of existing states or as new political foundations (Rattray 1932, 340–41).

The same pattern applies to the creation of the formations of Boulsa, Boussouma, Conquitênga, and Yako in Moogo (Skinner 1964, 10; Tauxier 1912, 55–75). New states were not just dismemberments of ruling lineages; they were also the making of unsuccessful candidates removed from the competition for power, such as marginalized brothers prone to exile, in order for them to realize their 'political call', which would be that of state-making wherever possible. This process meant that the *Naam* model could be found in various forms along a long spectrum of highly centralized to decentralized polities.

GRADATIONS OF STATENESS

Different modes of deployment and uses of tales of origin are crucially central to my argument. In the Mamprusi-Dagomba-Mossi region (I also use 'the Voltaic region' to refer to this zone) virtually all groups trace their origin to Mamprugu. This is true for all categories and types of states, political communities and centralized and non-centralized societies found in the region.

There were greater and weaker degrees of sovereignty; in other words, many core centres from which power emanated in concentric circles such that new peripheries overlapped and interpenetrated given that boundaries were neither rigidly demarcated nor stable.

The trajectories presented below are not meant to suggest an accumulative process whereby social formations moved from less centralized to more centralized forms. Far from that, centralization and decentralization were a function of particular historical circumstances: the same states could experience both processes at different historical periods. What I sketch below is a rather simplified account of state and authority types. Despite a dearth of historical accounts from stateless populations, there is something reassuringly familiar about the relatively abundant dynastic and state accounts. In what they depict in elaborate detail as much as what they leave unsaid—the heroic origin of the state being constantly reaffirmed, its principle of superiority firmly set—these produce narrative figures and tropes that often work as a substitute for actual facts. From these, it is possible to glean in turn diversity out of homogenizing discourses and resistance out of consensual rhetoric.

Early scholars of the African state, particularly in the West African region, worked on the basis of a distinction between kingship and religion and between politics and economics informed by the Weberian model that framed their perspective and their working questions. Some of these views have, however, been thoroughly revised. McCaskie (1995) for instance very convincingly brings belief as a metaphysical, ritual dimension of political rule to bear on the normative, spiritual and constitutional responsibilities of kings. But the Ashanti model was perhaps unique in the way it was framed and refined within an understanding of social realization through accumulation and status display.

If loose decentralization and the alliance of autonomous entities seem to have been the most common Voltaic model, the emergence and fall of the city-states of Segu, the Sokoto Caliphate, the Theocracy of Masina, the Mali Empire and other authority systems suggests a greater institutional diversity than has thus far been recognized in the history of state formation in Africa. Centralization seems to have occurred in response to a need for a concentration of power to capture trading opportunities, pre-empt external aggression, reinforce internal security and confront ecological and environmental change.

The state was structurally constrained by a requirement to store foodstuffs, stable horses and maintain people in fixed places. It was thus necessarily a short-lived experience, and it tended to be strongest around royal residences and villages. There were therefore very physical impediments to state expansion. These included the difficulty of traveling long distances within reasonable amounts of time due to uneven terrain and a lack of surfaced routes and reliance on basic means of transportation—horses were available only to a few— with limited access to fodder.

Moogo has largely a flat terrain with little variation. This enabled a coherent cultural-historical area. Opportunities and constraints were externally induced (this was the case with trade) but change could equally result from attempts to operationalize ideas, namely the Mossi's relentless attempt to realize the full ideal of the Naam.

On the other hand, decentralized authority structures could consolidate into centralized structures. The existence, among the Dagara, of a clan of *naayiile* (people of the chief's house) might in fact attest to an earlier experience of centralization. Resistance to centralization could well have developed out of the deterioration of the latter (Rattray 1932, 427). Like the order of elders among the Mossi, the *naayiile* had no actual political functions attached to their title. However, theirs was a crucial symbolic and moral role for they mirrored the authority of departed ancestors in a moral order configured to be governed by an intergenerational panel, so to speak, made of retired, incumbent and aspiring chiefs. Below I present a number of formations that emerged and developed variously between the fifteenth and nineteenth centuries. They share a common association with the *Naam* but developed differently according to different permutations of the *Naam/Tenga* dichotomy.

MAMPRUGU: THE CORE STATE

In Mamprusi foundational stories, the episode of an immigrant-ruler invited by an earthpriest to become rainmaker is recurrent. The most widespread foundational version recounts the saga of mounted conquerors from Fada N'gourma (in present-day Burkina Faso) who invaded the area between the Gambaga ranges to the north and the Nasia River to the south after having defeated autochthonous populations between the fifteenth and sixteenth centuries. At any rate, ruling *nabisi* (princes) trace their origin to Na Gbewa, the founder and first *nayiri* (king).

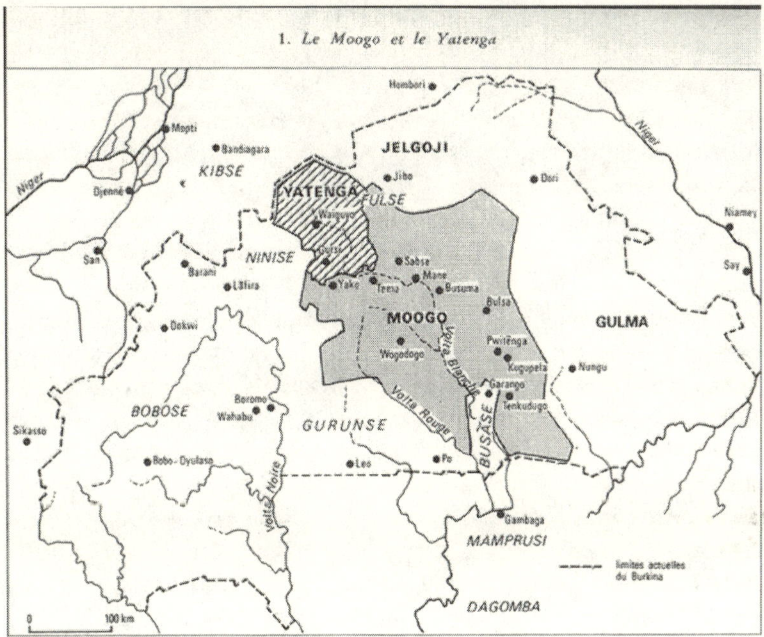

Figure 2.1:   Yatenga and Ouagadougou in the Sixteenth Century
Source: Izard, 1985.

A political order was constituted around the descendants of migrant-conquerors, the *nadema* (people of chiefs) while earthpriests were accorded the status of *na kpamamba* (elder) and the rest of the population became *tarima* (commoner-subjects; Rattray 1932, 546). Nalerigu was the seat of power and the residence of the nayiri; it was surrounded by the paramountcies of Kpasenkpe, Janga, Wungu, Yunyoo and Kurugu. Like Ouagadougou and Ouahigouya, Nalerigu was a thriving royal court organized around an intricate administrative structure.

The nayiri ruled with the support of a range of elders and servants; they included the *tarana* (the king's spokesperson), the *wudana* (chief warrior, linguist), the *sakpari* (the chief's personal assistant), the *maasu* (chief councillor), the *akara* (chief servant) and the *sakpanaba* (chief guard and executioner; Drucker-Brown 1975, 44–74). Most accounts concur on the fact that Nalerigu exerted limited control over neighbouring paramountcies (Drucker-Brown 1975; Davis 1984; Schlottner 2000).

From the beginning, Mamprugu operated like a confederation of autonomous communities of the *Naam* ritually connected to the Nalerigu *Naam*; there was considerable decentralization in contrast to Dagbon, Ouagadougou and Yatenga. Local chiefs recognized the primacy of the *nayiri* who in fact installed them. Political competition among a large pool of candidates resulted in increased centralization toward the end of the eighteenth century. The *kambonaba* (chief warrior), the *imam* (Islamic cleric) and a number of *nabisi* had councillor roles to the nayiri while the *nachinaa* (youth leader), the *magajia* (women's leader) and the *fongu kpamma* (sectional heads) had both structural and contingent responsibilities. The Mamprusi political structure was deployed around nodes of the *Naam* that mediated different degrees of rule.

Mamprugu and Nanun are often presented as 'loose' instances of diffuse centralization in the cluster of Voltaic states. Nanun in particular is often presented as a softer version of Dagbon, reputedly the most centralized and most powerful of the three Dagbamba states (Mamprugu-Dagbon-Nanun). In contrast to the original 'massacre' that validated the 'absolute' power of the Dagbon chiefs, peaceful collaboration and mutual integration were said to characterize the foundation of Mamprugu and Nanun. MacGaffey suggests that the confederation of Mamprugu may have been a loose alliance of independent chiefs that acknowledged the autonomy and the agency of one another as *primus inter pares* (MacGaffey 2013, 22; Kawada 2002, 32–33).

The combination of a flexible vertical hierarchy and complex horizontal structures organized the distribution and the circulation of power so as to prevent concentration. In fact, inherent to the legitimacy of the various administrators and councillors was the allocation of portions of the *Naam* or 'that which allows someone to rule over another people'.[25] The *Naam* was a quality of office that could not be captured, nor did it die with the death of an office holder for the *Naam* would have been 'eaten' by a body that fulfilled the role of a temporary carrier. Death mediated at once the 'transfer' of an essence that ensured continuity of office from a ruler to his descendants and sanctioned the transition of a chief from a mortal to a *badima* (ancestor; Davis 1987, 629).

At any rate, Mamprugu was to become weakly centralized because of the limited intervention of the state in the realm of earth custody. Mamprusi was never able to entirely subdue the indigenous (and decentralized) Tallensi and Kusasi. As the Mamprusi state drew these into its orbit of influence, it could nevertheless not incorporate them in the encompassing realm of the *Naam* (Fage and Oliver 1975, 187).

The core Mamprusi *Nam* was supplemented by the *nam yella*, a form of ancestor cult which was extended by the king and his *nayirii kpaamba* (councillors) to lineage elders and village chiefs. Political rule in Mamprugu was thus more narrowly determined by both reverence to the ancestors and to earth rituals. Three earthpriests were for instance involved in the appointment of a *nayiri* (Gambarana, Sagadugunaba and Bokunaba). Relative to Dagomba and Moogo, earthpriests had a degree of control over the central government (Drucker-Brown 1975, 131; 1981, 115–31; 1989, 385; Davis 1987, 629, 633).

In any case, Mamprusi established the basic *Naam* framework that was to inform political rule, the structure of office, and in particular the rules of office succession either on the basis of gates (Mamprusi), village-gates (Dagbon) or eligible dynasties (Moogo).[26] Other areas of common practice would include the Mamprugu-Dagbon-Nanun-Mossi states' reliance, to varying degrees, on captives and eunuchs as administrative categories and foreign mercenaries as well as Muslim advisers as the state sought to disentangle kinship from political rule.

The state's capacity to populate political cores with subjects was a constant preoccupation; it was in fact the motivation and purpose of war. If sovereignty over land could be distinguished from sovereignty over people, the former made little sense without the latter. It wasn't enough to just populate political cores with people; people had to be turned into subjects. The state thus cultivated multiple alliances based on blood, fictitious family ties, ritual relationships, intermarriage and alliances of protection.

I elaborate upon this specific point in chapter 4. Suffice it to say that in the case of Mamprugu, the rise of Na Atabia drastically changed the polity's configuration around the 1690s. Na Atabia (c.1690–1740) spearheaded a reform project that found support and sustainability in trading networks operated by Muslim merchants and more crucially in new offices only answerable to the *nayiri*. Political positions were entrusted to a eunuch administrative class, the *namaa'alis kpamba*, as well as Muslim advisers and a host of clients, predominantly stranger kin and an army of slaves, mercenaries and captives (Davis 1987, 630; Ferguson and Wilks 1970).

The constitutional basis of Mamprusi was compromised in the early colonial period when a British Colonel named Gibbs called a conference of chiefs at Gambaga and Nalerigu in December 1932 in order to draft a constitution based on codified rules and regulations, particularly with regard to succession (Davis 1987, 637). What was produced was a rigid 'tradition' that subverted the basis of contestation that underpinned pre-existing rules of office.

Where previously earthpriests played a crucial role, elders advised by colonial authority could now make and unmake kings in electoral courts. The codification essentially compromised the constitutional compact that had enabled cohabitation between political rulers and subject populations whose will could partly be represented in earthpriests' participation in the nomination of rulers.

THE MOSSI STATES OF OUAGADOUGOU/ YATENGA: STEADY STATIZATION

The break from Mamprugu articulated a critical turn in the steady statization process that modulated the formation of the Mossi states. If the foundational myth is built around a (Mamprusi) princess Yennenga and matriliny, the passage to Ouagadougou recalibrated the constitutive tale to fit the trajectory of Ouedraogo, putative descendant of Yennenga. Patriliny presumably fits better with a heroic history of state foundation achieved by dint of superior male technology and intelligence.[27] Mossi oral history makes numerous references to Dagomba horsemen as founders of Moogo. Their leader, Naaba Nedega, a 'Dagomba chief at Gambaga,' could have been a Mamprusi prince who broke away from the political core.[28] Wedraogo (Ouedraogo), the putative ancestor of all Mossi, was thus born from the union of a *na poko* (woman-chief) and a hunter.

Because of the uterine origin of Ouedraogo, the political links to Mamprusi had been severed to enable the *Moos bûudu* to set up its own branch of the Mamprusi model while maintaining some ritual link to it (Frobenius 1986).[29] If there was no break in the transmission of the *Naam*, there was a crucial rupture in its mode of transmission from a male chief to another male, through a *yennega* (female) agency.

The dialectic between continuity and break, early on, was also manifest in the institutional transmission of the *Naam* from centre to the periphery. Both forms of the *Naam* proceed from *Wennam* (*Wende* and *Naam*), the sky divinity common to both Mamprusi and Mossi. In contrast to the Mamprusi, *Wennam* was 'personalized' so to speak by the Mossi and integrated into an ideal hierarchy whose pinnacle it occupied. *Wennam* becomes Naaba Wende, a chief-divinity (Izard 1987, 63–64).

The desire for imperial expansion, in Ouagadougou and Yatenga, was undermined by the 'radically inelastic' nature of pre-existing sociopolitical mechanisms. The latter therefore had to be *transcended*. In Moogo, the homogenization process entailed kinship reform (from blood to alliance) and territorial reform (new political direction and content superimposed on existing ritual centres). But reform was more fundamentally framed in a new cosmological-ideological framework. The latter consisted of an ideological union between the earth divinity of first-comers and the high divinity of migrant-rulers. The new divinity turned an amorphous community into a moral community woven through an imaginary stock and 'the infinite extensibility of common symbols, shared cosmology' (Netting 1972, 233).

The elaboration of Mossi chronology was marked by notorious disagreements which have been sufficiently reviewed elsewhere (Saul

2007, 215). Suffice it to note that established chronologies were thoroughly challenged by Fage on the Ghanaian side and Izard on the Burkinabe side. Izard in particular attempted to re-adjust Mossi chronology by breaking away from former, uniform accounts. Facing the opportunity to collate references in the Ta'rikh with dynastical traditions collected in Yatenga, Izard made an informed move to break from the *continuity thesis*, which was up to that point accepted as consensus (Izard 1970 1:35–54, 56–78; Saul 2007, 15).

By Izard's estimation, Yatenga emerged from generation V while Ouagadougou emerged in generation III while earlier generations are traced around Tenkodogo and the southern limits of Burkina (generation I) in present-day Ghana.[30] Using Frobenius's master genealogy, Izard reworked the genealogy of Yatenga rulers in a matrix that reveals a tremendous amount of information on dynastic history and the intricacies of power, office and history. In any case, early writings on the Mossi therefore give pride of place to Mossi history and chronology and feed into the Mossi sense of superiority. This was not lost on Mossi intelligentsia, including present-day customary chiefs, who were well aware of these writings—some of which were incorporated in school textbooks.

In its strict sense, the term *Mossi* (*Moose, Mosi*, sing. *Moaga*) refers to descendants of warriors who originated from northern Ghana or 'somewhere east' and conquered swathes of the White Volta Basin around the middle of the fifteenth and beginning of the sixteenth century. The Mossi are the descendants of an agnatic group—the *Moos bûudu*—related to Mamprusi dynasts. Traditional Voltaic accounts commonly point to a region east of Lake Chad as the land of Tohazie (Red Hunter) the intrepid ancestor. Mossi scholars in particular have looked into linguistic connections to trace the origins of the Mossi-Mamprusi-Dagomba even farther afield in Chad, Nigeria, Niger, Mali and even Egypt (Simporé 2004, 561–71).[31] According to these, Kpogonumbo was son of Tohazie. He married Sohiyini, the daughter of Abdul Rahamani, king of Grumah. Gbewa, born of this union, is said to be the ancestor of all the Voltaic groups. The saga of Tohazie with Gur-speaking peoples and the Mande south of the Niger bend seems to have inspired Gbewa in his long peregrinations from Grumah to Pusiga. If little is known about history prior to Gbewa, both Dagomba and Mamprusi oral traditions recognize him as founder of the oldest of the Mossi-Dagomba states: Mamprugu.

A tendency therefore existed among the Mamprusi to equate Gbewa with 'the *fons et origo* in Mamprusi oral tradition' (Illiasu 1971, 96; Drucker-Brown 1981, 117). The ideology of the *Naam* is therefore crucial to the ritual processes that associated Mamprusi with Voltaic states as 'congregations to the cult of *Naam*'. Through a replication system and a process of saturation, '[the] *Naam* is continuously allocated, "returned" and reallocated to be embodied in successive kings and chiefs' (Drucker-Brown 1981, 117; Fortes 1940).

Mamprusi claimed to retain the original *Naam*, the master-model. But if any difference existed between offshoots of the Mamprusi state, it was necessarily determined by social and historical distance from Mamprusi. For the Moaga, the term *moogo* refers to the entire world (the common noun *moogo* means 'savannah' or 'bush' in the sense of wild, uncultivated space).

> When the princess Yennenga, mother of all Mossi, went to her father, the Gambaga chief, to introduce Riallé to him, the chief asked her, 'Who is this man? Where does he come from?' She indicated, with a gesture of the hand, 'From the moogo [the bush, the savannah].' So if you ask me if the Sawadogo [indigenous] are Mossi, I would say there is no more authentic Mossi than the Sawadogo because they come from the moogo, the bush. In fact, the Sawadogo say they come from the entrails of the earth (Vieux Karim, interview, Ouahigouya, 16 April 2010).

At any rate, all Mossi traditions trace their origins to Ouedraogo whose putative descendants became the founders of satellite states around Ouagadougou, Yatenga and Tenkodogo principally. The word *ouedraogo* (stallion) could have been the name of a real person as much as a (mnemonic) figure, that of the horse-riding conqueror that symbolizes the Mossi ruling estate.

Archaeological evidence also suggests that the Dogon (indigenous Kibsi), who mostly inhabited the north of Moogo, around Yatenga, used iron and pottery tools, as well as mortuary earthenware, for as long as they lived in the area. Kiethéga dates their settlement in Moogo to the thirteenth century and contends that they probably hailed from the cliffs of Bandiagara. They preceded the Kurumba and the Yônyôose in the middle belt of Moogo and the Fulse and Kurumba in Yatenga (Kiethéga 1993, 9–29; Marshall 1978, 122).

Ninsi would mean, from a Mossi perspective, 'those who were found there' (Ceux qu'on est venu trouver sur place)—in other words, *sẽn wa miki* (first-comers) according to Mossi accounts. The Ninsi were mostly concentrated in the central part of Moogo, particularly around Ouagadougou (Bouda 1986, 52; Simporé 2004, 544). The distribution of the population of Yoyonse and Ninsi suggests a gradual displacement of autochthons toward the north as Mossi 'conquerors' annexed populations along a south-north route (Simporé 2004, 556).

The Mossi use the generic term *nyonyonse* (*ninissi*, *ninisse* and *nionioisse* are used interchangeably) to refer to indigenous groups that inhabit pre-Moaga society. Their memories are by and large absent from Mossi historiography. From a Mossi viewpoint, *nyonyonse* were politically and civilizationally 'underdeveloped': they did not invent the state nor did they have the capacity to evolve sophisticated systems of rule. But even on the fringes of civilized order, the *nyonyonse* were known to control dangerous powers that were indispensable to the Mossi political project. A strong ambivalence therefore presided over Mossi relations with indigenous *nyonyonse*. The same ambiguousness applies to *gurunsi*, an appellation of widespread use in the Voltaic region. Many Mamprusi-Dagbamba-Mossi groups designate their neighbours, those they consider savage and on the fringes of humanity, 'sub-human' or 'men from the bush' (Liberski 1991, 54).

Mossi historiography recognizes two broad social categories in pre-Moaga society, *ninissi* and blacksmiths on one hand and *tengbissi* (sons of the earth) on the other. [32] The sons of the earth were in turn divided into two distinct groups of *nioniosse* that provided, and still do, the earthpriests invested with the ability to communicate with metaphysical forces and ancestors and the *sikomce*, or *sirkomce* (mask-bearers) who inhabit the realm of artistic creation and performance (Pageard 1963, 16). These latter groups are connected to two common ancestors, Tenghin-Poussoumdé (that which comes from the earth) and Bassi (leave him), who had three sons: Kellé-Tinga and Boud'yaré, the twins, are the ancestors of the *nyonyonse* while Zoalga, the artist-master trained among the *kînkirse* (bush spirits), was the ancestor of the *sirkomce*.

Mossi conquerors pushed the indigenous Dogon north toward the cliffs of Bandiagara while some of them remained under Mossi rule (Skinner 1964, 8; Tait 1955, 201). The Samo on the other hand are said to have opposed a more robust resistance against Mossi expansion although they were eventually defeated and incorporated into Yatenga. While the Mossi adopted pre-existing arrangements by juxtaposing the *Naam/Tenga* binary upon the Fulbe binary chiefs/gravediggers, they based the legitimacy of their newly constituted states on far-away sociopolitical constellations with which they shared the ideology of the *Naam*. Fundamentally, collaboration hinged upon an attempt to deploy the *Naam* over a territory beyond the control of the state.

The articulation of the structural distinction of political functions from other roles was meant to impress the importance of political practice as specialized technique in state formation. Specifically, the crystallization of models of cultural units in contrasting roles within political and social spheres contributed to expanding centre-periphery dynamics, a process that is crucial to institutional building.

The Mossi framework of power was a syncretizing and synthesizing design, an amalgamated state out of great diversity. Outside founding charters—which differ in some details across Ouagadougou, Yatenga, Fada N'gourma and so forth but have the same constitutive elements[33]—new genealogies were aligned with service, strategic alliances and personal achievements. The common trend was for conquering Mossi to incorporate the indigenous groups as first-settler groups into their new polities, regardless of their status in pre-Moaga structures and whether these were acephalous or organized with some degree of hierarchy. The constitution of these convenient alliances was to have lasting effects on the collective identities of 'conquered' groups. Mossi-centred narratives, however, project a self-contained history and culture that disregards the structural conditions that made political centres possible; for example, a slave economy that enabled the state to tap into a large captive population that was appended to the state; first-comer communities whose earthpriests were devoted to assuaging ancestors and gods so that kings could rule freely; and a system of delayed exchange in women and gifts that supported alliances within different state factions and between the state and neighbouring communities' ruling elites. Quite fundamentally, it became a project that sought to attain autonomy by instituting a divide between kinship and kingship for ideological reasons.

In both Ouagadougou and Yatenga, a reigning naaba expanded his territorial base through the creation of peripheral *naams* for his sons and allies who then formed a pool of *nabisi* eligible for the competition for the master *Naam*. Thus, collateral lines were progressively marginalized and excluded from competition because of a tendency by agnates of a single line to keep the *Naam* for themselves; continuous centralization entailed a limitation of office succession for sons and grandsons of former rulers.

The seeds of stratification and differentiation were thus sown in the production of *naaba/nabisi/nakombsé*. Thus royals who lost their right to compete for *Naam* 'fell' into the ranks of commoners (Izard 1985, 24). I expand upon the Mossi statization process in chapter 4. I specifically show the production of subjectivities in relation to the construction of a notion of power greatly constrained by the subjective experience of public will.

DAGBON: A MOBILE KINGDOM

The recognition of the primacy of Mamprugu went hand in hand with an effort to endow Dagomba history with an autonomous voice that marked its independent character. If Mamprugu oral traditions are relatively sketchy on many key aspects of Mamprusi society, in Dagbon there was a distinct keenness to record and recount history, to formalize and streamline the recording and recounting of history. This was achieved through the establishment of a corporate group of court historians or *lunsi* (state drummers), members of the nobility organized as titled officers under the supervision of the *Namoo Na*.

The *lunsi* underwent years of painstaking training; they were highly specialized artists handsomely paid and highly respected. The Dagomba thus developed particularly elaborate and efficient technologies of preservation and transmission of the past, of relaying the exploits of the 'upper class' and of preserving the memory of constitutional practices and the sources of belief (Illiasu 1971, 96–97). The quality and the scale of the Dagomba oral-traditions machinery, visible at every unit of the state, were an important element in assessing the authority of sources of knowledge and traditions often employed in sanctioning political and social practices.

A common story goes that when Na Nyagse occupied Dagbon, he exterminated earthpriests and replaced them with his relatives. Dagbon fought a great number of wars. Dagbamba rulers retained a few priests while eliminating many even though dynastic traditions make their original *total* massacre the constitutive justification for the concentration, in the hands of Dagabani rulers, of political and ritual power. There was, however, the interesting feature, common to both Moogo and Dagbon, of an order of 'ancient elders', figures often removed from both political rule and ritual practices but who nonetheless exerted great moral influence in both fields. It is no coincidence in fact that earthpriests were called the 'original elders of Dagbon'.

According to Dagomba traditions, they forsake their rights to rule. One can surmise that Dagbamba rulers captured a few priests to collaborate with the ruling class while arrogating to themselves the right to appoint new earthpriests. Whereas in Dagbon and Nanun these were reduced to ritual/ spiritual figures, in Moogo, they were very much part of the ruling class. They were to ensure respect and legitimacy/legitimation within the logic of dynastic rule. Their function was therefore a first layer of checks on state power of the kind that a first wife and a king's mother would play in different political arrangements (Kawada 2002, 32–33).

The history of Dagbon is transmitted through epic poetry recited by lunsi praise-singers through intricate performances. The core poem is the story of Na Nyagse, which provides the justificatory basis for an exclusive dynastic claim to political rule. Upon a succession struggle in Mamprugu, Na Nyagse, son of Sitobu, founded a *naam* in western Dagbon and imposed his rule upon indigenous Konkomba left with token power. The political centre of Dagbon,[34] Yendi-Dabari (ruined Yendi), was established as its capital along the White Volta in the middle of major trade routes that connected the Akan forests to northern markets, toward Jenne, and also along the Hausa routes toward Katsina (Fage and Oliver 1975, 187–88).

Reflections on Dagbon as an early modern state are both projections of twentieth-century understandings of the state and a unidimensional reading of early colonial administration. Lower-level office holders exercised different categories of function on the basis of which it would not be possible to conceive of hierarchy in the same rigid manner that colonial authorities later did. In fact, Dagbon was not a single political unit but 'a mosaic of chieftaincies, some of them subservient to Yendi, others independent' (MacGaffey 2013,

75). Some of these included shrines that 'escaped' the foundational mas-sacre of Na Nyagse. Dagbon's centralized nature, relative to Mamprugu and Nanun, was a consequence of its insertion in the Mande and Hausa trading networks after 1700.

An effort to contain the fissionary tendency of migrant-rulers led, in Dagomba, to new rules that limited office succession, specifically the *Nam* of Yendi, to the sons of previous rulers. A further requirement was that candidate-sons had to have held at least one of the three *gate-skins* (or lines) of Karaga, Mion or Savelugu (Duncan-Johnstone and Blair 1932; Ferguson and Wilks 1970, 340–52; Wilks 1985, 472). The restricted polydynastic system has been associated with the resolution of protracted internecine succession struggles following the death of Na Gungobile (ca. 1700) upon the arbitration of Na Atabia (c. 1690–1740) of Mamprusi (Ferguson 1973, 92–93; Ferguson and Wilks 1970, 352–63).

Such instances of reference to the Mamprusi core were not infrequent; in fact, the Mamprusi link ensured a mechanism of standardization of basic rules of succession that maintained—although increasingly altered in newly formed polities—the relevance of royal dynasties as the primary pool of recruitment of political rulers. The stakes of restricted succession were to do with the privileges and entitlements such as subsidiary titles accrued to members of a particular line when an incumbent from their ranks rose to Yendi.

Yendi on the other hand could be recognized as a seat of power in a way fully centralized after 1715. Centralization was spearheaded by Na Zanjina, an early reformer and wealthy trader converted to Islam who capitalized on the skills of Muslim clerics to develop Yendi as a trading centre (Ferguson 1973, 23, 97, 247; MacGaffey 2013, 31). In Ferguson's conceptualization of Dagbon history on the basis of a first and second kingdom, the trajec-tory of Dagbamba conquerors is well outlined although it is not clear how long, through what means and under what specific historical conditions they founded political entities along a north-south axis.

What we know is that these were loosely constituted given material constraints and the need for considerable resources (that were not available then) to maintain centralized polities. 'Both ambitious princes and "refugees", that is, people who did not care to submit to the exactions of chiefs, fled west'. In addition, 'the dates are uncertain, but Dagomba are said to have founded dynasties in Wa and Bouna, although Bouna tradition describes the Dagomba founder as a wandering hunter rather than a prince' (MacGaffey 2013, 31). The very trope of the wandering hunter as state-builder permeates all the foundational accounts of the Mamprusi-Dagomba-Mossi states, and it was an important element of institutional history.

After 1744, Dagbon became a junior ally to Ashanti and it capitalized on prosperous scholar-traders to strengthen the influence of Yendi. The seeds of centralization were sown in a succession dispute that occurred around 1700. Na Atabia of Mamprugu was asked to mediate a conflict between Na Zanjina, the youngest of Na Tutugri, and his brothers. Na Zanjina had become wealthy in the trans-savannah trade, and close interactions with Muslim traders led to his conversion to Islam. His wealth and new Islamic knowledge made a difference in the dispute and he was enskinned at the expense of his brothers, who had to accept a reform in succession rule that consolidated power among Na Zanjina's descendants. In fact, the roots of an endless battle among different royal factions—still ongoing today—are to be found in this specific episode of Dagbon history. Now a 'vassal' of Asante, Yendi was inserted in the north-south trade through Salaga and exchanged cloth, cotton, tobacco, butter, slaves, livestock, leather items and protective amulets in addition to imported goods from the Mediterranean for goods such as iron, guns, powder, cloth and gold. Yendi experienced tremendous prosperity; the Dagbon kings acquired horses, spears, swords and Western guns and established a corps of *kanbonsi* (Mossi *kambose*), an elite order of warriors professionalized in the use of Western guns (MacGaffey 2013, 51–52).

A variety of figures with more or less explicit functions and roles were responsible for the upkeep of shrines. Among the *tindanas* (territorial priests), the *buguli* (shrine keeper) and the *bugulana* (shrine owner) was a category that intervened in association with or for the benefit of the state. Thus the *kuga na*, a senior ritual chief who belongs to a line of priests that antedates the foundation of Dagbon, intervenes in successions, burials and funeral rituals and also acts as regent ruler. As the holder of an independent office with roots in the sphere of *Tengan*, he very much epitomizes the amalgamated functions of a priest in a context of intersecting jurisdictions (MacGaffey 2013, 76).

Among the Mossi, the rule of avoidance applied to the *kurita* (king's scapegoat). Among the Dagbamba, this rule often denoted an irreconcilable discourse of political primacy with the reality of multipolarity. Thus 'avoidance skirts the question of ranking between similars; it can be seen as finessing the difference between [the central state] dogma and the reality that many tindanas are independent, but it also responds to the belief that both parties control dangerous powers' (MacGaffey 2013, 76). Further, avoidance problematizes the question of power as a non-encompassing and specialized practice subject to the test of efficacy. Both political and ritual chiefs were believed to have access to the means of taming and assuaging the metaphysical forces that caused disaster, sickness, hunger, human anxieties and vulnerabilities.

DAGARA/DAGAABA/DAGAO: UNEVEN STATELESSNESS

Up to the middle of the nineteenth century, pressure for greater centralization was strongly resisted by the Dagara. From the north, the Dagara faced frequent raids from Samory and Babatu while Dagbon exercised tremendous pressure fuelled by its desire to centralize Wa, the seat of power. It was not until the arrival of British colonists that the Dagara started experiencing a degree of centralized authority. The British sought to promote traditional institutions, especially the institution of a contingent *polo naa* (war-chief) as the new bearer of centralized power for the Dagara.

Traditions of origin and settlement histories take pride of place in Dagara history, and they typically leave the *Naam* dimension relatively unexplored. Lentz documents the institutional flexibility that characterized the Dagara. Their institutional arrangements constituted, in contrast to rigidly stratified Dagbon, a model of *Naam/Tenga* dichotomy that did not prioritize the 'needs of *Naam*' but rather focused on the dynamics of land, ritual and history (Lentz 1994).[35]

Both Tallensi and Dagara are, in Kopytoff-speak, 'frontier societies' best understood from the perspective of forms of equilibrium between the political, the economic and the ritual as opposed to a trajectory of gradual and cumulative political centralization. Among neighbouring Tallensi in particular, political rule was not restricted to *namoos*; both ancestral affiliation and proven affiliation with *tindana* families could provide a basis for 'political' membership.

In Dagara accounts, the constitutive rupture with Dagbon is framed in terms of a rebellion for 'there was too much "dictatorship" and too little "autonomy" and "dignity", and therefore [the Dagara] decided to break away from the Dagomba kingdom'.[36] Inbuilt in the philosophical traditions of non-state societies was a normative inhibition against centralization. This could have been the result of a previous traumatizing experience of centralization; it could have been an attempt at instituting paradigms meant to inform methodologies of institutional rupture. Yelpaala identifies 'mythic, metaphorical, and mimetic negative images of kingship' among the Dagara. These often portrayed kings, rulers and chiefs as 'unimaginative, unintelligent, lacking common sense, and likely to use brute force' (1983, 357).

In this regard, oral narratives were meant to mould and inflect political conduct. Yelpaala provides an anecdotal example that, like many others in Dagara popular culture, exalts an ingrained ambivalence toward the concentration of power. 'An example of this is the narrative called *yeng gang naa* (intelligence is better than kingship). The king in this narrative, angered by the intelligence of his subject, tries to get rid of him by plotting a murder at a feast. The intelligent subject outwits the king, survives the plot, and invites the king for a feast in his house!' (Yelpaala 1983, 357).[37] Kingship according to this tale was a thankless, debilitating endeavour that was productive of many risks.

> In many accounts, particularly those of the tengansob clan which is usually the one claiming to be the 'first-comers' in a village, a hunter discovers a promising amount of game (and sometimes good farming land) during one of his expeditions, erects a temporary shack and later fetches his wives, children and possibly brothers, who all come and settle at the new location and start farming. Often, the new land turns out to be already inhabited. A further episode narrates how the new immigrants meet the original settlers and reach an agreement over sacrifices to the earth god, the distribution of game and the disposal of lost animals. In other stories, the newcomers meet not human beings, but dwarfs or *kontome* ('beings of the wild', 'spirits') and these have to be outwitted or pacified before the immigrants can settle there in peace (Lentz 1994, 465).

As for the motives for emigration, most stories are silent while others explicitly state that there were 'too many mouths to feed' or they give a combination of hunting activities and the search for farmland as reasons. Kopytoff has also looked into 'witchcraft' accusations in addition to the common dynastic, succession battles and segmenting patterns (1999, 88–96). Later under colonial rule, movements across international borders became a strategy to evade colonial taxes or compulsory labour as much as they continued to result from family conflicts.[38] Whether these accounts are used as justificatory strategies for present-day settings and disputes over scarce resources is beside the point.

Quite fundamentally, the piecemeal migration of kin segments has corresponding readings in a notion of *circulation* as organizing principle for close and extended alliance networks, the codification of relations and positionality among close neighbours and ultimately the normativity of diversity in settlement patterns, kin structures, ideological orientation and therefore epistemological possibilities. In this sense, while thwarting the possibility for the accumulation of power in a particular place, person, group or institution, stateless societies recognized the relative benefit of stable, centralized power as a pragmatic, problem-solving framework:

> [Stateless societies] recognized the tremendous advantages of centralized power during war and used a limited form of it only then. Leaders were given the power to command and carry out operations but during peacetime they became … common people and ceased to exercise that power (Yelpaala 1983, 357).

For this reason the Dagara had chiefly figures but political duty was often assumed by unlikely characters such as social dependents. The *tindana* could, upon consultation with elders, elect to appoint a *polo naa* recognized for proven qualities of 'valor in warfare, farming, and exemplary conduct', particularly suitable to lead in times of war (Yelpaala 1983, 263). Despite his potency, there was never much enthusiasm or need to constitute a centralized Dagara state outside what could be termed a contingent/extraordinary *polo naa*. In reality, the potency of the *polo naa* was delegated, and as such it was a limited power with an implausible capacity to generate the needed catalyst for centralization. And even when the British could muster, under colonial rule, enough centralized authority to monopolize power, they were forced to replace appointed chiefs at a frequent rate given popular complaints and rejection.

In fact, 'according to numerous oral sources, the first chiefs in the Lawra District in particular shocked everybody with the oppressive nature of their exercise of power. Several complaints were made to the British administration and most of the chiefs were replaced' (Yelpaala 1983, 357). Among the neighbouring Sisala, another 'stateless society', the familiar construct *sipaalaara* (one who goes first)/*tinteeng-tin* (earth custodian) was destabilized when they became the target of slave raidings. If the *sipaalaara* played the role of military and economic chiefs, their powers became enhanced during vulnerable times as a new class of warriors emerged to defend the community; they mimicked war leaders of the centralized states in military strategies and paraphernalia.

The basic unit in Dagara society is the *lineage*, made of members of particular descent groups and *yir* (house). The *kpiime* (spirits of departed ancestors) are fairly central to the daily life of the lineage. The latter is represented at the communal level by the *yidaadoo*, who is both head and spiritual leader. The Dagara recognize a mixed-clan system whereas the patriclan is a discrete political unit and the matriclan seems to command less political significance. There are also differences in the distribution of communally held land for the right to land for patriclans applies to a whole range of categories as opposed to the limited right attached to the *kukuri* (hoe) for matriclans, which is 'property acquired with the proceeds of farming'.[39] Clan members share a common name and a *dumo* (totemic cult) around which is articulated a strong ritual and spiritual commitment and to which rights and duties are attached.

Up to the nineteenth century, political authority among the Dagara was organized around the practice of *teng* (village units). The head of a *teng* (*tendaana*) and *nimbere* (lineage elders) were involved in political rule in a mixed, horizontal structure. While most matters of general interest were debated and deliberated within this structure, the *tendaana* was often the authority of last resort when consensus could not be reached. The oscillation between loose centralization, decentralization and delegated rule meant that existing offices could disappear altogether depending on relevance while new ones could emerge according to need. The office of the *kumbelo*, a messenger tasked with a vast range of errands and the mediation of communication between the *tendaana* and the lineage elders, once existed, and he executed sacrifice- and contravention-related duties.

Diffuse forms of authority could emerge among *taaba* (age group structures) in so far as these mirrored the authority of lineage groups. They constituted aspiring lineage elders. The various autonomous *teng* were linked by 'contiguity, consanguinity, historical ties' and other institutions which could be activated in times of distress such as war with non-Dagara groups or resistance against slave raiding for which these units would 'coordinate, cooperate, or deliberate as a larger central unit' (Yelpaala 1983, 364).

The benefits of centralization were thus occasionally activated to serve a specific purpose. The Dagara share some of these organizational characteristics with neighbouring decentralized groups such as the Tallensi, the Sisala and the Kusasi. Among Dagara, Tallensi, Kusasi and other stateless groups, both *tendaan* and *naam* offices could be held by the same chief or individual. Consequently,

> legality and power might be coterminous in some societies. However, the fact that they both reside in the same institution does not make them conceptually one. The implication of all this is that, among the Dagaaba, authority may be legal even when the power to induce or coerce obedience is absent or might never have been intended to exist (Yelpaala 1983, 367).

Until the advent of colonialism, the notion of a chief as a discrete political institution separate from ritual ruler was an unusual thing among the Dagara. The few instances that have been recorded were generally subject to the authority of elders and the *tindana* of a given locality. The late-nineteenth-century chief as a 'centralized and monopolized power and authority', therefore, 'constituted a significant and radical departure from the political organization of Dagao' (Yelpaala 1983, 372). Chiefs mediated colonial authority through administrative and judicial duties. They recruited and supervised forced labour and manpower on behalf of the colonial government, levied taxes and handed down arbitrary judgments. They were largely seen as an oppressive power that lived off the people and gave little in return.

Figure 2.2:   Moogo at the end of the nineteenth century
Source: Map drawn from Izard (1985: IX).

WHAT TO MAKE OF ALL THIS?

What I have sketched above is a dynamic history characterized by pluralism, diversity and complex and multiple models of political authority and
social order. The distinction state/stateless cannot capture the nuances, the
inflections and modulations inscribed in various groups' attempt at translation of their ontological commitments to realization of the *Naam*. Thinking
about authority as a mode of alignment of the *Naam* as an overarching

condition—in relation to the ways in which bearers respond to, and are challenged by pre-existing configurations—I have tried to argue for a notion of political order framed in an understanding of the constitution of authority and governance structures in networks of the *Naam*.

Arguably though, the *Naam* embodied different meanings, and it was equally made to do different things for different societies at different historical moments. In chapter 3, I show how in decentralized systems, particularly among the Kusasi, the Kasena and the Dagara, the principled binary was mediated in the absence of a rigid 'government'. In chapter 4, I show how in the centralized Mossi system, the distinction *Naam/Tenga* was hedged about with strategies of deconstruction at the different levels of governance. In these different forms of governance framed on a centralized-decentralized continuum, the point of governance was less the fulfilment of a model than *an imperative of deconstruction of power* on one hand and the realization of themes of solidarity and openness in a historical ecology characterized by mobility and movement as founding mechanisms on the other hand.

More generally, the diversity and complexity of structures and constitutional arrangements outlined above is indicative of a key concern, in many pre-nineteenth-century formations, to provide for the fragmentation and distribution of power within institutions that were not necessarily 'political' in design and orientation.

Two related features can be noted. On one hand, the fragmentation of power among different locations was a constitutive strategy against its concentration, be it in the hands of specific individuals or groups. Thus corporate formations retained prerogatives that were effective both within the restrictive realms of these groups and which extended into the elaboration of public spaces and order where members of the different corporate groups were also to operate. On the other hand, these provisions created mechanisms for effective resistance against (an excess of) power and ideology.

Four observations are crucial here. First, the force of the *Naam* is a metaphysical and mystic quality inherent in its constitutive matter. Its substance is embodied, and it lives in the person who bears this force. A Frazerian view (e.g., of divine kingship) would conceive of conquerors as those who seek the power of autochthons in order to hold sway and endure—that is, gain control over first-comers (MacGaffey 2013, 46). This dynamic constantly pitted the power of the *Naam* against the forces of *Tenga*. The first-comer/late-comer construct is not just a matter of historical contingency; its ubiquitousness throughout West and Central Africa suggests that there is more to it as a reality and narrative trope. At the least, if the conquest framework seems particularly attractive to anthropologists and historians, the process of settlement was less straightforward than a mechanical movement and waves of old and new conquerors (MacGaffey 2013, 69–71).

Second, despite an entrenched state discourse framed in binaries that allocated different functions to different groups, there was no possible separation between ethics, law, religion and morality as discrete conceptual categories that were embodied by different figures and imaginaries. Instead, these were built into sociopolitical organizations. This pattern is most stark in the ritualized transfer of sovereignty from territorial priests to political rulers: political incumbency was the responsibility of the territorial priest. Further, through this transfer, interdependence between power bearers and those upon which their rule was to be exercised was elevated to a normative principle. However, ideology inevitably sprouts where there is a stake to preserve, a power to expand, a position to defend and a future to elaborate. I further address these points in chapter 4.

Third, key to our theoretical dilemma is the manner in which time, in fact temporality, relates to social phenomena and how we might go about factoring this relationship into our analysis. One must take a view of social action as articulated at the intersection of intentionality, contingency and opportunity—as the very stuff with which history operates. Many scholars have written a great deal on notions of temporality in African philosophical traditions (Mudimbe 1985; Wiredu 1996), and it is a topic that deserves more attention than can be given here. An understanding of spatiality beyond territory and that of temporality beyond genealogical succession and linear time opens a whole universe of diverse conceptions of power and authority. I come back to this theme in chapter 3.

Fourth, an engagement with the conflictual actualizations of principles of order may serve as an antidote to descriptions of harmony that pervade the literature of the precolonial as a time of consensus. The plausibility of foundational accounts and historical trajectories must be subjected to a variety of hypotheses, narrative styles and tropes, evidentiary modes, regimes of intervention and the extent of historical imaginations. This is however not the place to attribute truth and veracity to one particular account against another. Despite variations in historical sequences, the role and prominence of key actors, the dynastic, biographical or ethnic location of actors and the relative importance and hierarchical positions of related prerogatives and so forth, the thrust of the historiography points to competing accounts constantly reactualized in the context of ongoing strategies of recognition and appropriation. While not denying that variations might have an impact on the direction of my interpretation, their importance is relatively neutralized by close similarities as regards origin, migratory routes and forms of sociopolitical alliances.

CONCLUSION

Trajectories to complexity were multiple and in no way limited to hierarchy/ egalitarian, centralized/stateless modes for there could also be complexity in horizontal 'systems of diffuse, decentralized, consensus-based, or horizontally counterpoised power' (McIntosh 1999, 9). Conceptually, therefore, a number of issues stand out from the foregoing discussion. First, the residentialist tendency (i.e., an uneven integration of migration in the analysis of state formation) obscures the cognitive dimension of mobility and movement in the development of fitting institutions of order and authority.

Second, an understanding of historical attempts to construct meaning outside state settings, hence of the possibility of statehood outside a Westphalian-type state and in many decentralized structures, spurred political experimentation that produced individuals as contingent ruler-figures meant to tackle exigent issues. The colonial obsession with classification and ordering of social species has distorted our capacity to understand differentiated groups by their capacity to mobilize different categories of resources, knowledge and skills in the preservation of balance and social order.

In so-called stateless or decentralized polities, the different aspects of governance and authority were kept in operation simultaneously so as to ensure balance and prevent despotism. Ideological distortions drove the development of various histories in a way that justified indirect rule for the British and direct administration for the French colonial regimes.[40]

Third, there is great difficulty in conceptualizing unfamiliar social phenomena. Where historical difference should stimulate sustained research and the elaboration of appropriate analytical tools, scholars of the state have instead shown great reluctance to engage with social experiments.

In West Africa, centralization in the full sense of the word occurred around the early colonial contact, and it was essentially achieved through imposition and imperial *dominium*. Centralization was made possible by the capacity of European powers to erase historical contradictions through the deployment of technologies of government, be they ideological, military, political or cultural. The codification of dynastic constitutions by colonial scholars and administrators and African governors did tremendous violence to precolonial history in imposing a unitary reading on a field of ideas, values and norms that were not the preserve of kings and the ruling classes. Furthermore, codification represented the articulation of figures of order, authority and morality which Dagomba and Mossi elites were all too happy to validate as it reinforced their position under colonial rule.

There is, however, a cautionary tale in centralization: the material and social impediments that undermined the possibility of a concentration of power in precolonial Africa still operate to a degree. In fact, it is no surprise that there is virtually no single African government that could not be overthrown by a lightly resourced dissident group. One valuable lesson to be drawn from institutional diversity in precolonial West Africa is that the state needs to establish its authority differently and certainly away from the authoritarian tendencies that have turned postcolonial states into predatory machines that live off their citizens. What is therefore needed is radical reform in the constitution of new imaginaries and new ways for people to relate to the state—in other words, the establishment of new linkages with the state without coercion and without purely interest-based alignments.

NOTES

1. For a critique of the model of the segment lineage system as expounded by functionalists, see M. G. Smith (1956).

2. *Rog-n-miki* is a tricky concept to translate. Mossi informants explain it as the system of values and traditions that ancestors transmitted to generations. They often translate it as 'Je suis né trouver'. 'For example in my family, we cannot eat the heart of animals or kill a lizard because it is our totem. We don't eat the heart of animals because we have to be strong in order to serve the *naaba* as warriors. Our ancestor in the past ate the heart of an animal in order to become a strong warrior' (Ila Ouedraogo, interview, Ouahigouya, 16 April 2010; see also Niang [2011, ch. 3]).

3. Except for the Kusasi who took refuge in the Agole Hills and the Tallensi in the Tong Hills. The latter were bombed by the British at the end of the nineteenth century as a demonstration of the futility of Tallensi resistance to colonial subjugation but the attack merely reinforced Tallensi belief in the power of the hill gods.

4. Vansina also finds similar governance patterns in interstitial areas between centralized polities in Central Africa around the Rund Kingdom (2004, 259).

5. The Oti-Volta-Group (also Mole-Dagbani) comprises Mooré, Frafra, Mampruli, Dagara, Dagbani and other Gur-languages.

6. Interview with Ousseyni Sogoba, Ouahigouya, 14–15 April 2010.

7. If the assumption of Voltaic state-bearers as a foreign category is accepted, their treatment of the Ninisi, Fulsi, Kipirsi, Kasena, Nunuma, Sissala, Ko, Kuasi, Konkomba and other first-comer groups thus accounts for the type of social formation later adopted. If the Mossi combined force and negotiation, the Dagomba are said to have been more radical in their treatment of indigenous peoples, hence the limited role accorded to earthpriests in decision making.

8. For further discussion of Gur languages, see Westermann and Bryan (1952), Arens and Karp (1989) and Wilks (1985).

9. On pre-Moaga groups, see Kiethéga et al. (1994).

10. De Heusch also maintains that the Kuba and the Lele of Kasai rejected centralization and hierarchy for similar reasons; see De Heusch (1971).

11. Report on tour of inspection, March–May 1905, Ghana National Archives, Accra (GNA), ADM 56/I/50. Public Record Office, London (PRO), C096/493, enclosure 3 in Gold Coast no. 41 of 19 January 19I0; Lt. Fabre, 'Monographie de la Conscription de Diebougou', January 1904, Archives Outre Mer (Aix-en-Provence), AOF, 16304, 14 Mi 686, 6, quoted in Lentz (1994, 468; emphasis added).

12. Captain Moutray Read, report on a tour of inspection through the 'Lobi country' in 1905, GNA, ADM 56/I/50, quoted in Lentz (1994, 472).

13. Chief Commissioner Morris to the governor of the Gold Coast, 6 February 1904, PRO, CO 96/417, enclosure in Gold Coast Confidential of 1 March 1904, in Lentz (1994, 472). The British identified Dagarti (Dagari) and Lobi either inter-changeably or bundled them together while the French tended to identify Lobi with stateless groups on the Burkinabe side and Dagari with those on the Ghanaian side.

14. Fortes and Evans-Pritchard (1940, 1–23) most explicitly conceptualized the dichotomy of state/stateless societies while Sharpe (1986) provided a pertinent critique of what became conventional knowledge on stateless societies.

15. The Dagara/Dagaaba group comprises subsets such as the Lobi, Mwelere, Lowire and so forth. This could be due to both a long history of intermingling and variable use of terminologies; see Jack Goody (1956).

16. It is not uncommon for Mossi rulers to trace their origin as far back as Egypt.

17. Wilks notes that as wars of expansion over Gonja, in the sixteenth and seventeenth centuries, 'extended the sway of its rulers as far east as the Oti river, effectively isolating the Akan from the Mossi … in the mid-eighteenth century, Asante armies were to thrust deeply into the savannah country and reduce both Gonja and Dagomba to tributary status' (1985: 466). See Skinner (1964, 7–12, 205) for a cogent review of the different versions of foundational traditions.

18. Variations of the ethnonym *Mossi* include *Moose, Moshi, Musi, Mossah, Mousi* and *Mossi-be*. The singular is *Moaga* (a Moaga, a Moaga society), and the plural is *Moose* or *Mossi*.

19. That much is suggested by both Izard (1985) and Skalnik (1978) even though the former demonstrates original unity only to further nuance its implications. For a recent account, see MacGaffey (2013).

20. Anthropological literature provides the bulk of what we know about political institutions in the region. For Mamprugu see Davis (1984, 1987) and Drucker-Brown (1975, 1981). For the Dagara/Dagao see Lentz (1994) and Kuba and Lentz (2002) and Yelpaala (1983) for legal and political perspective; for Dagbon see Tamakloe (1931), Ferguson (1973) and Staniland (1975); for Fada N'gourma see Kawada (2002); for Ouagadougou and Yatenga see Izard (1970, 1985, 1987, 1992); for the Kusasi see Liberski (1991) and Liberski-Bagnoud (2002); for the Gonja see Wilks, Levtzion and Haight (1986).

21. The institutions of the *dougoutigui* (earthpriest) and the *dougoukeletigui* (war-chief) are well known among the Bamana. In the Great Lakes region, the Alur are known as rainmakers, mediators of peace and endowed with other skills that can be mobilized in the work of preserving institutions, i.e., the possibility of (social) order and single (political) authority. In a sense the Alur are not a 'typical' stateless society;

their social structures allow a transcendence of the division state-like/stateless. See Southall (1963).

22. This precedence was in fact analogous to motherhood. If Mamprugu was the parent-state, it gave birth to a numerous offspring. Cognitive distinction between 'parent' and 'branch' or 'children' states did not however correspond to physical superiority or inferiority between the Mossi on the one hand and Mamprusi-Dagomba states on the other.

23. For a detailed study of the role of the horse in the political and military history of West Africa more generally, see Law (1980). The literature certainly suggests that the power of the early Voltaic states was enhanced by the possession of horses and the command of techniques of cavalry warfare. It is not however clear what role horse-riding effectively played in facilitating the expansion and consolidation of Mamprusi-Dagomba-Mossi states. There are also doubts about the systematic use of horses across the Voltaic region given their cost and upkeep and given environmental conditions.

24. See also Ivor Wilks (1975), especially chapter 7 for a detailed description of trading links between the Ashanti and the Mossi.

25. I use 'the *Naam*' generally to refer to the attributes of the master-idea, that naam attached to the highest authority and I also use it as an abstract concept whereas '*naam*' is generally for 'portions' of power allocated to various political offices. Administratively, provincial chiefships mirror the organization of duties and responsibilities in Nalerigu, the political centre of Mamprugu. The *naa* oversees a political structure in which the *kpandana* (senior earthpriest) and the *wudana* (linguist) play an important role. Installation ceremonies among the Mamprusi and other voltaic states are called 'enskinment' for *naam* holders sit on *gbana* (animal skins) while holding office.

26. The gate system is most likely a late-nineteenth-century innovation in Mamprugu; a rotational system ensured that the four gates of Na Bariga, Na Paari, Na Zori and NaNyongu (all sons of Na Salifu) would preserve their eligibility and access to the Nalerigu Na. See a discussion of enskinment/deskinment of chiefs in Mamprusi customary laws by Davis (1987, 643).

27. Very little is known of Riale, the hunter who 'won' Yennenga's hand. Kawada (2002) ventured the interpretation that he might be a member of the 'proto-Mossi'—son of a king of Mali. Other traditions make him a Busanga. In any case, the silence of oral traditions on Riale contrasts with the various versions of the story of Yennenga as recounted in Mossi traditions. The difference is all the more striking considering that the Mossi have prioritized a patrilineal system of succession. In adopting the continuity thesis, Kawada sees, following Izard, in the dynamics of formation and decline of a proto-Mossi group, the roots of the divergent trajectories between the Mamprusi-Dagomba and the Mossi groups.

28. The confusion of the name of the place of origin may have arisen from the fact that Mamprusi refer to *dagbamba* as *yoba* (or *yooba*, literally 'bush people') and call themselves *dagbamba* (anglicized into 'Dagomba') while outsiders refer to them as 'Mamprusi'.

29. The metaphorical existence of Ouedraogo, ancestor of all Mossi, is crucial to the reality of the Mossi political structure and to Mossi identity. The *Moos bûudu* comprises all patrilineal descendants of the agnatic group members who claim to be descendants of Ouedraogo.

30. Tenkudugu constitutes a hybrid example of political traditions in terms of variations of the *Naam* on the different Ghanaian and Burkinabé sides. As the central Mossi states emerged from around the Tenkodogo area, the latter 'provid[ed] a bridge to the patent political formations in present day northern Ghana; therefore its traditions possess critical importance for interpreting the rest' (Saul 2007: 4).

31. Simporé extensively quotes Ki-Zerbo (1978, 82–83). Kawada also discusses the confusion around references to Mamprusi and Dagomba, as well as the thesis of the Nigerian link, Kano in particular (1979, 288). For instance, a former Mogho Naaba, Naaba Tigré would say, with regard to the origin of the Mossi 'When I was in Bordeaux, I read documents according to which the Moose came from Egypt and they transited through Chad; from there they moved to Ghana and finally to Burkina Faso'; see Diallo (1996 in Simporé 2004, 565). Such a reference could be a result of a reworking of the colonial Hamitic hypothesis, thus the absorption of written accounts, some of which are fraught with a number of misinterpretations. All this makes it difficult to reconstruct the trajectory of Mossi migrants into what was to become Moogo.

32. The distinction between 'people of power' and 'earthpriests' is a close but inappropriate translation, and this is discussed in the history of many African societies. The translation of *tengsoba* as 'earthpriest' can be misleading. Earthpriests are believed to be individuals who are endowed with key insights into the workings of nature. These insights are unavailable to ordinary individuals who thus need their mediation for sacrifices and prayers dedicated to nature, ancestors and the earth divinity. Although a chief of the earth/earthpriest is generally opposed to a political chief, the same person may be at once earthpriest and village leader, and sometimes the earthpriest is the only authority in place, in which case he cumulates many capacities. At any rate, there is a conceptual separation between the two functions (thus duality and structural dichotomy) even in instances where the same person plays both roles. The major distinction is the fact that political power is hereditary/lineage-based or gained through elections. It is given by men whereas spiritual power is given by the earth. Among the Tallensi, the distinction between the two offices of the *tengdana* expressed the two complementary aspects of authority exercised over men and over the earth—as well as a ritual link between the local community and the material earth. The term *Tenga* designates the earth, territory, a powerful divine benediction and many other things; see Rattray (1932, 339–44), and Verdier (1965, 333–59).

33. The focus of narrative and the specific details incorporated in formal stories generally serve to explain how a satellite state came to exist and how certain practices were the result of key historical moments. For instance the *'faux depart de La'* becomes an explanatory account of the split between Ouagadougou and Yatenga.

34. Tait (1955, 201) contends that some of the Konkomba who chose to remain were 'rewarded' with the position of bowmen within the army.

35. Continuity and change are conceptualized on the basis of the critical interaction of economic, political, identity and territorial dynamics.

36. Oral tradition recounted in Lentz (1994, 458).

37. For a comparative discussion of the production of history among the Dagara and the Gonja kingdoms, see Goody (1978).

38. On Dagara-Sisala relations, see Lentz (1994).

39. Yelpaala (1983, 373) recounts a familiar West African tale according to which a mythical uncle wanted to reward a deserving nephew and punish an undeserving son. The uncle decreed that all property derived from his farming activities would go to his nephew. Whereas elsewhere the patriclan was a mere expansion of the lineage, among the Dagara the latter was not always a group that could trace an origin to a common male ancestor.

40. This is similar to an account of the Tutsi/Hutu divide whereby a conquering pastoralist group (Tutsi) was promoted as a superior, more 'enlightened' ruling class over the Hutu.

Chapter 3

The Time/Space Dynamics of the Constitution of the Political

INTRODUCTION

Dominant political discourses in the Voltaic region have made the binary of state/stateless, political/non-political and the distinction between the underlying imperatives of the 'sphere of politics' and a 'sphere of rituals' more generally a founding construct for state-society relations. However, these distinctions were never constitutive to the societies and peoples of the Mamprusi-Dagomba-Mossi states system. The divisions were instead gradually instituted through processes of differentiation; they came to acquire something of a historical fact particularly for the more centralized groups.

In the loosely centralized and decentralized societies, these categories of social action and their bearers were part of the same structure of government and governance, and they drew on different sources and modalities of power. As intimated in the previous chapters, the duality discourse has crucial implications not only for the construction and justification of the institutional structure in centralized societies but also for the articulation of ideological discourse and the constitution of social relations. It was therefore often 'theatrilized [*sic*] in as much as a series of rituals are staging the opposition and complementarity of these two figures of power' (Liberski 1991, 72).

The duality discourse produces two distinct, ritual and political figures alongside supporting structures: a category of historical entrepreneurs, equipped with revolutionary ideas and techniques and a drive for change, as opposed to a category of the conquered portrayed as static, timeless, passive and steeped in ancient beliefs. The implications of such a distinction for the possibility of apprehending the operations of politics and the political are too important to be accidental to history. Historical deconstruction therefore requires that we collapse this dichotomy and imagine a frame of understanding whereby centralization does not have to be the sole reference framework. In this regard, the elaboration of political rule among decentralized societies offers key insights for further analysis. Important among these is the recognition that 'both [spheres are] necessary components of a single social system in which locality and descent express the relationship between the spatial extension of society as a productive system (land) and its reproduction from generation to generation (descent)' (MacGaffey 2013, 71). In fact, among the Dagara, Kasena and Kusasi as among other decentralized Voltaic groups, ancestors are not just human beings and divinities, they are also kin and affines, men and women, and therefore at once historical, ritual and ideological categories that are dissolved in a way that renders structural oppositions and binaries inoperative.

Decentralized societies were organized according to a system of ritual jurisdiction: *tengdana* for southern Voltaic states and *tengsoba* for northern Mossi, with an authority over the custody of earth shrines and the preservation of the integrity of social morality (Goody 1971, ch. 4; Wilks 1985, 470; Law 1980, 13–15). Decentralized societies were characterized by 'mobility, overlapping networks, multiple group membership and flexible, context-dependent boundaries' (Lentz 1994, 459).[1] Their organizing structures offer key insights into the processes of sociopolitical genesis for the underlying sociohistorical moments. The 'events that shaped them were not rare' and were very much embedded in the organizing principles of everyday life, essentially in two ways: 'in the everyday flow of African social life and in the traditions of origins of established … African societies and polities' (Kopytoff 1989, 5).

Decentralized societies could adapt to the dynamics of change, particularly within a context of expansionist tendencies of centralized polities, by creating, for instance, nominal political functions for immigrants or performing enskinment rituals that were very similar to those of Mamprugu, a centralized model. Kaboré (1962) relates Nuna and Kasena traditions according to which autochthonous groups invited hunters and dejected chiefs from neighbouring centralized polities. In doing so, they 'loaned' some of their amulets (*kwere*, *kwárá*) to the newcomers, who used them as regalia. By keeping the secret of the fabrication of the regalia, autochthons were able to control political power and its potential for encroaching upon ritual jurisdiction (Gomgnimbou 2009, 338).

This chapter contends that at stake in the constitution of social order among decentralized societies is the mediation of the overlapping, competing control of (sacred) divinities and political agents over the determination of the contours of social experience as they take shape spatially, temporally and historically. From this, three general issues structure our inquiry into the procedures of decentralized systems of governance.

First, at stake in (mis)representations of authority and order is the fundamental question of the relationship between society and nature on one hand and that between different social components/constituents on the other hand. More specifically, beyond the *Naam/Tenga* division, questions of ancestral continuity (descent), territorial (dis)continuity (land and locality), historical discontinuity (centralization) and how they concurrently inform the construction of social order would need to be explored.[2]

Second, the abstract forces that are commonly mobilized in procedures of territorial occupation say this much: the battle of gods and humans unravels in ordinary interventions in both the formally divided sociopolitical and socioritual spheres as spaces of action and possibility. Consequently, the space of rituals in decentralized societies was an active zone of political action. Even as it is commonly presented in the literature as an ahistorical, atemporal and apolitical field, *Tenga* and other ritual fields actively produce categories of knowledge wrought in the multiple permutations of nature/culture formulations. The extent of interdependence between this and other domains derives from the structuration of (settlement) stories that provide schemas and frames of thought for thinking coherently about metaphors, analogies, allegories, figures of speech, prohibitions and moral codes. If references to *Tenga* make it seem like a singular entity/deity, it is very much engaged through a 'plurality of ritual territories and a multitude of competitive ritual actions' (Luning 2007, 93). Variations in foundational stories determine and validate the distance between the two main poles, political and ritual. Among the Kasena for instance, the notion of historical precedence as a source of ideas about rights is fundamentally problematized. Whereas elsewhere in Moogo *the chef de terre* provides the migrant-ruler with the means of his rule, among the Kasena, the two figures are often coeval and historically contemporaneous. The point therefore is that in making visible the strategies of political action contained in the ritual field, a conception of ritual interventions in the landscape needs to be further examined.

Third, this chapter seeks to bring into productive conversation on the one hand the distinction between 'politics' and 'the political' variously conceptualized by Carl Schmitt, Jean- Luc Nancy and Philippe Lacoue-Labarthe and on the other hand the implications for social action of such a distinction. The distinction itself reveals two fundamental problems with a liberal conception of politics. The first problem is the idea that the location of power in the hands of a sovereign is a prerequisite to the possibility of order; in other words, that power is something that exists and circulates in fragmentary forms. A further implication is that in the absence of power's monopolistic concentration, there can only be danger, uncertainty, hostility and ultimately disorder. The second problem is what the distinction suggests, that there is something of a special *quality* in the political that can be isolated and opposed to the social and a whole range of nonpolitical purviews.

This chapter challenges this view in three distinct ways. First, it shows that among the Kasena, the Kusasi and other decentralized Voltaic societies, space is a social-referential domain that produces its own normative and ethical requirements as individuals and groups solicit and confront natural forces and constantly re-enact the past/future to make a present possible. This form of interaction produces its own configuration that is necessarily informed by a particular ecology of life. Second, in the Kasena, Dagara and Kusasi examples I explore specifically in this chapter, the ethics of state inhibition essentially operate as an inhibition against a concentration of power. This is however no rejection of the political per se. The constitutive vigilance against power derives less from objective constraints (even when these are real) than from an ethical posture, although the very idea that people may not desire to be part of centralized structures may be inconceivable to state-bearers.

This chapter looks into the different temporal and spatial modes of structuring at work in the transposition of the division between 'the sphere of power' and the 'sphere of rituals' as a division between the political and the nonpolitical, and the operation of authority and order resulting from an understanding of time in relation to social reproduction, personhood and historical process versus a conception of space in relation to social production, personhood and institutional order. In doing so, the chapter introduces a dimension of multiple temporalities in the conception of sovereignty, not least in the complex interactions between the temporality of kinship in the sequentiality of generations and the spatiality of rule in the fragmentation of space.

Third, hybrid autonomous communities were articulated around a commitment to specific shrines and ritual spaces, and such membership typically intersected with kinship in so far as kin, clan relatives and strangers were (also) recruited as 'constituencies' of ritual locales. The nature of 'the political' that is produced out of these lines of engagement forces us to rethink politics in the very manner in which individuals engage each other in daily modalities and produce intricate forms of sovereignty as closely connected to individual and collective interactions. These different arguments structure the organization of the chapter.

SPATIAL OCCUPATION AND/AS THE
ETHICS OF BEING/RELATING

This chapter re-conceptualizes the inhibition against political centralization that characterizes decentralized societies in terms equivalent to cultural practice and/as political experimentation. It specifically draws on Liberski's work on notions of time/space/territoriality among the Kasena; Mather's work on the Kusasi land gods; and Yelpaala's and Lentz's work on the Dagara's politico-legal organization. The Kasena, the Kusasi and the Dagara are three decentralized, Voltaic societies whose sociological and cultural practices of authority say much about the contours of social phenomena and social thought.

Three aspects of decentralized politics are here of interest to me: (1) the spatial translation and performance of the complexity of social phenomena, (2) social structuration as deployed in the oscillating spatial and temporal poles of social reproduction in the constitution of kin, lineage and society, and (3) the institutional translations of the ethico-legal thinking that underpins social action. These different aspects broadly shape the epistemic conditions that lend political substance to social and cultural practice on the one hand and a philosophy of ecological preservation on the other.

What the imposition of administrative jurisdiction and by extension the imposition of a blanket administrative catalogue does to concepts of self in the validation of subjectivities through rituals is to undermine crucial aspects of agency. One of the arguments I make in this chapter is that decentralized societies went a long way in staging the complexity of the mutually bounded nature of being-as-dwelling and the dynamic character of 'nature'—this includes an undefined historical process—that make being possible. What I'm saying here is that in light of the implications of the spatial occupation strategies for self-constitution, selfhood and social thought outlined below, the very conception of (what is) 'the political' needs to be reworked.

There is something at once emancipatory and constraining in the various modes of spatial occupation among the Kusasi for whom social organization is discussed in terms of spatial *locations*. Social groups are primarily ritual constituencies attached to, or revolving around, discrete ritual territories. The primary dwelling place is the *yir*, an earthen-wall compound inhabited by a *yirdim* (residential group) and typically headed by a *yirana* (senior male). The *yir* is in turn subdivided into *zak* (courtyards). These are generally headed by brothers of the same mother and are inhabited by a residential subgroup made of a mother and her *zadkiim* (offspring). A *dabog*, or lineage, is a house made of lineal segments, or rooms. The *dabog* is opposed to the 'wild', the dwelling space of a wide range of antithetical invisible forces, suspected threats, neighbouring patrilineages, and so forth. Kusasi generally refer to family relations in terms of belonging to the same 'house' or the 'same room' (Mather 2005, 45).

Liberski-Bagnoud describes Kasena settlement patterns along almost the same lines.[3] In fact, one cannot think *community* among the Kasena beyond or outside the notion of a house, or *songo*: 'For the Kasena, one's life is intimately bound to a *songo*, signifying both home/house and belonging to a house. The Kasem feels fulfilled if he founds a house or builds a room' (Abasi 1995, 465).[4] The point is to stress the nature of social constituencies but also the realization of subjectivity as constitutionally linked to residence, location and space. This concept is liberating in so far as it cuts across administrative and political affiliation; it is, however, constraining in the way it defines social inclusion on the basis of spatial-ritual location.

The articulation of patterns of social action and thought in spatial configurations denotes at least one fundamental principle which is that the formation of the political takes root in the interaction between individuals and space. In fact, among decentralized societies, the generation and reproduction of meaning is enabled through this very interaction.[5] Central to this interaction is a basic attempt by individuals to tame or to domesticate potentialities of threat from nature in the very process of human and social formation. This domestication is ritual in form and it is typically deployed in shrines and ritual sites as spaces of encounter and production. Mather for instance remarks that among the Kusasi, 'shrines are sites of mediation where the ambiguity and unpredictability of relations are harnessed to generate meaning' (Mather 2003, 23). In fact, land is never just 'occupied' in an unthought and a random thrust; it is very much conceptualized, engaged and articulated. This engagement is always and necessarily dynamic for it requires the rethinking of being and action, of being and becoming, and therefore self-constitution as an act of interaction and a contribution to past and present signs and memory-making.

If the 'traditional' nature of African experience, the dimension of the 'past' in the African experience, has often been reified, it has also been the case that such reification tends to conceal the prospective(ist) nature of social action even when it builds on the past as a culture and normative frame. The ontological basis of the articulation of social action is by necessity a field of enactments of memory and imagination as inseparable categories. Spatial engagement thus becomes a process of knowledge-making that is pregnant with historical imaginaries. In the investment in traces for future use/consumption, subjectivities are thus projected. The formation of existential selfhood is here indistinguishable from this interactive process.

I insist on the significance of individuals' engagement with their surrounding environment, the interactive process of the constitution of selfhood within this frame and the ritual requirement afferent to this recurrent, historical cycle in order to suggest that both group membership and social structures are a function of these iterations. Insights from Ingold's 'dwelling' perspective and his notion of *taskscape*, elaborated in relation to Kusasi conceptions of space, suggest that the essence of sociality is this. In the performance of everyday tasks, people 'also attend to one another'; they do so in a mutually attentive manner which conveys the particular quality of the 'unfolding of a field of relationships' (Ingold 1993, 160–61, 152–53; Mather 2003, 25).

In the examples I describe, one could even go as far as to contend that people in fact constitute each other in the very making of culture not just because of the inevitability of being bound up to others but also because of an *ethics of being for others* as a matter of responsibility. There is great resonance between such ethics and Judith Butler's insights on the fundamental precariousness of human life. Precariousness is an 'existential condition' that enables individuals to cultivate the referential force of interdependence so as to render the mutual attention adumbrated above not only inevitable but also productive of positive mutuality. Such mutuality is only possible through a context of 'dependency, contiguity and unwilled proximity' of the kind the Kusasi envisage as underpinning individuals' interaction with both ritual spaces and each other (Butler 2010, xxv–xxvi).

In both centralized and decentralized Voltaic societies, there is great tension between the tendency of political authority to assign fixed categories to individuals and groups and the complex process of being-as-becoming through the intertwining of living individuals and ancestral beings. The tension is therefore one between an administrative requirement for social roles to be fixed in a recognizable manner and the ethical requirement for individuals to be 'here now' but also 'there then' in a present-past-future continuous reference (Mather 2003, 26).

The Kasena, the Kusasi and other decentralized Voltaic groups share a practice of founding settlements around shrines, land gods or ritual locales. The next section seeks to understand the dynamics between individuals and groups with ritual sites as a corporeal mnemonic of social action. If territorial use is articulated around ritual zones attached to specific shrines or ritual cores, the limits of ritual areas do not coincide with administrative and political divisions. The overlapping but distinct notions and experiences of territoriality denote original frames of rapport between subjectivity, ritual commitment and territory.

The constitution of governance in a decentralized system becomes conditioned by concepts of territory and space as differentiated categories: the territorial translation of political and juridical fragmentation affects the nature of the spatial expression of principles of belief. An important question that arises from this is What is the relationship of spatial configuration as an expression of social norms with the nature of collective representations?

LAND GODS AND TERRITORIAL
OCCUPATION: MEDIATING SOCIAL PHENOMENA

The relation of human and society to earth/soil/land is shaped by the knowledge that the (work of) the earth is no sinecure. The earth is transformed through hard work, pain and the violence of (re)production. Through this relationship, the articulation of the rapport of human and the earth posits the permanent jurisdiction of the latter on people's horizon. It is this very process of accumulation and restitution of 'debt' that endows people with different degrees and forms of personhood (Marie et al. 1997). In this way, social agents participate in a constant recoding of the social frame through earth rituals. In centralized societies, the very possibility of social life is greatly defined, and constrained, by a variety of rules and institutions, and the absence of these in decentralized societies in no way lessens the weight of obligations and constraints woven in secrecy, dissimulations, anxieties, taboos, cautionary measures and countless prescriptions and proscriptions (Journet-Diallo 2007, 9–52).

At the heart of the production of meaning in everyday settings, every component of social life is committed to the permanent interaction of the living and the expired, the present and the past. The Kasena for instance have a rich repertoire of ritualized daily routines that involve the making of pots and calabashes, the decoration of walls with geometrical patterns, the practice of rock art, all of which are defined by specific rules of precedence and the cadence of life in large homesteads. At the heart of this farmstead-based cultural frame looms the figure of the head wife as key to the fertility link, both literal and figurative, maintained through ritual connections (Fiedermutz-Laun 2005, 260–63). Her mundane acts are codified by the primary requirement of attention to ancestral and household precedence but also to the spirits and invisible beings that populate and participate in the life of the household. The Kasena specifically stretch the requirement for meaning-making as the basis for the construction of life-worlds to radical logics.

While acknowledging the mammoth task of 'making a meaningful life-world out of what is beyond meaning: death', a task at which ancestors have severally failed (*nabara ge tuum pa a wari wongo a ta* [The ancestors have failed to conquer (domesticate, understand) and so I can say nothing (about death)]), the Kasem relentlessly confronts death with brave and necessary questions.[6] Among the Tallensi but also the Builsa, the Kasena and the Nabdam, the cattle yard plays a similarly important role in doubling as a private meeting place for men. The cattle yard links to the *zong* which is the only room in a Tallensi compound that opens onto the cattle yard. The *zong* is a ritual structure where communing with ancestors takes place, along with funerals and fertility (Gabrilopoulos et al. 2002, 230, 232).

According to Mather, land gods or ritual locales among the Kusasi—a notion better rendered in the French translation *aire rituelle* used by Liberski-Bagnoud in relation to the Kasena—configure prevailing 'patterns of social action and thought' as sites of mediation of 'established meanings' (Mather 2003, 23). This process of mediation is at once unending and disciplined for it has to harness the contradictions and antagonisms, the ambiguities and insecurities of a vulnerable life, all under conditions of uncertainty and unpredictability, in order to engender 'stable' meaning and therefore 'stable' life. In the anthropological literature, attempts to conceptualize a landscape beyond its physical attributes have often looked into its capacity to generate meaning.

According to Luig and Van Oppen, historically in Europe, landscape denoted 'a set of social norms (customary law) that apply to a specific settlement' (Luig and Van Open 1997, 9 in Mather 2003, 24). Its restricted reference to topography was thus stretched to reveal its influence on social conduct. In fact, the consolidation of the term 'landscape' from 'an area covered by a set of social norms—a bounded space or territory in which a particular set of norms predominated' (Mather 2003, 24) to a political waste-land that provided an antagonistic frame to processes of statization, urbanization and industrialization indicates an active history of erasure and silencing, in Europe and elsewhere, of the ritual-spatial dimension of political power. Among the Kusasi and the Kasena, 'ritual territory appears as a common good that cannot be owned, not even by ritual officiants, but with which *precarious relationships* should be maintained. However, this inheritance does not apply to a general common good, nor to the future of all generations to come' (Luning 2007, 93; emphasis added). The precarious nature of this relationship presumably exhibits the vulnerability and the texture of the sort of inevitable interdependence discussed above.

At stake here is the particular relationship between landscape and social thought. For the Kusasi, space is not 'occupied' for occupation implies an unthought, unarticulated process. Space is rather engaged in a dynamic, interactive process that produces an indefinitely flexible history as well as flexible social meaning. Space is constituted in the act of *impregnating* it with present and past traces, thus with temporality and meaning:

> The division of the world into a mosaic of externally bounded segments is entailed in the very production of spatial meaning. Just as the word, for Saussure, is the union of a concept with a delimited 'chunk' of sound, so the place is the union of a symbolic meaning with a delimited block of the earth's surface. Spatial differentiation implies spatial segmentation (Ingold 1993, 155).

Space is constituted in an active investment by individuals as 'tenants' of a particular historical period and in the elaboration of material and symbolic traces that are provisions for use by future generations. In other words, space becomes the frame for existential subjectivities construed through projective conceptualizations through a past-future movement. Thus the very conceptualization of occupation, living and dwelling, the turning of land into 'social space' as residence and physical frame of demarcation, is subject to a specific ecology that structures an inclusive ontology. Among the Kasena in particular, 'local social life … is about the right fit between social presence and the bush. This bush is tangible but also a projected space. Accessing and protecting this projected space requires great care in how to place sociality, as is emphasized in narratives and rituals' (Luning 2007, 101). Here, what Luning is gesturing toward is the possibility of a moral community defined by a particular political culture of space-time.

Kasena architectural patterns and dwelling structures reflect the sociopolitical dimensions of the interaction between space and culture. Kasena farmsteads are fortified mud structures organized in circular patterns. The houses themselves are cylindrical buildings narrowly clustered together and surrounded by a protective wall. They are windowless and are 'linked to each other by an apse-like, protruding wall' with entrances looking inward.

In addition, farmstead dwellers share their living space with deceased elders: their graves together with a ritual 'refuse pile' are typically found in the inner courtyard by the entrance to the compound (Fiedermutz-Laun 2005, 252–53). Fiedermutz-Laun gives the example of the farmstead of an eastern Kasena *pe*, or district chief, which contains 'ancestral graves in the inner courtyard, a sacral sphere in the form of an outer court or *mationgo*, a circular mud-throne bearing insignia such as sacral trees, and a ritual rubbish pile' (2005, 253). In the mid-twentieth century, 'the elevated political status of the *pe* came to be expressed … through architectural elements such as the house of worship, *koara dige*, containing ritual objects (*koara*).' Upon assuming power, the *pe* is required to spend a month at the *koara dige* with his first wife so that she can conceive (2005, 253).

Aires rituelles in turn reflected normative structures and established normative conduct and categories. This meant that their greater alignment with the sociological contours was an asset in the possibility of thwarting attempts at political centralization. They could reinforce these normative categories, but there was an ambiguous latency for they could also 'be put to practical use, for performing actions and proposing alternative categorizations that contradict, refute, and challenge the norm' depending on the perceived potency of the supernatural power mobilized in the performance of rituals (Mather 2003, 28). The hidden nature of the knowledge that lends authority to the *tengdana* (officiating priest) is such that it leaves much room for interpretation and manipulation. But this knowledge is susceptible to decline and alteration; its relationship to the efficacy of ritual intervention and the competence of officiating agents articulates and reflects the dimensions of social change.

Following Colson, Mather makes a distinction between 'shrines of the land' as representing and symbolizing the founders of a particular settlement and 'places of power' as representing and symbolizing a covenant between first-comers and land spirits. The latter denotes greater recognition of the integral 'power' of ritual sites and by extension the land as an autonomous agent. The Kusasi land god *Agole*, residing on a hill that juts over Yarigungu, is a good example of a 'place of power'. The Kusasi of Agole territory (also referred to by the same name) do not conceive of themselves as a discrete social group outside this reciprocal relationship and covenant with the spirit of the land. This covenant is underpinned by a principle of mutuality. The loyalty, but also the kin membership of spirits, comes under question when the spirits fail to deliver assistance in times of need. This often results in their shrines being neglected by living kin (Colson 1997, 52). The senior earthpriest in his dual role of chief and priest to an extent embodies this principle of reciprocity.

The constitution of the Kusasi as an autonomous group is associated with a Mamprusi retaliative expedition in the early nineteenth century. In an attempt to avenge the killing of a cruel Mamprusi prince ruling over Bawku (Mahama) by Kusasi and Bisa, the Mamprusi sent an armed cavalry. According to Kusasi legends, a swarm of bees from the Agole hills—where the Kusasi had taken refuge—overcame the Mamprusi army, thus consolidating the very covenant that underpinned the Kusasi's attachment to the land god. Sacrifices and rituals performed for Agole serve many purposes. They are meant to revisit the covenant that binds people to the land, and they are a recognition of the inherent power of Agole. In the sense that 'the spirit of the land is fused with the spirit of the founding ancestor, this attachment provides the ultimate rationalization for establishing and maintaining reciprocal relations with the lands' (Mather 2003, 33).

Drawing on examples from the southern African context, Schoeffeleers categorizes shrines as territorial cults 'whose constituency is a territorial group identified by common occupation of a particular land area, so that membership of the cult is in the final instance a consequence of residence and not kinship or ethnic designation' (1999, 50 in Colson 1997, 48). If we were to extend Schoeffeleers's designation to ritual sites in general, it is obvious that the singular appeal of ritual practice is that it cuts across and transcends ethnic, political and other boundaries, and this is crucial for my argument. Ritual sites have the quality of 'timelessness' in that they predate communities, residential and sociopolitical arrangements. Their 'non-human origin' means that 'their cults override parochial political considerations' hence their appeal to communities of settlers of old and new stock, but also to migrants (Colson 1997, 48).

In fact, as Werbner surmises with regard to the Mwari cult of southwest Zimbabwe, the contours of this sort of ritual order can be seen as 'underwriting the idea of a moral world order, guaranteed by the understanding that those on religious errands should have the right of free movement across communal boundaries' (1989, 246 in Colson 1997, 48). Not only that, but ritual devotion as a mode of individual and collective constitution necessarily has to relate to ancestors and land spirits as entities that operate both inside and outside history.

Among the Kusasi, the *tengbana*, or land god, is 'skin of the earth' and ritual authority is conceived of as covering 'the land and human relations with the land' (Mather 2003, 33). Given that each clan and maximal lineage has its own land god, the implications for territorial organization, the possibility of group membership and the nature of social action are too important to be ignored. The rituals and various performances associated with Agole and lesser gods have to be seen as mapping the contours and revisiting the terms of a charter that governs society at large. In fact, Kusasi society draws a framework for settlement, mobility structures and the modalities of social recruitment from the configuration of land gods. In other words, equivalences between ritual, spatial and social divisions make land gods discrete spatial markers that orient people's movements and activities. One important implication is that any additional markers such as administrative divisions are necessarily grafted onto this first layer of social organization for throughout history, land gods are the most 'permanent features of the landscape regarded as inherently sacred or as the loci of spiritual power' (Colson 1997, 48; Mather 2003, 34, 35). The tending and dynamization of land gods mobilize all segments of Kusasi society. To participate in specific rituals, to tend specific land gods and to organize specific festivals all become enactments of group identification, a performed claim to particular territories and a demarcation of social differentiation, in addition to being an eminently political act.

The modalities of the social order thus delineated are informed by, and infused with, the intellectual and spiritual force of the land gods. Land gods could be trees, caves, mounds, hills, river shores and similar fixtures which are bearers of the traces of historical occupation and a reminder of the interconnected nature of past and present.

As mentioned above, there were many occasions, in Kusasi and Kasena daily endeavours, that showcased the imbricated nature of dwelling as a mode of engagement with different notions of space, but there were more specific moments of communion that dramatized this dynamic even more starkly; enshrinement was one of these. Enshrinement can be seen as a strategy to domesticate land spirits and tame their excess emotions and their whims.

These spirits are thus so to speak re-integrated in the human order in the discrete categories articulated around blood and locality.

As social authorities, land gods intervene in the regulation of social order, and they palliate the ills and disasters that strike society. In order to influence the direction of their action, the Kusasi must seek to 'capture' spirits and this is the essence of enshrinement (Mather 2003, 40–41). In repositioning ancestral spirits at the summit of the hierarchical order through enshrinement rites, the Kusasi both recognize and endorse 'the transition of a social persona from living member of the community to ancestor' (41). One can also see, in this very process, the normative transformation of a 'human community' to a 'community of land dwellers'—that is, a community fit not only to occupy the land and to cohabit with ancestral spirits and land gods but also to negotiate with them social and political frames and categories.

Ritual sites themselves become the sites of the formation of discourse, protest and dissidence in the performance of rituals and in the displacement and transfer of ritual places, the erection of new sites and the mobility of members between different spheres of ritual influence such as neighbouring village and localities. The modalities of everyday life are shaped by these transactions in what they denote of the ambiguities and uncertainties mirrored in the desires and wills of gods. Mobility here articulates spatial continuity and discontinuity; it is built, structurally, in the production of social, political and ritual order. But also germane to the epistemes of Kusasi was the way in which space routinized movement. Specifically, the integration of new cults by newcomers or cults borrowed or 'bought' from neighbours constituted productive interference in the way they subtly displaced pre-existing practices.

In considering the effects of enshrinement on social action, Bell's study of the link between ritual and temporality offers key insights as regards the notion of validation in relation to memory and by extension to historical construction and social change. Bell contends that the purpose of ritualization is to 'structure a space-time environment through a series of physical movements'. The frame thus produced moulds social actors and 'both validates and extends the schemes they are internalizing' (1992, 109–10 in Insoll 2009, 290).

The temporality of rituals suggests that individuals can project and inscribe changing constructs of selfhood and (human) potentialities as many sediments onto space/land. It also suggests that change cannot be an adjunct to ritual time but must be very much inbuilt in *movement* as the principle that underpins ritual practice. For Insoll, movement enables stability rather than stasis for it is informed and articulated in a broad 'ritual reservoir' (2009, 291). Change is also a function of knowledge that fluctuates on the basis of memory and capacity. This is most evident in the 'anticipated effects' of the ritual of earthpriests in so far as agricultural production and human productivities were concerned. If the earthpriest's role was to enhance 'the fertility of the crops in his territory [to ensure] abundant and fruitful harvests,' his success was contingent upon the power of neighbouring earthpriests to 'deliver' (Luning 2007, 92–93). This competition was therefore a structuring mechanism of the distribution of knowledge of history and historical practice, but also of the earth and spatial configurations. The bigger point remains the heterotemporal nature of the principles that cohere in the articulation of social action across the social, the mental, the cognitive, the political, the material and the existential between language, codes and symbols (Schoenbrun 2006, 1403, 1418).

What is missing in this configuration, however, is a narrative of sovereignty and self-constitution. The juridical principle of sovereignty established by Westphalia in relation to European states remains ambiguous in its applicability to non-European states and nations; it is not clear for instance how it might apply to the precolonial Kusasi, Kasena and Dagara. In the following section, a conception of sovereignty is explored in relation to a notion of subjecthood at the intersection of space, belonging and ritual operations.

RITUAL LOCALES AND SOVEREIGNTY

Thus far, I have tried to show how spatial configurations and categories of temporality create a frame of reference that is crucial to institutions and practices of mutuality and order. At the interaction of space and time, human action is constrained by ecological imperatives. Sovereignty under these conditions is enacted in a variety of foundations and through ontologically operative mechanisms. *These are at once ecological, spatial, historical, ritual and economic, all operating in conjunction rather than separately.* What I have tried to demonstrate in the previous section is that a common view of human constituencies as either articulated around genealogy or territory does not critically capture the nature of the territoriality as enabled by adherence to ritual communities. Such a distinction has often motivated a functional division between the utilitarian (genealogical governance) and the 'moral' (ritual governance) as distinct terrains of possibility. Among the Kasena, this kind of distinction is rather difficult to make (Liberski-Bagnoud 2002, 19).

In effect, the different ways in which people relate to space and land, and the manner in which they divide and demarcate territory, offers an interesting if alternative view of the practice of mutuality. This principle binds individuals' action toward each other and in relation to their environment to an ethics of *mutual attentiveness* as adumbrated above. Socially, this principle is operationalized in the deployment of norms that weave a number of obligations and responsibilities among members belonging to the same *aire rituelle*. These may be clans that are ritually allied to the same *aire*.

The Kasena, the Kusasi, the Dagara and their decentralized neighbours formally experience two forms of rule, ritual and political, both of which are often amalgamated in the same individual.[7] This is neither unusual nor surprising given the uncertain boundaries between different categories of action for such a distinction would have limited constitutional effect. Among the Dagara, the title *naa* (chief) was also used to refer to a rich person (*bundaana* or *terasob*, both synonyms of *naa*). This could mean a number of things—for instance, that a ruler provided sustenance and protection to those who worked for him (Yelpaala 1983, 361) or that there were lines of structuring out of accumulation as a marker of achievement.

The differentiation thus created—by gratitude, need and (inter)dependency—would become a basis for the constitution of political power that is also a translation of economic power. In this endeavour, social precedence is primarily a function of one's culturally defined and ritually expressed power. Among neighbouring Tallensi, the Namoos claim descent from Mamprugu whereas the autochthonous Talsé claim the status of first-comers. While political rule was not restricted to the Namoos, access was determined by an individual's capacity to demonstrate affiliation with earlier chiefs. Among *tendaana*-holding groups, this meant an attested ritual bond with the Earth or one of the ancestral cults (Fortes 1945, 39, 184), and for this latter group, a non-linear type of sociality applied 'in the double sense of that which precedes the start of social time, as well as that which is outside of social space' (Luning 2007, 100).

At the heart of this chapter is the vexing issue of cohabitation for it poses ontological questions for communities on the nature of the relationship between individuals and nature and among groups sharing a natural space given their diverse origins and commitments. Communities were to come to consensus (multiple consensus) on the nature of the world they lived in and to reflect on the means of engaging that world as they might be brought to see it (Stahl 2001, 6). Cohabitation also poses the problem of how different communities relate to nature and to the land/space/territory they share and depend on in more or less equal measures. It ultimately points to degrees of complexity as regards 'African aspirations for moral community and the forms of collective action they inspire' (Schoenbrun 2006, 1403). These are aligned with ecological diversity and the shifting possibilities of social forms.

In relation to the above, I wish to understand the dynamic interactions of the *political* and the *territorial*—specifically, the role of propitiation not only in mediating the natural and the material but also in linking competence of action with the potential of adherence. In setting aside, conjointly, a view of territory as purely or eminently political, and a propensity to reify blood/

family relations over other crucial types of co-constitution such as those generated by a common commitment to sacrificial cults and also to earth-skins, I like the way Liberski-Bagnoud is able to demonstrate, among the Kasena, the originality of *aires rituelles* as social borders spawn by the lineage system but which intersect the latter in a peculiar manner. In theorizing belonging away from what Glissant calls 'terriorialized filiation' outside the lineal mode (of filiation) and the territorial mode, one is able to locate productive agency and promise in identities 'of relation' (Glissant 1990, 27, 57).

When we pose the relational dimensions of spatial layouts, the role of ritual as political *governor* cannot be eschewed (Niang 2014). If modern theory, the exclusion of numerous forms of knowledge from theoretical engagement, does not allow a ready translation of ritual knowledge into fixed paradigmatic functions, unfamiliar forms crucially need to be integrated in our attempt to apprehend the spatial and temporal dimensions of political action.

Sovereignty as we understand it becomes a poor vehicle for grasping such complex structures of interaction. From the Kasena example, it would be misleading to conceive of sovereignty only as a modality of rule. Sovereignty was a function of knowledge—in other words, the capacity to make visible that which is sacred thus mysterious. Every *aire rituelle* generates so to speak a specific kind of spatial subjecthood and a different kind of sovereignty; members of particular *aires* perform propitiating acts and develop a cult to specific groves (earth-skin) under the supervision of a celebrant and according to changing terms and the purpose of propitiation.

Among the Kasena, the earth-skin produces three distinct but overlapping forms of subjectivity. First, it is the place where members of an agnatic lineage belonging to the same *aire rituelle* symbolically 'come into reality'—it is in fact the place where they 'breathe'. Second, the earth-skin provides a vital breathing space for isolated individuals with no agnatic affiliation but who dwell within the same ritual boundaries. Thus the earth-skin constitutes both a historical and a common mythical referent for all groups that cohabit in the same *aire rituelle* (Dacher 2005). In doing so, *aires rituelles* produce at once communities and spaces that problematize conventional territorial divisions around villages and other territorial units.[8]

Ultimately therefore, the type of sociality produced under these conditions is not entirely territorial, or lineal, or residential, or structural or political but all of these at once. Such a sociality essentially brings out more starkly the significance of notions of parenthood and social affiliation, culture and territoriality, belief and subjecthood.

This leads me to an essential discussion of the place of 'religion', 'belief' and their many inflections as well as different orders of belief in state/society relations, particularly the interpretation of secularism as a space that would be distinct, in value, distance, function and quality from the space of belief which can be pushed back to some 'private' realm. The very notion that the 'secular' is indispensable to a balanced political life is itself a nineteenth-century revisionist argument that found credence in Europe but was never sufficiently tested. It is a doubtful argument.

Moreover, the opposition of the secular and the religious makes little sense in light of the multiplicity of human experience of social authority. Even in so-called modern republics, the binary religious/secular does in no way exhaust the many dimensions of the state for there is no contradiction, for instance, between being republican and non-secularist at the same time. The Kasena and others have always operated outside this type of distinction and this line of demarcation anyway on the basis of modes of regulations that are not mutually exclusive. What the Kasena example shows us, therefore, is first, the impossible distinction between these spheres, and second, in the imperative that people modify and adjust rituals in order to accommodate new 'political' institutions, ritual innovation is invested in the service of political experimentation and not the other way around.

SUBJECTIVITIES OF INTERSECTION

I'm interested in those ideas *from* and *about* the sacred and ritual from which public morality seems to be derived. Among decentralized societies, whenever there was a need to modify the political setting—such as for the creation or allocation of new roles of authority; the demarcation of territory as politically useful; the nomination of people for actions and roles they did not have before (e.g., a contingent war-chief in a non-centralized society), ritual practices and configurations had to be changed. This element is crucial for my argument. Periodically, the political needed to be accommodated or *normalized* in the way that people relate to each other and to the constitutive mechanisms of productive life. Therefore, if 'every significant structural differentiation has its specific ritual symbolism, so that one can, as it were, read off from the scheme of ritual differentiation the pattern of structural differentiation and the configuration of norms of conduct that goes with it' (Fortes 1970, 91), it is precisely because adjustments have to be made so that the changes incurred by political innovation can be properly integrated.

In both centralized societies and stateless groups, lineage structures were only one way of formulating relationality and positionality, authority and continuity; these elements were also distilled within parallel institutions that crosscut and intersected lineage, residence, descent structures such as age groups, title societies, technician and artisan groups, secret societies, cult groups and so forth. Equally, it was not unusual, among stateless societies, that the two roles of political and ritual ruler should be combined.[9] This was in fact the norm rather than an exception even though the two spheres were presented as two modes of intervention in the world made at once antagonistic and complementary: one that protected and healed (ritual) and one that appropriated and destroyed (political; Liberski-Bagnoud 2002).

The Kasena example I used above is instructive on so many levels, not least in the manner in which solidarity was routinized, within lineages, in the frame of courtyard spaces and across lineages through commonly held *aires rituelles*, and the way in which it was performed, steadily, in rituals attached to particular *aires*. The centrality of cultural spaces is undeniable in establishing the terms of living between communities.

The imbrications between blood relations and 'soil relations', territorial dynamics and lineal dynamics, point to the fact that ties on the basis of territory (*jus soli*) and blood (*jus sanguini*) can find different and innovative interpretations. If in the world of human descent, generations succeed each other in a linear order, in the configuration above, such linearity makes little sense (MacGaffey 2013, 71). The idea is not just to establish that 'space' is as crucial a category as 'time' in deciphering the parameters of lineal relationships; the sacred grove is at once a space of exception and a differentiated space in the same manner as the *lieu de souffle* of a lineage is the repository of the 'breath' or 'soul' of all members of a lineage. The multiplicity of 'spaces of breath' that dot an area territorialize social groups but can also be seen as autonomous entities inscribed upon the body of the earth, limitless and undifferentiated.

In relation to this discussion, Deleuze and Guattari expand upon Jean-Luc Nancy's reflections on statelessness to make two important suggestions. The first is that there is a constructive ethics in fighting the state. Second, they note that the state as development and trajectory cannot be made sense of as a self-contained process that is independent from, and uninfluenced by, its interactions with non-state forms and processes (Deleuze and Guattari 1987, 360). However, one should not read in Deleuze and Guattari the romanticized statelessness of philosophical nomadism that extolls the deterritorializing forces of stateless thinking. In fact, stateless thinking has great appeal for postmodern thinking because of its potential to deconstruct absolutisms and undo institutions, notably the centralized state, though postmodernists are stuck at the level of discourse and transition and rarely do they engage the life-worlds of the peripheries that provide fodder for European theory (Cresswell 1997). The latter are, so to speak, suspended from history, time and contingencies. The possibility, here, to bring into the conversation Nancy's and Deleuze and Guattari's views and the Kasena, the Dagara or the Kusasi's practice of decentralized politics is developed below in an attempt to further explore the distinction of 'politics' from 'the political.'

The issue of mutuality discussed previously prompts the question of how human processes emerge out of a temporality that is neither chronology nor history for 'the notion that we can stand aside and observe the passage of time is founded upon an illusion of disembodiment' (Ingold 1993, 157, 159). In the very culture of dwelling, we 'effect' time in a manner that allows us to capture at once past and present (as possibility or vista) in that unique moment of action (Merleau-Ponty 1962, 421 in Ingold 1993, 159). This possibility allows Ingold to maintain that 'the present is not marked off from a past that it has replaced or a future that will, in turn, replace it; it rather gathers the past and future into itself, like refractions in a crystal ball' (1993, 159). Durkheim long ago recognized this quality (to bridge time so to speak) as inherent to rites, festivals and various types of ceremonies. His conception of temporality is fundamentally social. In engaging the world, people also engage each other; in other words, people 'attend to one another' in conducting their tasks (Durkheim 1976, 10 in Ingold 1993, 159). And they do so verbally, or silently through codes, symbols, body language, mimetism, creativity and so forth. Temporality thus must be seen on the one hand at the intersection of 'event', history (as passage of events) and historical agents and on the other hand in the relations between these elements. In Evans-Pritchard's words, temporality is '*the succession of tasks* [as much as] *their relations to one another*' (Evans-Pritchard 1940, 101–2 in Ingold 1993, 161; emphasis added).

Ingold proposes we think about temporality in terms of an analogy with an orchestral performance whereby the musician has to match his play to the movements of fellow musicians and of the conductor so that his music can *resonate* with that of others. Social life is equally made of repetitions, cycles and rhythms and an intricate interweaving of these elements. Social life is also 'a dense fabric of concurrent tensions' in which the foundation of sociality lies 'in the resonance of movement and feeling stemming from people's mutually attentive engagement, in shared contexts of practical activity' (Ingold 1993, 160).[10]

CONSTITUTIONAL PRACTICE AND AUTHORITY IN A DECENTRALIZED SOCIETY

The Dagara constitutional order can be seen as operating at two levels that correspond to the main regulatory frameworks of social life. First, there is the order that governs the relations among individuals and groups within broader community models. Second there are rules and codes that govern people's engagement with nature. The Voltaic groups under study are mostly sedentary horticulturalists, their corporate groups often articulated around a patrilineal segmentary organization.

Leadership is provided in the complementary offices of a 'political' chief with limited authority over various units, clans, communities, lineage and an earthpriest whose jurisdiction extends to land allocation and the preservation of fertility. The *chef de terre*, closer in meaning to the notion of *tengsob*, supervises the sacrifices required before important endeavours or for the restoration of broken linkages. He also controls the distribution and the transfer of rights to land. This gives him control over valuable material resources. The territorial element of the *chef de terre* is therefore important for it denotes the political and administrative dimensions of the ritual ruler's responsibilities and his regulatory power within the boundaries of a given *ten-gan*[11] (see below).

Despite a common tendency to confine the realm of the ritual ruler to that of 'tradition', constitutional entitlements were guaranteed not in an abstract *tradition* as a vast experiential imaginary that could be filled with a wide variety of experimental practices but by practices that constituted contingent settlements even when they seemed rigidly coded. The 'village' is only the visible expression of a structure of interdependency spatially articulated, and which has been made more complex by the constant flow of migration out of Central and Western Africa starting in the seventeenth century by people looking for land (M. Somé 1999, 74–89).

Among the Dagara, *ten-gan* is held to mean two things. First, *ten-bàalo* is the lifeblood that sustains human and natural life as it is fecundated by *saa* (rain) and *namwin* (sky-divinity). It also receives the remains of human and natural life at death. Clan members affiliated with a specific *ten-gan* describe it as the repository of their 'breath', as 'the place where [they] breathe' (Liberski-Bagnoud 2002, 92). Second, *ten-gan* is a living spirit, a membrane covered by a *gan* (skin; hence the notion of earth-skin) over which all living things move (M. Somé 1999, 75).

A first level of ritual governance is articulated in a collective subscription to the cult of *ten-gan*. In the second level of governance, social action is influenced by structural mechanisms articulated around *ten-gan* and affiliated entities: *baa* (stream), *man* (river), *tanw* (mountain) and *wiè* (nature) as well as others. The various operations of these entities impose codes on human and social action especially as regards the exploitation of natural resources. In case of a violation, the *ten-gan sob* has to perform propitiation rituals. People therefore resort to a *ten-gan sob* as a mediator, 'not an owner of something, but a caretaker of a particular engagement' that consists of seeking to redress broken equilibriums (Luning 2007, 99).

Once the commonly held traits of decentralized government, namely egalitarianism (limited or no social hierarchy), freedom and isogamy have been identified, a recurring concern with the implications of 'fragmentation' seems less to do with a concern for disorder than with the administration of violence.

Obviously, a state-centred focus is at work here which ultimately locates sovereignty as the capacity to distribute violence by a 'final locus of juris-diction', therefore a head (here opposed to a 'headless' or acephalous group; Spruyt 1994, 35). The Dagara however seem to make a distinction between *government* and *custody*. The former predisposes a structured, centralized use of violence while the latter negates the necessity of a 'head' for efficacy and coherence for the acquisition, use and transfer of land as well as its adminis-tration because the benefit of clans or localities was subject to certain rules and codes (B. Somé 1969, 19–20).

Across the groups under study, the inflections of decentralized government were by and large determined by (1) a fundamental distrust of coercion and a strong desire to limit its possibility; (2) a practice of independence—corol-lary to a rejection of centralized rule—enacted in the architectural tradition; (3) an efficient cooperation between groups, whether related by blood or not for every clan had a ritual alliance with at least one other clan, and intergroup (re)alignments were often codified by soil charters; and (4) diffused authority distributed across *yir* (families), *dog-lu* (patrilineages) made of clan elders of first-comer groups who mediated conflicts and supervised sanctions linked to contraventions of moral codes,[12] and the *tenga yele* (chieftaincy of the land) represented by the *ten-gan sob* who was both earthpriest and political chief before colonial rule and the subsequent split of the two functions (Evariste 1998, 84–95).

The dual authority figure was responsible for the administration of peace and justice, for invoking *ten-gan* for rains and for keeping harm away through propitiations. Next to the *tengan sob*, the *suo sob* performed sacrifices and acted as *tempèlu sob* (mediator) between populations and the *ten-gan sob* and between them and *ten-gan*. Recruited from a lineage different from that of the *ten-gan sob*, he found support in the council of elders and served as a counter-power to the *ten-gan sob* (M. Somé 1999, 76). In the absence of a centralized state apparatus, the system of ritual constituencies, corporate and compound structures and age-sets among other mechanisms therefore provided, with the council of elders, a governance by committee for acephalous societies in the Voltaic region (Anafu 1973, 27).

Contingencies such as conflicts, war or extreme distress could mobilize corporate groups across linguistic and cultural divides. For instance, in the absence of a standing army, the Tallensi and Builsa pooled forces in times of war. Interclan solidarity was enacted in sacrificial events concerning birth and especially death whereby 'relatives of exterior yard' (as were called ritually allied clans) would perform rituals to a common 'exterior altar' (Liberski-Bagnoud 2002, 92–93).

The apparent demarcation between an 'interior' and 'exterior' altar, or yard or room, thus far characteristic of a manner of defining, identifying and ordering individuals' position within clans and lineal groups, here does not have the same ordering principle. The use of the same language for a different normative imaginary, therefore, requires some explaining. On the one hand, there were limits to action—or the possibility of action for a singular group facing conditions either cyclical (locusts, disease) or contingent (the emergence of eaters of the soul, witchcraft, etc.) that exposed the group to 'technical' and ontological challenges.[13]

The practice of extending the language of genealogical affiliation to those lineages to which a particular group is ritually allied, marks a concern to articulate a specific distress as general and common to groups. This serves to articulate a 'territory' as a terrain of support, both physical and metaphorical, for the possibility of action. In fact, modes of ritual engagement are defined by subscription to a common 'altar' (*nawuuri*, or 'territorial section') rather than belonging to a core cult of origin. Contiguous territorial occupation is therefore the norm rather than the exception for ritually allied groups.

Further, although the construction of fictitious relations is complex and their logic not apparently accessible to lay observers, clans and groups are said to engage in 'collective plant-seeding'. The making of 'community' among the Kasena therefore is a conscious endeavour that has to be apprehended on its own terms.[14] The attempt here has been to show that this consciousness participated in the model of governance. In addition to the genealogical fiction model, there also were other types of relations based on a convenient and pragmatic 'ritual work'. This further confirms rather than deflects the idea of the making of community and therefore of the constitution of the political as primarily an engagement with the sacred through various means.

For Liberski-Bagnoud, 'the complex theory that articulates the notion of "plant-seeding" (*dwi*) to that of territory' has to be understood as fundamental to intergroup collaboration most effective in *bagr*, or funeral rituals (Liberski-Bagnoud 2002, 102). The model of fictitious genealogy that locks people in a common frame of mutual assistance—manifest in the metaphorical use of 'room'—is therefore only partially captured in the common use by social anthropologists of the notion of 'ritual parenthood'.

In a system that was not strictly matrilineal, the succession of ritual rulers was however determined on the basis of connections through women: the son of an acting earthpriest, a grandson through a daughter, was often designated. As a result, the power of the priest was constantly fragmented and widely distributed; it was necessarily diffuse and de-concentrated. If the power of the *tengan sob* to adjudicate on economic, legal and political matters was expressed and enacted in ritual terms, it prevailed over religious motivations—necessarily so because (1) ritual knowledge was specialized, and

(2) the mediation of the relations among humans and those between humans and their environment was an eminently political endeavour.

The location of these multiple roles and functions in the person of the *tengan sob* or the *tindana* should not be a surprise. The yields of harvests, like other aspects of the sustenance of life itself, were believed to be enabled by conjunctive cosmological forces. As such, the preservation of their continued possibility required continued propitiation of *ten-gan*. The *tindana*'s intervention in the market system for instance was not only necessary, it was an onto-logical imperative that posed the very possibility of life for if interferences were left to endure against proper moral alignment, the capacity of *ten-gan* and other cosmological forces to keep on providing would be compromised. This imperative has an environmental corollary in the injunction for humans to balance consumption/usage with resources. At work here is a singular mechanism of control over the public good as that which is not the property of any particular person, group or institution but as something that belongs to an unconditional collective. As such, it was not to be hoarded, defiled or appropriated for limited use.

Equally, the constitutional 'charter' that governs social life among the Kasena applies to 'localities' made of webs of filiation among relatives linked by blood and among distinct lineal groups that occupy the same territorial confines. Strangers, both those who have assimilated and those who have kept a discrete identity, are included in this model. According to Liberski-Bagnoud, 'the tendency to code most social relations in terms of blood relations is expressed in many ways, but it is most salient in the fact that in the (governing) charter are introduced names of ancestors that are strictly speaking "ascendants"' (2002, 63). One can see in the common preoccupation with the constitutional orchestration of family-like systems of obligations a desire to compensate for the limits of precarious alliances.

To stress the specificity of this key determinant, and the relation to the land of the person who rises to the place of chief, his body is marked by a series of prohibitions. The chief is the guardian of the *kwárá* (the horn of an animal), symbol of power. One component of the *kwárá* is soil taken from various groves. The *kwárá* is 'daughter of the soil', with protective attributes that complement those of 'earth-skins'.

This is not to say that stateless societies *also* had government but to stress the internalization of the key functions and attributes of government in the coding of social and bodily rules. For instance, the ethics of hospitality and solidarity often evoked in relation to decentralized communities is not neces-sarily a measure of the fundamental goodness of the Kasena or Tallensi above other societies but rather an instance of livelihood strategies designed to curb potential destitution and isolation. In the absence of an ideology of order and a textual anchoring, social authority in decentralized societies was woven in invisible entanglements. Thus taboos abounded, with regard for instance to the making of noise at certain areas; sexual intercourse in the bush; pouring water in certain areas; shouting at night; the cultivation of 'wild' areas and the cutting of certain plants, for example.

The description above, the functions of social and bodily rules, barely resonates with conventional conceptualizations of power and authority. Despite its limits however, post-structuralist methodology imposes a certain rigor and forces a sustained effort to find coherence and logic in the configurations above and to refuse the idea of disorder and of the unfamiliar though less that of 'timelessness' and 'tradition'. It brings the possibility of philosophical reflection to the intersection of anthropological trivia and historical depth. If the anthropological 'fact' or 'event' cannot constitute a basis for laws, the anthropological fact as history and collective experience is not just useful but necessary to understanding the linkage between morality, politics and government.

For the longest time, the characterization of stateless societies as anarchical resulted more from methodological shortcomings and epistemological flaws—that is, a narrow understanding of 'government' as the location of politics. Early explorers and anthropologists were presumably baffled not to find familiar European social organizations in Africa. In an edited volume, Susan McIntosh broadens the field of applicability of the frame proposed in this book. She conceives of knowledge-based political economies as a conceptual and practical response to social diversity, the challenge to institute hierarchies both vertical and horizontal, and therefore the need to embed complexity in decision-making structures. The mobilization of ritual authority concurrent with that of the resources of political power points to a conception of power in terms of effective action rather than any perceived inherent properties (McIntosh 1999, 4, 17).

One cannot conceive of ritual spaces such as graves, shrines and altars as 'timeless' places. If the Earth has been here 'forever' and if it has no chronological history, if it is impersonal, as the Tallensi believe, it is also very much 'alive—that is, a controlling agency in the lives of men' and their surroundings (Fortes 1940, 255).

> First of all, the presence of new social life at a place requires the establishment of a relationship with the local, with the bush as a beyond. The first earth priests were literally made to assure a good articulation of a place and a social presence through ritual. Second, social life is portrayed as a temporal process in which movement in space and the filling of space are central. Sociality implies processes of fission and migration in which more and more places in the bush serve to accommodate social presence (Luning 2007, 89).

Colonial authorities in fact understood some of these spatial-temporal dynamics for they destroyed dwellings and the physical architecture of the Lobi (1921–1922) and Dagara (1923–1924) in order to break their sources of refuge and resistance as they proceeded to force villages together under new and centralized political units. To fight against the policy of clustering human dwellings, the Lobi and Dagara retreated farther into the bush and turned their temporary shelters (generally put together during the rainy season) into permanent structures (M. Somé 1999, 80, 82). Further, as the *chefs de terre* became increasingly marginalized under colonization, new forms of defiance, cultural and non-confrontational, were enabled in the importation of new cults across the Voltaic region, especially in formerly acephalous societies.[15]

The focus in this section has been on the nature of process relations across groups, the stuff that makes communities possible in a decentralized system architecturally, ritually, discursively and politically. The above analysis suggests that accumulated practice and invocation become a symbolic capital upon which both recognition and respectability can be bestowed.

OF POLITICS AND THE POLITICAL

Without suggesting the radical view that everything is political, Kasena's and similar decentralized models can be deployed as a critique of theoretical engagements on the perceived fading, limits, fragmentation, instability, or disappearance of 'the political' variously articulated in the works of post-foundational scholars such as Giorgio Agamben, Carl Schmitt, Philippe Lacoue-Labarthe and Jean-Luc Nancy.

For the proponents of the *Naam* in centralized societies, the peoples governed by the laws of *Ten-ga(n)* were by and large apolitical; they evolved *outside* the realm of the politically conscious. As such, if they could be recognized in any political consciousness at all, it had to be intermittent, irrational and aberrant. The 'political' is precisely defined as a discrete category of action and appropriated by the state as a marker of identity. However, in a context whereby markers of identity proliferate and do not follow any set typology, state ascriptions of identity are reduced to no more than provisional stratagems designed to support specific claims. This is particularly true for the use of foundational stories, place names, clan denominations, migration narratives, economic activities and so forth—as flexible and malleable as these are—as markers of identity. I elaborate on this topic in chapter 4. For now, this chapter attempts to articulate the challenge in recognizing and theorizing 'the political' as framed and articulated in unfamiliar guise and in unfamiliar sites.

The particularity of the Dagara, the Kasena and the Kusasi and similar decentralized groups is to recognize the open nature of cultural arguments. Their plurality fosters an environment of dissension, rupture and uncertainty. They also recognize that to tame plurality and dissension requires processes of ordering that could lead to the sort of centralization that would eventually repress these possibilities, hence a cultural preference for taboos and ritual prohibitions as adumbrated above.

SCHMITT AND THE THEOLOGICAL STATE

In the political thought of Carl Schmitt and the post-foundational thought of Philippe Lacoue-Labarthe and Jean-Luc Nancy, the distinction between 'politics' and 'the political' suggests the possibility of a critique of politics in its state-centredness and its imaginings of politics as order, rule and power. The attempt to expand an understanding of 'politics' in 'the political' is fraught with many difficulties, not least because it generates further suppressions of possibilities, both inside and outside 'the political'. Ultimately though, this difficulty comes down to a quasi-impossibility to think about politics outside the state as an overarching frame of reference and an organizing principle.[16]

Schmitt weaves a notion of 'the political' close to the essence of being and therefore to *humanity*. In fact, he takes this conjunction to an extreme position in intimating that an understanding of the human is inseparable from an understanding of 'the political' and vice versa. By extension, membership in a collectivity of humans coheres precisely because one is able to push this political-ness to an extreme, and to clarify one's humanity becomes an endeavour to identify what is not human, hence *unpolitical*, the enemy being the quintessential manifestation of this un-politicalness. For Schmitt, ultimately, 'the political' boils down to an imperative to distinguish self from enemies (1975, 79). What is apparent, in Schmitt and others, is a political ontology of identity constitutively imagined and articulated around a simultaneous recognition, silencing and erasure of *Other*—exposable to hostility and conflict, dismissal and exclusion. An immediate account that comes to mind is that of Giorgio Agamben's notion of 'bare life.'

A notion of 'the political' associated with ultimate authority, and ultimate sovereignty (Schmitt), can here be contrasted with a notion of 'the political' as both a critique of a state-centred notion of politics, a conception of the modern, secular state as well as a familiar tendency to disaggregate political rule from other terrains of possibility. For one thing, being together is an ontological condition that is most commonly experienced, in liberal thought, with 'the political'. This implies two things. First, that there is no possibility of community and togetherness outside 'the political'. Second, that those elements deemed *unpolitical* tend to be excluded from the community of 'the political.' If the shift toward 'the political' (in the strict sense of the state and its representative institutions) enables a break from a rigid analytical frame and a retrieval of the repressed in the way it has integrated conflict, contingency, uncertainty, disruption and agonisticity, there remains a constitutive suspicion against an unformulated 'apolitical' that is hardly an improvement on the classical distinction between nature and culture.

Schmitt has often been criticized for presenting a one-dimensional understanding of 'the human' in variations of the binary friend/enemy, disregarding the possibility for a human to be shaped by other spheres of action such as religion, culture and economy—and the relational possibilities contained in permutations of these. I think, however, that Schmitt's distinction is deliberate: it does not discount the significance of these fields but merely subsumes them under an institution that is to be recognized as having the greatest competency for organizing social life, the state. Such a tendency seems central to Western political theory. It resurfaces in the writings of Jean-Luc Nancy and Philippe Lacoue-Labarthe among others in the form of functional oppositions against 'the political' as substance or instrument that reverberates back on the critique of the state.

According to Nancy, ' "the political" seems to present the nobility of the thing—which thereby implicitly regains its specificity, and thus its relative separation' (Nancy 2008, 25). What Nancy finds totalitarian in the use of the political to qualify every social action often becomes also the result of a tendency among bearers of the political—understood as a superior endeavour endowed with a high quality of value production—to bring various social spheres and fields of action under the control and domination of 'the political'. Nancy proposes a manifesto of *specificity* for 'the political' as the most political in politics and for a return to the *essence* of politics.

In the debate to which Nancy, Lacoue-Labarthe and others sought to contribute, the question of the relationship between democracy and legitimacy—in other words, what becomes of the *void* left by the decapitated king—looms large. The banalization of 'the political' is constituted at once in its disappearance and in its obviation: if everything is political, the latter is no longer locatable. Nancy's critique is directed at two forms of withdrawal (or disappearance) of 'the political'. First, that effected by legal abstraction, precisely in the manner in which formal abstraction ' "does right" by every participatory and every relation, but without giving this right any meaning other than itself'. The role of the law here is that of a cipher for 'the reality of the relation of forces—whether economic, technical, or the forces of passion' (2000, 47). Second, the political has withdrawn into the society of the spectacle in situational speak; that is, 'a self-representation that no longer refers to an origin, but only to the void of its own specularity' (47). The society of spectacle basks in voyeurism and self-exposition in the sense that only representation matters for achievement, 'absorbing entirely both the transcendental and the concrete' (49, 52). For Nancy, therefore, both objectivized abstraction (legalism) and surfeit voyeurism (spectacle-ism) produce the same result of obfuscating 'the political' that therefore would need to be retrieved.

How do elements of spatial occupation and overlapping (temporal and spatial) dimensions of social reproduction translate into working relationships and operational structures? One can see the operations of 'the political' through overlapping temporalities and spatialities. What makes the strength of 'the political' is rather its elements of dislocation, dissonance and vulnerability, and further the manner in which time is rendered contemporaneous when anxieties are turned to one another. Two views of 'the political' can here be contrasted: an emancipated conception as typically found in Benjamin, Arendt, Levinas, More, Buber, Machiavelli, La Boétie, Leroux, Saint-Just and Adorno as opposed to a rigid, at once Cartesian and Platonic, anti-Hobbesian pessimism, and therefore rational, autonomous and centred view of the political. For some of these scholars, 'the political' is that thing that is best left to those who are capable and *conscious/cognizant* (have the know-how) in the work of governing. 'The political' from this view is not something that can be subsumed to the all-powerful will of a superior force that would be responsible for everybody's happiness. 'The political' comes alive in conflict, in encounters no matter how disorderly, in the plural condition of individuals and events—in other words, history. These views, however, operate within a Western canon that depends on the self-other delineation of a human relationship.[17]

With regard therefore to a notion of 'the political', post-foundational scholars suggest essentially two things. In the end, both Schmitt and Nancy gesture to 'identity' as necessarily existing and articulated against something (alterity, exteriority) rather than as a relationship or a rapport. First, they maintain the idea that categories of people can be pushed outside 'the political' into terrains where all attachments are severed. Second, they suggest that in the terrain of the 'unpolitical', the possibility of human experience can potentially be envisioned outside any relationship to the world. I find the latter problematic in light of my account above of Kukasi, Kasena and Dagara conceptualizations. For these groups, relationship to the world weaves the fabric of human experience if not in relation to other human beings, at least in relation to nature and its endless manifestations. If earth-skins, for instance, are portions of land withdrawn from common use and not subject to the production of immediate material goods, they produce both morality and anxiety.

To offer an alternative understanding, therefore, of the usefulness of the distinction above, I wish to offer two specificities. First, I have suggested that the idea of human experience outside a rapport with the world is a theoretical fiction that merely supports an argument for a positive account of the 'unpolitical'. If one can conceive of social life as 'a dense fabric of concurrent tensions', individuals can be seen to dwell in an intersubjective space in which man and nature are never opposed in binaries such as object/subject, operational/cognitive, material/ideal, etic/emic and so forth (Ingold 1993, 154). In the examples I provide above, what matters seems to be less the form (stateless) than the mechanisms in place designed to stem excessive tendencies associated with a concentration of power. The rejection of the juridicization and the technicization of social relations points to an apparent desire to preserve a different social morality.

Second, I wish to suggest that the eliding of temporality from discussions of 'the political' prevents a full and consequent exploration of the elaboration of 'the political' precisely out of interactions of various fields. The account above, of temporality among Kasena and Kusasi, suggests the possibility of an ethics of temporality that is neither grounded in nor motivated by an obsession with taming and controlling nature and living things. This suggests a context where every aspect of social action involves a 'dialogue with the materials and means of execution' (Lévi-Strauss 1974, 29). With regard to Dagara political culture, Yelpaala for instance seeks to link the rise and fall of communities to a specific conception of time, found in many African societies, that is circular. Time is a circular movement that is recursive but never in the same way and therefore generative of a past, present and future. This suggests that if 'events or phenomena may be seen as linear in relation to other similar phenomena' from a metaphysical and cosmological sense, time 'is not linear either to itself or to any other phenomenon' (1983, 358–70).

While such a statement might seem a tad bit essentialist, what interests me here is a two-level engagement with a frame of interactions that is not just vertical or horizontal but is inscribed in a temporality that places the living and the dead, the past and future (ancestor-us-children/past-present-future), 'the political' and the unpolitical in a common field of interactions. If 'scholars have only recently begun to acknowledge that political power in Africa is not reducible to what the modern world regards as its rational, secular elements' (MacGaffey 2013, 32), such a recognition has failed to translate into a sustained reflection on the *link between time and politics*. A first difficulty to overcome therefore is necessarily a better discerning of constitutions and commissions with regard to social codes and their bearers. When we ask questions such as What is a political ruler, what is his role? What is a ritual ruler, what is his role? we are still wedded to a language of politics-as-authority.

At one level, political subjectivity among the Kasena was not only conceived beyond oppositions, it existed in complex structures, networks and

imaginings. There is no ontological difference between a conception of political subjectivity in a statist and sedentarist perspective and in a decentralized
'mindset' except for the way in which it could be strategically redefined. The
equations 'stateness equals political' and 'non-stateness equals unpolitical',
therefore, become quite problematic. Regardless of the proper sequence of
the constitution of the Dagara/Lobi, or the Kasena or the Kusasi as discrete
groups, the making of community among these groups was very much a *political project*. Some anthropologists have attempted to apply an 'invention
of ethnicity' model to this phenomenon. While there are limits to this model,
what interests me in this constructionist process is the relationship between
foundational stories, ascribed or self-assigned identification, *intra-* and *inter-*
group relations, and narratives about various rights and obligations.

At another level, the literature on decentralized societies does not
altogether ignore the political dimension of ritual rule, nor is there necessarily a lack of recognition of the 'politicizing' effects of complex systems
of land occupation and mobility. Anafu in fact speaks of 'collateral political
institutions' among the Tallensi as indicative of the impossibility of any particular institution and authority, be it ritual or political, to lay claims, whether
juridical, executive or otherwise, over localities and peoples. Rather, 'soil and
political equilibrium was maintained by an intricate network of genealogical
ties and ritual interdependence' in a manner that was 'not centralization but
decentralization, devolution and local independence' and that constituted 'the
keynotes of Tale (Talensi) political structure' (Anafu 1973, 28).

An original response to the question of how do we produce law without
sovereignty resides in the manner in which everyday life is regulated and
legally and ethically sanctioned without the intervention of an overarching
body, and therefore the possibility of law and of politics without the state.
State discourse that catalyzes a politics/rituals distinction is meant to hide
a danger that threatens the very fundaments of power. It is among stateless
societies that alternative possibilities to the state order are the most apparent.
Among the Tallensi, Dagarti, Kusasi and other decentralized groups, a conception of social order and morality is translated through spatial and temporal
modes of structuring. Such a conception displaces political rule—in fact,
social order—more broadly, from a strictly 'political' reading, by revealing
the overlapping possibilities that are deployed in a view of time and space
beyond and outside a linear assessment.

Given the common cultural foundation shared by both centralized and
decentralized social formations in the Voltaic region, the salience of the division between the two spheres in centralized polities is a result of ideological
structurations of time and space. Where this division is tempered, the political
implications of spatial and temporal structures are more obvious. Thus 'the
complementary principles of social organization which are variously called

lineage/locality, kinship/residence, ancestors/Earth, descent/territoriality can be abstractly and heuristically polarized as a distinction between temporal and spatial modes of structuring' (M. Jackson 1977, 24 in MacGaffey 2013, 70–71). Given that there is no single temporal and no single spatial conception, the implications of their overlapping effects have to be sought in their very multiplicity.

CONCLUSION

How to understand 'politics' in the production, the projection, the circulation, the transfer and the interpretation of symbols and signs? Beyond the argument of nature as a source of life-generating powers, the cognitive dimension of self-government as a practice of freedom requires a more sustained theoretical engagement than has thus far been possible. To say that the field of the political goes beyond practices of political rule and institution is too obvious a statement. The domain of sociality and the domain of nature cannot be separated. There is no conceptual or conjectural area of life where the political does not have a place: it pervades the very texture of social life.

The argument in this chapter has not been to maintain that 'everything is political' for that might negate the possibility of locating those spaces to which tend to be attached specific political claims. Without advocating a fencing off of politics from other domains, scholars such as Turner ask what to do with those special areas of social life that uniquely represent politics for many people (Turner 1994, 42–43). There is no straightforward answer to this question, but in so far as there is no possible separation between history and geography, the implications for political agency flow at the least both from possibility or potentiality and *experimentation* with uncertainty.

The discussion above partly articulates a fundamental mechanism at work in the making of political subjectivity in decentralized societies. First, it seeks to demonstrate that if the condition of power for a shrine lies in its very locationality, its interactional situatedness, then space as location is too narrow a frame to apprehend the determinations that ensue in the way in which land gods and ritual sites are actively mobilized in the projection of a historical and social production, the delineation of order and the generation of meaning and the moulding of personhood. The way they are invested in multiple ideological and sociopolitical processes denotes fragmentary commitment to loose fields for one cannot decant the political into the social; the other way around would also be impossible. Second therefore, *ten-gan (Tenga)* among the peoples of the northern Voltaic states is believed to be both *force* and vital source; it guarantees material and spiritual resources and controls fertility and productivity; it restores the proper order when morality and norms have been violated. If its 'power is pervasive and ubiquitous', it is also 'differentiable from location to location' (Yelpaala 1983, 369).

The cosmological framework of ten-gan as constitutive of core ideas of being, origin, nature (Earth) and (re)production and as informing the metaphysics of life is universally shared among Voltaic societies regardless of the type of social organization. The power of *ten-gan* is believed to be located in the *tengantug*, from which spreads its radiating influence until it meets the effects of neighbouring *tengantug*. This primary act feeds into a continuous duty to monitor land use, land encroachment and the exercise of land rights, land use and occupation by particular families.

Among the Dagara, the *tindana* also adjudicated allegations of acts of destabilization of the social structure where resort to a prohibited substance (poison for instance) could incur normative disruption. The release of a *kongteng* (curse) against perpetrators is commonly read as a ritual sanction without any concrete implications other than the phenomenology of ritual utterance. I agree with Yelpaala, however, that 'though this function certainly has a religious flavour, its legal importance in dispute settlement and its importance as a powerful means of non-coercive control and influence over the society cannot be overlooked' (Yelpaala 1983, 370). In fact, the act of healing cannot be seen as merely a restorative endeavour discrete from, and unrelated to, a political mechanism of preserving civil consent through mediation.

Further, the destruction of ecological resources is seen as a moral transgression that mobilizes and frames individual qualities such as shame, integrity and moderation. There is something about the way in which shrines are anthropomorphized, something about the way they are thought 'to be sentient and wilful; to have emotions and behaviour' that is striking (Mendonsa 1979, 397). Like humans, their referential character is transitory (Colson 1997, 54). A propitiation ritual is meant to calm ancestors, the living spirits in things and animals, for it is a historical fact that 'culture was derived from a hostile nature that constantly needed to be placated or reckoned with' (McCaskie 1995, 43). However, contrary to prevalent analytical orientations, the primary purpose of ritual intervention is not *domestication* per se but rather an attempt to mediate people's will, anxieties and selfhood. Rituals cannot impose an order on nature. From this, the practice of rituals confronts a fundamental paradox in the sense that it must draw coherence from the immutable dimension of the sacred even as its deployment is necessarily subject[ed] to variations, uncertainty and subversion. It is precisely these paradoxes that are exploited by political agents in an attempt both to share in the sacrality and power of ritual forces and to contain the effects of ritual operations.

This chapter has attempted to reconstruct the conditions that presided over the possibility of laws and social coherence in the absence of the state.

Political claims were not always territorial and institutional, and statelessness can be reconceptualized as a mindset that rejects the tendency to amalgamate while erasing subjectivities and mental constructs and redefining human collectivity under the sway of a 'final locus of jurisdiction' (Spruyt 1994, 35) as one of its markers.

Concomitantly, a notion of territoriality that is linked neither to residence nor to genealogy clearly offers a flexible framework for rethinking the possibility available to individuals and communities of reinventing 'communities' as 'cultural communities' that can operate in democratic settings. If this form of territoriality is not necessarily opposed to other forms—for instance, linked to blood or lineage—it certainly problematizes these and subjects their usefulness to categories of action and belonging within a *space/identity* nexus.

NOTES

1. For an analysis of the internal workings of non-centralized societies and their mechanisms of social control in the Voltaic region, as well as varied accounts on their pre-colonial configurations, see Lentz (1994), Goody (1957) and Yelpaala (1983, 349–85).

2. This dilemma poses the question of the use of two fundamental resources in the sustainability of life and the possibility of social order: nature and history. The first provides or withholds sustenance and needs to be placated; the second relates to the place of ancestors in the determination of subjectivities and the value and temporal substance of the present.

3. Liberski-Bagnoud (2002), especially chapter 2 'Architecture Lignagère'.

4. For Abasi, 'the Kasena house is a living organism, capable of growth and continuance, or of decline and death'.

5. See Mather (2003, 23–45) on the importance of landscape as a frame for human interaction, rituals, spatial occupation and society among the Kusaki.

6. Abasi (1995, 472–73) presents a beautiful and informative parallel between terms and the rituals of meaning-making in birth and death rituals among the Kasena.

7. As the chapter demonstrates, the political organization of decentralized societies was more complex than this. However, its lack of apparent dynamism is a reason why its study has been the preserve of anthropologists and not historians, let alone political scientists.

8. Dacher also notes that networks of relation woven into clans, cults and lineages may overlap but rarely become superimposed upon each other.

9. Among the Tallensi, one finds *tindanas* among migrant Namoos.

10. Ingold also speaks of 'resonance as the rhythmic harmonization of mutual attention' (1993, 163)

11. *Ten-gan sob* (earthpriest) and *naa* (rich man, chief) are clearly distinguishable words but sometimes the word *teng-naa* is used, suggesting that the earthpriest is 'a chief in his own right'.

12. A key figure in this seniority-based governance was the market supervisor. When the double condition of voluntary interaction and competition in market transactions was violated and said to lead to *fao* (robbery), the *tindana* could intervene to restore fairness even if this could result in another form of robbery and confiscation of the seller's goods; see Yelpaala (1983, 370–71). Also important in this setting is the *bodeme* (society of secrets) characterized by practices of secrecy, bodily connections with various terrains of existence, gender-transgressiveness (said to include both ritualized sex and same-sex desire), and knowledge of plants and healing methods. The *bodeme* are mediators of conflict (especially involving men and women) and of perceived antagonisms (e.g., gender categories not as 'anatomic' but rather 'energetic'). Their status as 'gatekeepers' positions them as interpreters of ills, boundaries, anxieties, disorders and the ancestral world. See a most interesting dissertation on the *bodeme* by Hameed Herukhuti S. Williams, 'Our Bodies, Our Wisdom: Engaging Black Men Who Experience Same-Sex Desire in Afrocentric Ritual, Embodied Epistemology, and Collaborative Inquiry'. Fielding Graduate University, 2006.

13. This section is based on Liberski-Bagnoud (2002, 92).

14. Long-term neighbours as much as captives could thus become fictitious genealogical relations: 'une fiction généalogique, un discours sur la 'semence', et un lien sacrificial au bosquet sacre eponym du village sont les trois traits qui donnent leur unitee aux lignages constitutifs de la communauté de Kaya. Ces trois traits viennent a leur façon construire l'origine de cette association de lignages hétérogènes, origine qui n'est pas loin de se confondre avec l'engendrement de l'espace villageois' (Liberski-Bagnoud 2002, 101).

15. These included the *Dieu de San*, the *Boro*, and later the *La'ho* (Duba) and the *Dén Djugu*.

16. See Inna Viriasova (2013) for an engaging exploration of the theoretical usefulness of post-foundational notions of 'the unpolitical', 'the impolitical' and the 'bare life'. She holds Massimo Cacciari's and Roberto Esposito's categories of 'the impolitical' to be a promising critique although relatively confined.

17. For an insightful discussion, see Nayar (2013).

Chapter 4

Statization and Centralizing Processes in Eighteenth-Century Moogo

INTRODUCTION

Kopytoff posits an idea of the *frontier* as the production of similarly structured polities out of a complex 'political core' (1989, 3). The frontier thesis debunks evolutionary theories that conceptualize states as stemming from hypothetical archaic bands evolving into small polities and then into a variety of centralized states. The process of fission conceptualized in the frontier thesis resonates with Sahlins' 'heroic mode', which attempts to explain the territorial expansion of core polities as a consolidation of the influence of ruling dynasties as they deploy power and cultural practices across outlying territories—in other words, physical and sociocultural frontiers (Sahlins 1983, 522).

In the Voltaic region, fission happened in an uneven manner, spreading lineage clusters across what would subsequently become Moogo. While the somewhat deterministic outlook of the frontier thesis does call for some relativization, it provides a usefully broad scaffolding for thinking about the fragmentation of the *Naam*. The fission of the *Naam* was primarily a strategy designed to make room for the countless contenders to a *naam*.

The Mossi *Naam* is characterized by a structure of authority which projects power as a tool of diffusion internally to effect a homogeneous political system replicated at all levels of authority, and externally to endow the state with greater territorial and political resources. At the core of this chapter is the widely perceived problem of *how* complex political systems emerged in West African societies, and therefore how political science may lay claim to the precolonial past and how through theoretical engagement with oral histories it can account for the nature of continuity, change, diversity and divergence and can cut through flawed accounts of the contemporary state in Africa. It does so using the politico-ideological logic of the *Naam* as a core principle of state formation in Moogo.

This chapter further shows how social integration, both a condition and product of the consolidation of state legitimacy, was a function of ritual, blood and political alliances within a historically diverse society. It also shows how the state negotiated territoriality, 'ethnicity' and social differentiation in its attempt to consolidate and stabilize state institutions through the elaboration of new rules and the implantation of new capital cities in the middle and end of the eighteenth century.

This historicity of the *Naam* in turn informs identity and the assimilation process of non-Mossi groups into wider Mossi society. I explain the making of *mossiness* (homogeneization and assimilation) not through bureaucratization or state-led ideology alone but through the penetration of the realm of *Tenga* by that of the *Naam*, in other words, the colonization of culture by politics. In the absence of technologies of effective enforcement, Mossi ideology spread into pre-existing society progressively and gradually.[1] This development was a combination of intentionality and more or less deliberate propagation.

In exploring the making of political identity in Moogo, this chapter argues that the *Naam*'s confinement in things political does not prevent state ideology from 'spilling over' into the realm of *Tenga*. In fact, the very logic of political competition and territorial claims converged, and these drew *Tenga* into the realm of the *Naam* and vice-versa. The sentient path to identity (mossiness as self-referencing) or the elaboration of a corporate identity, therefore, operated along shared consciousness. In contrast to the previous chapter, this chapter focuses on the orchestration of power among centralized Voltaic formations, especially Moogo (Ouagadougou and Yatenga) in present-day Burkina Faso and Mamprugu, and to a lesser extent Dagbon in present-day Ghana. It seeks to demonstrate that beyond the horizons of order and formalization of power put forward by state promoters, the basis of political imagination was only superficially eroded by the imposition of the *Naam* as an overarching framework over and above pre-existing ideas and values.

Implied in the previous chapter is one key principle. It is that epistemological possibilities over the nature of the political necessarily had to be placed under the control of the state or what amounted to it if the latter was to preside over its conditions and content, or to shape its boundaries and orientation. The same imperative extends to the state's capacity to control political expression from other categories of representation. There are three important aspects to this endeavour tackled in this chapter.

First, Mossi political discourse sought to alter the constitutive characteristic of encounter by constructing the state *as different*, thus severing organic continuity and coherence in relation to pre-state Moogo. The *Naam/Tenga* model thus essentially yields a systematic opposition between civilized/uncouth; reason/unreason; feminine (matrilineal)/masculine (patrilineal); political/ nonpolitical; society/anarchy; rational/irrational; and migrant/autochthon. The construct state/civilized/subject versus non-state/barbaric/self-governed as a recognizable reading grid of a social division of labour in this history may have been taken for granted. In reality, it is merely the ideological (re) production of a social phenomenon made to be purposeful, persuasive and necessary and its promoters turned experts in political practice. Where for instance the *tengsoba* (earthpriest) as political and economic regulator was directly involved in all processes of production and subsistence, the Mossi state introduced a formal structure of control and appropriation of agricultural products as an attempt to undermine his power.

State discourse was a means to consolidate *the fact of* the state and to naturalize its necessity. It also served to tame and stigmatize the contingency or the *fear* of anarchy contained in the uncharted nature of statelessness. The *Naam* discourse achieved a unique feat in that it expanded exponentially the grandeur of the state—which in reality had only limited physical reach. Its account of state goodness, the divine origin and power of the Mogho *naaba*, the king of Mogho—whose apparition is likened to the rising sun—built a conceptual and symbolic world meant to enthral the imagination of Mossi and non-Mossi alike. The legend of Yennenga, pregenetrix of all Mossi, became in particular a dependable, normative stock in Mossi cosmology, one that engraved her extraordinary journey in a narrative of achievement, revolution and promise. The *Naam* was positioned as the only valid constant source to which all memory had to be anchored and from which all morality had to proceed.

Second, the process of statization was underpinned by an ambitious, two-pronged, ideological project of transformation. The state sought to reformulate the terms of social membership by subverting the principle of kinship by blood into one of *kinship by alliance*. Consequently, it endeavoured to turn the three pre-existing conventional orders, namely the segmentary order, the order of elders and historical categories respectively into the category of 'state', the category of 'chiefs' and functional categories (Izard 1985, 64–68).

The ultimate purpose of the Mossi state was 'the embedding of culture, the increase of society, [and] the articulation of political authority' (McCaskie 1995, 48). In this endeavour, the state was condemned to interplay with the structures that mediated the resources needed for its realization. In effect, the union *Wende/Tenga*, emblematic of Mossi attempts to insert themselves in the pre-Moaga social landscape, was not a political expedience designed to counterpoise the occult powers emanating from *Tenga*. It was to serve the mobilization of various resources in the consolidation of power. The accumulation of sources of power was underpinned by a relentless struggle for immigrant-rulers to capture or co-opt the mystical power of the earthpriests. Even when they did not or could not incorporate them, states maintained a contrapuntal relationship with stateless groups through trade, intermarriage, ritualized family relations (hence stranger-kin), enslavement and other forms of exchange.

The state was keen to control choke points along important trading routes but it could not do it on its own. This relational network explains the edifice of command occupied by the *Naam* in both centralized and decentralized societies across Moogo.

Third, however, state design collided with the production of social thought, and conceptions of socialities elaborated outside the sphere of the state, among earthpriests, artisans and technicians such as metalworkers, smiths, potters, woodcarvers and even bards. The state's attempt to institute an intellectual division between law-giving, political rule and the intercession of divinities was at once a strategy to tame dissonance, to repress the potential for transgression of those whose craft was invested in social intervention during critical junctures, and it was therefore indispensable to the elaboration of culture and the construction of human subjectivities (i.e., different stages of the life cycle). The aim was consequently to thwart the very making of a political community capable of confronting contingencies in the articulation of social transformation. Continuous Mossi efforts to particularize portions of the political community conflicted with the possibility of technical discourse and practices susceptible of interfering with the political discourse.

In sum, in the centralized state system, the *Naam* was a formidable lever. It was fully exercised by the Mossi as such, as an argument for mediation and of the pertinence of stateness as a new *cultural order*. What is interesting in this process is the arrangement of structural rapports created by a specific logic. That logic needs to be understood; it needs to be understood through the resources provided by an ideological reservoir. As a commentary on statehood, this chapter seeks to do just that.

The chapter successively explores myths of origin and links them to the formation and expansion strategies of the Mamprusi-Mossi-Dagomba states and the progressive rupture between kinship and kingship as fundamental to centralization processes across Moogo. Furthermore, the chapter examines *rog-n-miki*, or *jural corporateness*, as a form of cultural jurisprudence that informs and contains state and social ideologies. In particular, the chapter dwells on the role of earthpriests and blacksmiths as central figures in the articulation of a relation of equilibrium between the realm of political power and that of ritual. The next three sections show how a state definition of identity through the constitution of a 'royal class', the practice of deferred exchange of women under the care of the king (*pogsiure*) and strategies of integration of strangers including captives participated in the *Naam*.

FRONTIERMEN AS STATE-BUILDERS

Myths of Origin in Moogo

While mass displacement of people such as take place in times of war, famine, extreme violence and natural disasters have a more salient and dramatic form, less visible and smaller movements are constantly and continuously taking place in the midst of systemic change that informs and shapes sociopolitical cultures across the African continent. As a result of this, 'the formation of new social groups as offshoots of old ones has been a constant theme in the histories of African societies—histories filled with the movement of the disgruntled, the victimized, the exiled, the refugees, the losers in internecine struggles, the adventurous, and the ambitious' (Kopytoff 1989, 18).

A very common story says that horse-mounted conquerors subdued first-comer groups across the Voltaic region in the early sixteenth century thanks to their technological and civilizational superiority but also because of the first-comers' ritual figures' apparent disinterest in *things political*. These first-comer ritual leaders—*tengbiisi* or *tengdanas*, were gradually marginalized in favour of a new political elite and a new political system complete with its bureaucratic structures, its military apparatus, its hierarchies, its institutional language and its demarcation of various socio-professional categories. The ritual leaders became confined to the task of preserving the moral order and things spiritual. State discourse made the first-comers' withdrawal a *voluntary* one from activities conspicuously political. This account is not fortuitous. It derives from a convergence between dynastic history as formulaically propounded by the relatively centralized Mossi, Dagbani and Mamprusi polities and a search for African sociopolitical forms that could validate the evolutionist or structuralist ideas that animated, and blinkered, early European anthropologists.[2] In Mossi accounts in fact, non-Mossi groups are represented as a vague grouping of the *nyonyonse* (indigenous) made up of Gurunsi (Kibse), Lobi, Kusasi, Nankani, Builsa, Busasi, Nabdam, Kasena and so forth. However, in alternative accounts, Mossi rulers emerged in contexts of fragmented specialization and were typically 'invited' to act as conflict mediators and rainmakers. This meant that their power was always going to be limited in practice.

A function of the first-comer role was to counterbalance political power, but the first-comer was not the only source of regulation of political conduct. A chief was accountable to the living and the dead, to ancestors and to forces of nature. These structuring forces inculcated restraint and humility. A chief was also responsible for maintaining reproduction, keeping droughts and famines away, and the continuity of prosperity. Accountability thus evinced a powerful symbolic character insofar as kings bore the burden of providing coherence and hope to communities.

All Voltaic societies, whether organized as centralized states or acephalous societies, relate to Na Gbewa through his descendants. The principle of fission as normative application is here crucial to the reproduction of the *Naam*. The sixteenth and beginning of the seventeenth century saw a proliferation of established states with different degrees of centralization around political nuclei.[3] State formation in Moogo spanned three centuries, from the beginning of the sixteenth toward the end of the eighteenth century. The cluster of Mossi states covered as much as 100,000 square kilometres, extending from the Ghanaian-Burkinabé border (11th parallel) in the south to the Malian-Burkinabé border by the end of the nineteenth century. Nacanabo notes that under the rule of Kumd'mye, 'the most important scission[s] in the history of Moogo' (2003, 346) took place. The proliferation of petty states gave rise, in the northern Mossi region of Kupela alone, to the kingdoms of Bulsa, Kayao, Yako, Risiam, Mane and Tema. One informant explains the formation of these satellite states in the following way:

> There was a hierarchy of status: first came the Yatenga *naaba* [*rima*, or sovereign], then came the *nabisi* [princes], then *kombere* [provincial chiefs] and then the *tansobnanamse*, etc. In the authenticity of things, the chiefs of Ratênga, Tatênga, and Busu were *kombere* or *nabisi* who depended on the Yatenga *naaba*. They could be his sons or brothers of men he trusted. He appointed them at the various frontiers and corners. Nowadays, they are more or less independent. They can come pay respect to the naaba or can also choose not to come and greet. But if they do come to pay respect, then they have to doff their hat. Even if these states were independent, if there arose an issue that they felt were beyond their capacity to solve, they would come and consult the *naaba*. In this way, there were still relations between them.[4]

This is a common account that explains the formation and autonomy of satellite states that emerged from pre-existing formations, namely Ouagadougou and Yatenga. The Mossi settled in areas that were previously occupied by a range of *nyonyonse* (*ninissi* or *nyonyose*). These included the Dogon (*Kibsi*), who occupied the north of Moogo, what later became Yatenga. Kiethéga dates their settlement to the thirteenth century and contends that they probably hailed from the cliffs of Bandiagara. He bases his investigations on iron and pottery tools and mortuary earthenware that have been used by the Dogon as long as they have lived in the area (1993, 9–29; Marshall 1978, 122). They preceded the Kurumba and the Yônyôose in the middle belt of Moogo and the Fulse and Kurumba in Yatenga. *Ninsi* would mean, from a Mossi perspective, 'Those who were found there' (Ceux qu'on est venu trouver sur place)—in other words, first-comers (*sẽn wa miki*). *Ninsi* were mostly concentrated in the central part of Moogo, particularly around Ouagadougou (Bouda 1986, 52; Simporé 2004, 544).

The distribution of the population of *Nyonyoose* and *Ninisi*, as well as the Dogon, seems to confirm, in addition to the disposition of the archaeological remains, the gradual displacement of autochthons toward the north as Mossi conquerors annexed populations along a south-north route (Simporé 2004, 556). Gurunsi were pushed toward the south and the west, and the Bisa toward the southwest while indigenous *Ninisi* and *Nyonyoose* were gradually assimilated into a new 'Mossi society' made of new (migrants) and old (indigenous) populations. This was achieved both peacefully and violently. Around Ouagadougou, Oubri, a founding ancestor, established the most centralized and largest Mossi state as Mossi migrants intervened as mediators in the conflicts that prevailed between different groups. They also contracted ritual relationships with first-comer groups while subjugating the populations that resisted their domination. This at least is the Mossi version of history (Ki-Zerbo 1978, 249).

The most constant motivation for the large numbers of Mossi migrants was the desire to hold a particular *Naam*, to deploy its possibilities and to exercise it for themselves and for the good of the people who knew 'no organized' form of community. For the Mossi, *gurungo* (pl. *gurunsi*) is shorthand for 'uncivilized', 'uncouth', 'backward'. The term 'first-comer', if it is a recognition of the primacy of *gurunsi*, *nyonyonse* and others in the lands of Mossi migration, it is also a reference to the primitive stage of civilization to which they were still confined and from which they needed to be emancipated. However, a fixed, static and essentialist understanding of cultural and civilizational difference is at odds with the intense history of interactions between the *Naam* and *Tenga* populations, including gurunsi and other groups.

There were degrees of stateness in the various permutations of the working contradiction between the sphere of politics and the sphere of rituals, and one should be able to argue this without falling into an evolutionist bias—there were in fact various degrees of centralization and decentralization. The latter was key to royal accountability given the lack of developed technologies of violence up until the early nineteenth century. A political structure organized like Dagbon with a hierarchical logic and different subordinate structures could be easily likened to a statelike institution because the state is the closest thing we can compare it to. However, it was not statelike. MacGaffey (2013) contends that there was a logic that drove the ingathering of kin and the constitution of communities of interest in this particular polity.

In Dagbon, there were trading routes to be captured and mineral deposits to be exploited; alliances of interest were therefore necessary. Like elsewhere, amalgamation was a second stage, a 'counter-process' that followed fission, and its outcome was typically the absorption of small clusters into larger, more centralized groupings (Comaroff and Comaroff 1991, 127). In so far as a discussion of stateness goes, forms of centralized and decentralized statehood that do not confirm the European model should point to the possibility of recognizing different *species* of statehood (of which sovereign statehood would be one) as opposed to the genus as common political unit or *polity* (Eckstein 1979).

The Ends of Power

According to the Mossi narrative, a nomad conqueror civilized the 'uncouth autochthon', and he borrowed the autochthon's practices only in so far as these were also the means to penetrate autochthony in order to better control it. The autochthonous character of pre-Moaga societies is therefore crystallized by the political will of the conqueror. State power was underpinned by a social ideology based on socio-professional particularities and a division of labour. This division was integrated into a political discourse and a historical trajectory that asserted the evidence of political power. A second phase in state building consisted of erasing the distinctiveness of socio-professional associations. While these groups were flexible in their membership, the state's assimilationist policy undermined their capacity for self-reinvention.

Manifestations of state power amounted to episodic incursions in the form of the enthronement rituals which every *Naam* ruler had to perform in order to achieve the status of *rima* (see chapter 5), the messenger who collected taxes and the state representatives who partook in various harvest rituals. If anything, the state was an intruder in the lives of most populations. The very idea that power could be unilaterally imposed by an individual was not only normatively unsustainable, it upset the formulation and the subsequent internalization of the social order.

Given continuous migration and intricate clan and ethnic affiliations, loyalties could not be determined by the logic of political centres alone. Environmental change and natural disasters such as drought, divinatory injunctions and family fortunes were determinant factors in the constitution of alliances, fragmented subjectivities, multi-linear political patterns and, crucially, the way people related to centres of power. In the end, political authority was reduced to dynastic politics and the interactions of a handful of people. In fact, outside Ouagadougou, Ouahigouya and Yendi, which consolidated as unitary sovereignties only toward the end of the nineteenth century and following colonial expansion, state sovereignty owed much to what officeholders had to say about it. One can easily imagine that their representation of state power was a purposeful attempt to give it more grandeur and substance than it actually had.

The configurations of power were very much contained by the ordinary activities of corporate groups, including age-sets, descent groups, secret societies, cults and other sodalities. The latter constituted spaces productive of social action that resulted in 'regulating power, creating systems of meaning, and articulating ideologies' (McIntosh 1999, 19). State terminology is telling in this regard. For instance, three words intervene in the semantic make-up of authority: *na-am* (power), *so-ba* (possessor) and *kasma* (elder, head). Zoanga contends that political authority consists of *ziiri* (prestige) and *panga* (strength), both of which are contained in the formulation of the *Naam* (1978, 216). If in discourse, therefore, the *Naam* was promoted as a new necessary edifice of hegemony, it emerged and co-existed in a context of plural cultural practice.

The ends of power were in many ways culturally embedded. As Walter Benjamin once contended, they consisted of foregrounding and ritualizing the inevitability of, and necessary goodness of, the state: 'to naturalize the progression and necessity of the state in general and the nation-state in particular' (Scott 2009, 350).[5] Material resources are its most visible but not most significant aspect; power is both material and ideational, visible and non-invisible; the capacity to produce and manipulate these aspects in the creation and circulation of meaning participates in building the political base of rulers.

The introduction of firearms under Naaba Piiyo I (1750–1754) was crucial to the centralization of northern Moogo. Succeeding Piiyo, Naaba Kango (1754, 1757–1787) established Bambara mercenaries, *kambose* (fusiliers), *bobose* and *ninissi* archers. His peregrinations took him beyond the borders of Yatenga and across Kong, Segou, Mau and Gomboro in search of alliances. The hunt for captives intensified during this period and was extended to Fulgo and Kibgo (Fulse and Kibse countries in northern Moogo). Kango was a radical reformer. He refused, for instance, to perform the *ringu* enthronement ritual and trampled on many other conventions. He went against the established practice of rotating royal towns and established a permanent capital in Waiguyo (Ouahigouya, literally, 'Come and submit to me'). These reforms had tremendous consequences for the concentration of power and for state capacity to draw capabilities from within and outside political society.

Naaba Kango was the most feared of all Mossi kings. Dynastic accounts intimate his ruthless grip over the state even though they tend to be silent on the cost of his obsession with power and control. Kango held power for a long time, and twice in fact. The first term was fairly short (1754) and the second fairly long (1757–1787). The instrumentality of force was deployed over the limited reach of state centres, and residents of these centres bore the brunt of violence that would have otherwise been deployed against neighbouring polities. The state's capacity to populate political centres with willing subjects was a constant preoccupation and also the motivation and the purpose of war.

Conquered populations often preferred to stay away from the close vicinity of kings and princes except for those that desired to be part of state action—that is, to become 'members of the state'. The strength of the state was measured by the capacity of a ruler to concentrate manpower and his capacity therefore to gather large followings made of voluntary or recalcitrant dependents, namely slaves, captives and women received as part of *pogsiure* (a system of differed exchange of women; see below).

From the perspective of the Mossi state, the division of labour between the *Naam* and *Tenga* was both rhetorical and instrumental. It served to dramatize the distance between the ruling class and the rest of society. In dealing with difference, the Mossi state had two options. First, it could assimilate all forms of differences, cultural, social and ideological, by subsuming them under the state project by producing a new subject who bore the mark of the *Naam*. Second—and this was no less violent a process—the state could pursue a homogenization project that treated ideological recalcitrance as versions of anti-state practices; the exclusion of the latter from the field of the political simultaneously suppressed all possible recognition of their cultural and social significance. The Mossi system was an unsuccessful attempt at implementing the first option.

The *Naam* produced a specific history of accountability, an enabling framework for the engineering of compliance, assent and desire. This accountability was however locked within the *Naam*'s own logic. The *Naam*'s foundational stories can in fact be seen as intellectual discourses and as 'myths of constitutional accountability and betrayal' (Lonsdale 1986, 135). The production of meaning was central to the political process. It was also productive of risk in revealing the very foreignness of the language of those who purported to introduce 'political rule' as a revolutionary practice. Conquest politics in a foreign language had to be translated into the local language for its power to be efficient.

In the neighbouring Dagbon polity, *tindanas* (the equivalent of the Mossi earthpriest) were responsible for social (re)production. They were 'expected to ensure collective economic well-being by appealing for rain and fending off pestilence' (MacGaffey 2013, 102). Their work was to preserve a balance between forces of nature and the production of livelihood. It therefore affected and inflected the weather, economic production, agriculture (fertility) and the supply of goods for human consumption. *Tindanas* also oversaw market activities (102).

STATIZATION AS DIVORCE OF
KINGSHIP FROM KINSHIP

It was believed that the *naaba* could never adequately exercise political power unless he was free from all forms of lineal tutelage. The *tom yugri* (ritual of allegiance) thus marks the break between a life permeated with lineal obligations to an existence articulated by the requirements of the *Naam* (Izard 1980, 768; 1995, 415).[6] Divorcing the king from the kin group was the condition for his passage from an ordinary royal to the sacred institution of kingship.

The marker of chieftaincy was that it was made to embody an occult power (the *Naam*). The Mossi state thus turned the axiomatic character of kinship ideology, the very notion that 'no other model can explain emergent social relations and new structural alterations so new forms are interpreted as a reproduction, rather than a destruction of kinship' (Mendonsa 1979, 392). Successive Mossi *nanamse* thus proceeded to populate the state's core with non-royal allies and various dependents, retainers and followers.

The disarticulation of power from kinship was effected by *panga* (force or violence—a form of travesty, a violent materialization of the *Naam*) which intervened by isolating—and exempting—the *naaba* from all forms of loyalties. In Yatenga, the chief *pangsoba* was the chief of Ula, a captive turned war-chief and the second personality of the kingdom. He took liberties with the *naaba* and needed no intermediaries in dealing with the latter. During the *napusûm*, the annual greeting ceremony for chiefs of war, he would ask the *naaba* to indicate 'where to take the (next) war' (Izard 1985, 51). Equally, the *naaba*'s extended kin, particularly *nakombsé* (princes) embodied a coercive potential in their demeanour, their language and their disregard for rules that applied to common people. They stole cattle and poultry from people's homes and administered a form of private justice in the name of the state.[7]

The *naaba*'s aversion to the constitution of dynasties extended beyond the royals he actively marginalized. For chiefs of strategic localities who had received a personal nomination from the *naaba*, their families had to be relocated and their houses burned down at the time of their death. Statization developed as an anti-dynastization struggle whereby war chiefs and people of the royal household were placed at the heart of villages or nominated in an individual capacity by the *naaba* himself, to whom they were thus answerable.

In Yatenga, this policy was pursued by Naaba Kiisum (ca. 1690–1720). Statization also consisted of turning territory into *political space*. This policy translated into the creation of six territorial units across Yatenga headed by war chiefs, four precolonially and two after colonization: Ula, Kosuka, Ramba and Windigi in addition to Kalo and Barelego in the eighteenth century (Izard 1985, 50).[8] The role of non-dynastic chiefs and war chiefs around the *naaba* was crucial. The four war chiefs of Gursi, Lago, Ula, Kosuka and Tange[9] took part in the nomination of the *naaba*. As in other centralizing processes, the tension between space and place was inherent in the widespread conception of a state as territorially bound. The subjection of space into territory as a con-stitutive criterion for state formation undermined relativizing views on space and the reaffirmation of people and spatial identities in differentiated ways.

The tension between space and territory was further exacerbated by the fact that royal capitals were always mobile and temporary. No true capital city was established during the formative period as successive rulers sought to make their mark by founding new capital cities, and they used these cities to keep an eye on the activities of officeless nobilities: Tangazugu (Naaba Yadega); Waiguyo (Naaba Kango, 1757–1787); Komsiliga (Naaba Kaogo); Bulese (Naaba Nyambemeogo, 1825–1834); Zia (Naaba Totebaldo, 1834–1850); Sisamba (Naaba Sanuum); Zemba (Naaba Kiisum, ca. 1690–1720); Pirgo (Naaba Ramiga); Tang (Naaba Lambwega, ca. 1630–1660); Bsisigi (Naaba Nabaasere); Ziya (Naaba Piiyo I, ca. 1754; Somnyaa (Naaba Vanteberegum); Bugunaam (Naaba Sugunum); Ziya (Naaba Saaga, 1787–1803); and Komsiliga (Naaba Kaogo, 1803–1806). In fact, between the seventeenth and eighteenth centuries, many more royal villages and capitals would be set up across Ouagadougou and Yatenga. The *natenga* (royal residence) was a place of power. No royal prince or member of *Tenga* was admitted into it, and no sizable market could be established in its vicinity given that the *naaba* was forbidden to engage in commercial activities.

It is interesting that almost all those excluded from the competition for power from the political cores of Dagomba, Mamprusi and Tenkudugu would found their own ruling clans. The framework of state formation that results from the transfer of ideas through migration is best illustrated by this pro-cess (Sedogo 2010). In contrast, succession 'wars' and courtly rivalries were intense electoral competitions. Conflict was dramatized as a foundational fea-ture that ran through royal rituals, nominations and various commemorations. Political competition was the only time the use of *panga* was permitted.

For Mossi princes, the spirit of competition was an integral part of their political culture, and all available means were mobilized for the purpose of power. Very crucially, succession wars dramatized the investing of kings 'with power over production and their followers with control over kings' (Lonsdale 1986, 147). At the same time, such constitutional rituals served to distin-guish the distinctive nature of the royal 'class' from other social categories, and the enacting of the language of class formation imposed an imperative of mutual respect and mutual control across various jurisdictions—that is, the intercession with divinities, political rule over people, the adjudication of legal conundrums and so on, as chapter 5 will show with the *ringu* ritual which shielded ritual resources (productive forces) from kingly access.[10]

In so far as the *Naam* ideology of power was exempt of almost any reference to land, it is important to look at the significance of ideology (belief, ritual practice) over its institutionalization. It is therefore understandable that royal actors endeavoured to 'secularize' the state away from ritual jurisdiction and for kings to surround themselves with servile allies against both kin and rivals.

The *naayiridemba* (royal compound) was divided into a *moose* section and a *bin* section. The former was predominantly made of *talsé*, or commoners, but also a mixture of old families and individuals who stood out because of a specific quality or skill. A number of youth were placed here as well by their parents as an 'investment'. The *bin* was a compound of war prisoners, victims of raids, individuals pardoned from a death sentence and people who joined the royal service voluntarily.[11] Captives were shaved and socialized as *Ouedraogo* (literally 'stallion'—the surname of the king). They married among themselves, the king's family, or the Mossi royals.

Further, *nayiritese* (servant villages) were extensions of royal compounds. They comprised, other than captive quarters, *saadogo* (blacksmith quarters), *bobose* (mercenary quarters), and quarters for all that participated in *pogsiure*, the system of accumulation and distribution of women that was fundamental to the reproduction of captive groups and the state more broadly (Skinner 1960, 20–23). To recapitulate, Moaga society proper was made up of the three distinct groups of *nakombsé* that provided kings, *tasobnamba* (dynastized orders of warriors) and *nayiridemba* (courtiers) made of *moose* and *bin* captives who provided a varied range of court servants as well as non-dynastized orders of war chiefs. These different orders were demarcated on the basis of the mode of exercise of the *Naam*. From the perspective of the *Naam*, the remaining population, a largely undefined category of *talsé*, thus existed in a state of relative political uselessness.

At any rate, the rule of the *naaba* was in no way absolute. His action was hedged about with many prohibitions. In Mamprugu, the performance of rain rituals—in fact the coming of rains—was the responsibility of the *nayiri* (the Mamprugu equivalent of *naaba*, or king).

In Dagbon, the *Ya na* is *bimbiegu*, 'a bad thing'. This means he is imbued with dangerous metaphysical powers. He is also said to be a lion, thus imbued with formidable physical force. Like earthpriests, he possesses *tim* (magical power or medicine; MacGaffey 2013, 82; Mahama 2004, 95). In Dagbon for instance, there were three types of ritual centres: household, territorial and dynastic. MacGaffey contends that the configuration of the dynastic shrine; its centrality in the operation of political power and legitimacy and the conduct of the sacrifices performed during and in relation to enskinment (enthronement); its location in dynastic history as counterpart and counter-point to centres of power; and the formal rules that governed the interactions between royals and earthpriests 'suggest that chieftaincy was once much more like the earthpriest or *tindana* office than it is [in the contemporary period]' (MacGaffey 2013, 108).

Skalnik notes that in the neighbouring Nanun polity, *tindanas* must have played the role of warriors (1987, 310).[12] In this particular polity, there was no monopoly of power by a single entity—in fact, there was no power to speak of but rather diffuse forms of authority. *Tindanas* do not compete for succession; they are 'chosen' by spirits and ancestors through coded signs and other manifestations. Theirs is not the most attractive function to hold. It is a tedious and dangerous activity that consists of 'manipulating' the forces of an unruly nature. The larger point here is that the authority of a ruler is hedged with ritual constraints, public morality and most crucially by the principles of *rog-n-miki*, to which I now turn.

The *Naam*, Jural Corporateness and *Rog-n-miki*

Rog-n-miki is a difficult notion to translate. Mossi informants explain that it is a system of values and traditions that their ancestors transmitted to later generations. They translate it as 'Je suis né trouver'. According to one informant, 'In my family, we cannot eat the heart of animals or kill a lizard because it is our totem. We don't eat the heart of animals because we have to be strong in order to serve the naaba as warriors. Our ancestor in the past ate the heart of an animal in order to become a strong warrior.'[13]

If the *Naam* often appears as if it were superimposed on pre-existing structures, in reality it is woven into diffuse elements having to do with *rog-n-miki* as customs and cultural heritage of Mossi society whereby social action is performed in the context of binding forms of interdependency between members of collective units. According to Maurice Bazémo, *rog-n-miki* is 'that force that perpetuates the past. It enacts history. Through [*rog-n-miki*], the past and the future are lived in the present. It is a force that creates dur-ability in favour of a socio-political order the biggest beneficiary of which was the royal [family]' (1993, 199–200). *Rog-n-miki* is a corpus of imme-morial custom—what McCaskie calls 'jural corporateness'—that governs and organizes the coherence of a community. If it is not subject to alteration; it is susceptible to adaptation (1995, 87). It is adhered to based on the premise of its fundamental integrity as 'a culturally determined jurisprudence, uni-versal in its aims but particular in its exercise' (Lalu 2009, 161).

In Moogo, the *Naam* makes the state, differentiates it from society and elevates it as the source of normative conduct. The reproduction of the state and the reproduction of the *Naam* are therefore closely interconnected. As the

Naam model was reproduced in places far from its Mamprusi core, a more literal and blunt version prevailed, which stuck more closely to the ideological construct while the anatomy of the state had to be constantly reinvented.

In the process of expansion of the state, the *Naam* became an ideological reservoir that framed state structurations and attempts at structuration 'within the lexicon of a knowledge derived from a close reading of cultural experience' (McCaskie 1995, 74), of achievement, vision and revolution. If the *Naam* came to be elevated as the source of knowledge, its promoters struggled to elaborate a Mossi culture solely informed by its ideology. Mossi promoters tenaciously pursued the realization of an encompassing frame of knowledge and experience capable of subsuming all pre-existing formulations of cultural experience, including *rog-n-miki*. Even as this endeavour thickened and intensified, the need for equilibrium—ever present in the elaboration of a community of diverse subjects—required compromises in the marshalling of *transformation within continuity*.[14] Given that territorial priests mediated the reproduction of the essential quality of political rule, the *Naam*, and in particular its legitimation process, inevitably fell under their control.

When arguments are congealed into statements, they codify knowledge in a way that generates new epistemic clusters regardless of their ontological and subjective validity. Whereas oppositions, hierarchies and status demarcations are framed in conjunctions within particular age groups at a particular time and place, and within kin relations at a particular time and place—in other words, where statuses are relationally *particulate*—the state seeks to institute relatively rigid boundaries and to ascribe positions of subordination and related modes of emancipation depending on the will of different rulers (Wolf 1982, 95). This is obviously a familiar configuration which is very well sketched by Wolf in his comparative assessment of the broadly defined kin-ordered mode against the tributary and capitalist modes of production. The first mode 'inhibits the institutionalization of political power, resting essentially on the management of consensus among clusters of participants' (1982, 95), thus making room for the reshuffling of relationships and commitments, when conditions require, in the form of retraction, extension and complexification. In contrast, Wolf links the history of statization with demands for surplus, the attendant requirement for the regulation of labour and mobility and the coercive apparatus that enables both:

> In contrast to the kin-ordered mode, both the tributary and the capitalist modes divide the population under their command into a class of surplus producers and a class of surplus takers. Both require mechanisms of domination to ensure that surpluses are transferred on a predictable basis from one class to the other. Such domination may involve, at one time or another, a wide panoply of sanctions based on fear, hope, and charity; but it cannot be secured without

the development of an apparatus of coercion to maintain the basic division into classes and to defend the resulting structure against external attack. Both the tributary and the capitalist modes, therefore, are marked by the development and installation of such an apparatus, *namely the state* (Wolf 1982, 99; emphasis added).

The particularity therefore of kin-ordered societies in contrast to the tributary and capitalist modes resides in the very inhibition of naturalization or an absolutization of cultural places (Cheyfitz 1997, 5). In contrast, the process of statization is inseparable from the invention of ethnicity: modernization and homogenization become the two pillars of an alignment made ineluctable in the institutionalization of difference—initiated already in precolonial state formations and consolidated and routinized in colonial bureaucracy.

Administrative technologies thus enabled the reproduction of disparate groups identified by colonial rulers on the basis of cultural and linguistic traits. Postcolonial elites in their turn instrumentalized ethnic differences in a bid to consolidate political bases and to create political figures along the lines of hardened ethnic boundaries.

The configuration of the ethnicity and normative order in precolonial and postcolonial times helps make sense of the very complex interactions between the *Naam* and *Tenga*. They underlined and framed the structuration of order in which the state was to be historically engaged. In fact, the state's outsiderness did in no way limit or stem the fact that the discrete purposes of the state had to be formulated on the basis of 'precedent imperatives, norms and values that underpinned society, and so framed, described and otherwise qualified its ordering' (McCaskie 1995, 74). As a result, the *naaba*'s authority was impermanent because it was caught between the requirements of *rog-n-miki*, the necessary intervention of earthpriests in social action and the mutable configurations of the *Naam* order.

Frames of Interdependence

Once established in Ouagadougou, Ouahigouya and elsewhere across Moogo, Mossi rulers had to figure out a way to secure the cooperation and consent of conquered populations. Michel Izard argues that 'the peculiarity of state control is to produce consent with violence' (Izard 1985, 556), so to the question Why did autochthonous groups 'accept' Mossi rule with an apparent readiness? Izard's response is that the indigenous subjects 'did not revolt openly but rather responded to Mossi rule through a kind of resigned acceptance, a withdrawal into themselves' (1985, 555).

I wish to problematize Izard's argument here by introducing cultural elements of resistance. Izard describes at length these cultural forms without attaching a dissident value to their motivation. At no point in the history of the Mossi state, even in the middle of the eighteenth century when it reached its apogee, was the state able to impose standardized cultural forms. This incapacity to subsume existing cultural orders under a Mossi framework meant that state hegemony was always partial and fundamentally challenged in the area of culture. Two socio-professional categories in particular whose role was crucial to state and social processes produced forms of knowledge that constrained state action. These were the earthpriests and the blacksmiths.

Given that my own antinomic analysis of the object/subject dichotomy is tainted by creeping elements of a statist mindset whereby a state actor is necessarily at the heart of action, whether he or she is an object or subject only giving alternative possibilities of action within the same perspective, what Bourdieu called a 'state-think' (2014), some of these arguments will serve—as will be clear below—to relativize the stress too often placed on the distinct development of centralized states in precolonial Africa as a sure marker of these societies' advanced political culture.[15]

Earthpriests

The terms *tengsoba* and *tindana* (pl. *tengsobdamba* and *tendeme* or *tendaama*) are often translated 'owner of the land' or 'guardian of *Tenga*'. This particular office and its related responsibilities was inherited by male descendants. Among other prerogatives, the earthpriest granted permission for newcomers to settle and farm the land. The most apparent roles of the *tengsoba* were ritual: the performance of offerings to the *tengantug* or *Tenga*, thanksgiving, harvest rituals, purificatory and expiatory rituals for the restoration of order and so on. However, the *tengsoba* was never *just* a ritual ruler. Or to put it differently, the ritual rule was never just about the performance of ceremonial acts. In fact, the *tengsoba* not only distributed land for settlement, he also administered its use and preservation, oversaw the regulation of markets and settled disputes among the people of his village. He also adjudicated cases of violations of moral rules and ordered the expulsion of individuals found guilty of irredeemable acts. As the main administrator of the land, a duty crucial to the establishment of new village-communities, his role was to determine 'unoccupied' or 'empty' land, and therefore boundaries—an assessment that was not only technical but highly political and which had broader implications for the constitution and ascription of identities.

The articulation of a relation of equilibrium between the realm of political power and that of ritual comes up against divergent visions of *space, historicity* and *temporality*. The social reproduction of ritual sanctuaries, familial burial places and so forth (the material support of specific settlements) was central to the lives of segmentary groups. That is to say, in the non-political realm, memory and identity were very much engraved on the land, the territorial and material support of the community.[16] The Moaga on the contrary had no such attachment to 'land'; claims of the political power of land embraced a multitude of tracts of land brought together in a unitary territory.

The Mossi state's claim to historicity entirely lay in genealogical history and migratory trajectories. Yet even narratives of mobility and un-attachment are enfolded in the landscape through acts of remembrance, and the latter mobilizes individuals' capacity—both putative migrants and putative first-comers—'[to engage] perceptually with an environment that is itself pregnant with the past' (Ingold 1993, 153). Thus the Moaga state imposed a different temporality on the experiential duration of pre-Moaga groups in the same way that the colonial state was later to impose a new time—the time of a 'modern' and centralized—government on African societies.

As an ethical field, *Tenga* is a system of significations that bears on intricate relationships among different groups; it is the vehicle through which people are able to make sense of these relationships. An examination of meaning-making exercises is crucial if we are to make sense of how particular subjects can apprehend an experience of political authority.

The construct *Naam/Tenga* as a working pair of antagonistic references and life-worlds cannot be understood as delineative of distances but rather as productive of positinalities and relationalities which are indissociable from the projection of mental charters. Elements of subjectivity are encoded in frequent adjustments of group identity in rhetorical frames. Distinctiveness and connectivity are encoded in lineage bodies, genealogical formations, initiation milestones, household dynamics and micro-authority structures, all of which are underpinned by a sociology of togetherness characterized by flexibility and freedom.

Mossi ascendency over *Tenga* could not have proceeded without the integration of narratives produced in the realm of *Tenga*. The frames of this accommodation are indispensable to an understanding of procedures of erasure and invisibilized oppression. Fundamentally, the *Naam* exists in a condition of ontological interdependence with *Tenga*. The stranger-king overwrites first-comer claims to precedence in religious and ancestral authority in aggressive and transgressive demonstrations of superior power.

Typically, then, there is enduring tension between foreign-derived royals and the native groups. Invidious disagreements about legitimacy and superiority may surface in partisan renderings of the founding narratives, each claiming superiority over the other (Sahlins 2008). Thus the 'code of arrivals' (Murphy and Bledsoe 1989, 123–47) as foundational narrative allows a reaffirmation of *Tenga* as the crucible of the 'atoms of culture … the signs and relations from which the social fabric was woven' (Comaroff and Comaroff 1991, 132).

In the state of Yatenga, the beginning of the Mossi year is typically inaugurated by the drum-chroniclers' recitation of the totem-names (shibboleth names) of the six constitutive groups of the polity as well as the *siimde*, the greeting ritual.[17] On one hand, the recitation re-enacts a closely staged structuration of state society relations; on the other hand, it provides a state-centric perspective of the social order. The state presents a very lucid, ideologically oriented social charter that lays the basis for a constitution. It constitutes groups in naming them and confirming their role in the state-building endeavour. There are those who cultivate the land (first-comer *tengbiisi* and *tengdemba*) or provide the instruments for cultivation and for the transformation of earth products into food—for example, *saaba*, blacksmiths, make tools and their wives make pottery while *silmiise* herd cattle, and *setba* (artisans) make the tools necessary for transforming and preserving the food. A third group is made of royal captives and drum-chroniclers who constitute the state institution both in words (*benda*, or chroniclers) and action (*bingdemba*, or warriors). This recitation is therefore fundamental in the way it lays claim to the historical imaginary of groups present and absent.

The recitation of *sonda* (patronymic names) defines the limits of history and forecloses all possibility of modification of the nomenclature. The implication is that any new group will have to be subsumed under this formal frame. If *yarse* and *marase* traders are not evoked in this nomenclature, it is partly because their spatiality (nomadic, transnational) poses a problem for the state reading-grid. The apparent diversity of Moogo (ethnic, religious, historical) conceals an instrumentalized and reductionist view of pre-Moaga groups. Through this process and many others, the state exercises great cultural competency while making discursively effective claims about history, subjectivity, belonging, morality and change.

The bearers of the *Naam* do not envisage the latter's intrusion in pre-Moaga society as an interruption of an ongoing historical course. State ideology in fact makes that course both illogical and unsystematic. State ideology is superimposed on established 'stateless' communities characterized by an egalitarian economic orientation. What Goody terms 'contrapuntal paramountcy' implies a distinction *in* equality between political and ritual rule (1996, 5). Political rulers ascribed a non-political status to people of *Tenga* so that they could turn non-participation into a cultural deficiency, thus deliberately denying the possibility of non-normative participation—or non-participation—as a cultural disposition. In other words, the capacity, the skill or the art to rule was a birthright and therefore an attribute of a given community—in other words, the Mossi.

Blacksmiths

Blacksmiths were a socio-professional group whose knowledge and technical skills (i.e., the handling of fire and raw material) was at once crucial and dangerous to social life. Seen as a group socially and civilizationally removed from the rest, blacksmiths were at once indispensable to the possibility of social life and productive of harm given the threat that their occult knowledge constituted for the social order. Common attitudes toward them were therefore a mixture of distrust, contempt and fascination. Theirs was an intriguing, even baffling condition. Their capacity to transform iron and wood through their knowledge 'gives smiths important roles in everyone else's professional, social, and spiritual lives, thereby putting them in a surprisingly prominent position, given their enigmatic status' (McNaughton 1988, xiii in Haour 2013, 87). McNaughton also notes the 'confusing social spaces', the paradox in which smiths were generally confined in Africa. Among the Mande for instance and in West Africa more generally, '[smiths] are at once glorified and shunned, feared and despised, afforded special privileges and bounded by special interdictions'.

Fundamentally, blacksmith identity was mired in ambiguity, paradox, fascination, awe and contempt for they were 'facilitators, articulators and transformers' intervening in physical and invisible realms (McNaughton 1988, 151 in Haour 2013, 88). Pottery-makers, often the wives of smiths or belonging to the same endogamous groups, also provided similar specialist services during initiation rites, marriage and funeral ceremonies.

Despite that—or precisely because their art and skills were crucial for the maintenance of life through the confection of cooking utensils—their role in burial ceremonies and during enthronement rituals, the provision of healing and divinatory services and so on made them indispensable to the physical and spiritual well-being of society. The very survival of the collective depended on their provision of equipment of war, food and protection. Crucially, therefore, without their technique, social life was impossible.

The marginal position of smiths and potters made them susceptible to various policies of containment, including endogamy and spatial segregation, and the elaboration of many taboos associated with pollution, impurity and filth. The *mise-en-perspective* of blacksmiths, therefore, rests upon an othering that throws them out of history altogether and out of historical temporality. Policies of containment against smiths, potters and other artisans and technicians also became the means through which the state interfered with social process more generally as it intervened at every level and stage of the life cycle.

The capacity of smiths and other artisans to derail state design lay in the potency of their knowledge but also in the elusiveness of their intent. The transgressive potential of their power was a looming threat to the very possibility of the state. Smiths produced the thing that the state envisaged only in rhetorical discourse. They produced civilization by manufacturing culture from nature, by turning persons into humans through their intervention at various stages of the human development cycle. By and large, technicians were believed to have captured the vital force from ancestral spirits whose injection in the trans-formative work (clay, fire, tree, minerals) was the essence of civilization.

Deeply entrenched myths about the polluting power of artisans find a compelling resonance in the destabilizing force contained in the possibility of misuse or dissident experimentation. Ideas about impurity and pollution were produced in the process of centralization as the state sought to contain and neutralize the dangerous powers of technicians that imperilled its hegemony. Nonetheless, the state continued to depend on the specialized knowledge of artisans for the realization of state power.

A preliminary conclusion here is that if there was always the recognition, throughout the history of state formation in the Voltaic region, of the need for different functions to be carried out by different individuals, there was also the recognition that power could never be entirely removed from the ideational world that underpinned it lest it become alienated and cease to make sense to those who found themselves under its sway.

Second, political rulers and priests are presented as avatars of different worlds. The idea, therefore, is that *they are made of different stuff*: one is the vehicle of ideas waiting to be implemented, the other is the product of the earth; one belongs to the past and one inhabits nature. One operates on a mobile spatiality, the other belongs to an atemporal world and his spatiality is nature itself. There is arguably a good amount of state ideology in such a caricatural representation and it serves specific purposes, one of which is to conceal the fragmented nature of authority and territoriality in the Mossi state. The very existence of ancestral residences (*tasobtese* and *kiimstese*) points to the existence of different and overlapping forms of territoriality.

The fact is, autochthony becomes an inevitable category in the sense that every new order had to supplant a pre-existing one. Rather than deny the fact of autochthony, however, the state proceeded to pervert it by creating a new form of autonomy which it was able to populate with various categories of dependents. It was able to do so through policies of integration of strangers in its midst, a topic I now turn to.

OF CODES OF HOSPITALITY AND
SOCIAL INTEGRATION

A political history of *encounter* was foundational to the elaboration of social formation in Moogo; it implied that the status and role of outsiders was crucial to both social formation and the construction of categories of subjects. The notion of outsiderness had to be naturalized through ritualized and fictionalized alliances. The disposition for dialogue, in fact the need for negotiating the terms of engagement with outsiders, became a test of ritual literacy. Craft specialists and artisans were for instance invited so that their 'supernatural' power and their skills and knowledge could benefit the community. They were ambiguous strangers looked on with suspicion and distrust as to what use they could potentially put their power. Blacksmiths specifically were seen as closely connected to, and in constant conversation with, nature for they could extract ore from it unharmed.

In Moogo, normative references were distilled in the everyday practice of appropriate behaviour. In pre-Moaga society, normative principles included an obligation of hospitality to neighbours close and distant. In all foundational stories of encounter, a stranger always finds a host to provide food, a plot of land and a wife to enable him to settle. In fact, the axiom of hospitality was elevated to oppressive levels for a stranger could not be turned away. He was not only treated as a future member of the host community, but the propitiatory rituals performed on his behalf were meant to gain ancestral approval or assuage their disapproval.

The principle of appropriateness thus encompassed solidarity in the form of cooperative disposition, fraternity and sorority cultivated within age groups; the right of access to ancestral mediation; the right of consultation and arbitration in moments of anxiety and conflict. These principles and norms have been thoroughly documented in ethnographic accounts.[18]

However, it is also true that centralization of power consisted in a legalization and codification of principles and values of solidarity, (re)distribution and equity. For instance, the formalization of a defence corps inaugurated under Naaba Kango produced contradictory outcomes in that on the one hand it introduced a model of meritocracy that enabled the integration of non-Mossi in the state structure, including captives and war prisoners; and on the one hand, it consolidated mercenary practices that displaced solidarity models based on kinship and neighbourliness.

The new meritocratic mercenarianism became a contradiction, however, with the massacre of *kambonse* warriors by Kango when the former demanded they be given their share of war spoils. However, such turns were also moments of articulation of a quest for new bases and the renewal of the terms of a new compact between state and subjects. The massacre is therefore to be understood as a necessary purge, and the occurrence of similar massacres was cyclical in Yatenga and other Mossi kingdoms.

BEING AND BECOMING *MOAGA*

The structure, the enactment and the inevitability of the interdependence between the *Naam* and *Tenga* built up to one relentless, crucial question: How do you give space to and contain (power) at the same time? Within these parameters, power as such is not something that exists intrinsically but something that needs to be cultivated, if not manufactured.[19] Both the *Naam* and *Tenga* acted concurrently on the social existence of the Mossi and indigenous groups from different temporal frameworks. *Tenga* designates the space that provides a place of dwelling and a source of livelihood. It is the place that connects people to ancestors and mediates access to the sources of their personhood.

As the crucible of collective identity and social action, and also the place where the dead are buried, *Tenga* embodies an impossible ontological divide between the natural and the supernatural, the material and the spiritual, the natural and the social. *Tenga* produces reflexive subjectivities in so far as internal cohesion necessarily has to rely on all aspects of ethics, morality and religion. The self-understanding that obtains is challenged by 'outside' ideas of subjective qualities that are to be recognized in people on the basis of descent and not an innate capacity to tame natural forces, a capacity to ensure re(production) and the preservation of the social order. For the centralizing Mossi state, however, the very condition for hegemony was that it succumbed to that which it had set out to possess, namely, *Tenga*. The state thus sought to extend its hegemony through ritual association with indigenous divinities, ritual sites, land gods and so forth. It also extended influence through the commonerization of royal princes who could not be accommodated in state structures.

Royal princes who had lost the *Naam* or the right to compete for a peripheral *naam* were reduced to the category of *talsé*, or commoner (sing. *talga* from the Arabic *taraka*; also, *zemse*, sing. *zema*). Every state of this 'commonerization' gave birth to an exogamous lineage, so much so that Mossi-talsé descendants came to make up the majority population.[20] For a royal, to be downgraded to a commoner was the worst kind of outcome: 'If you ask a royal *nakombga*, he would say he would rather die [than become a commoner]. Because the *nakombga* needs the *Naam*; and if he does not have it, he has to be a *naaba* of something, for example a *saab-naaba* (master blacksmith) or even *tengsoba* (master of land) but never a *talga*.'[21]

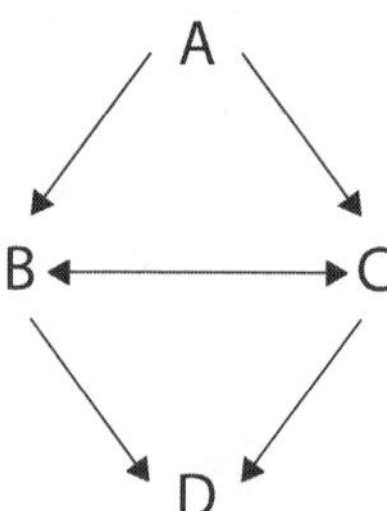

Figure 4.1:   Identity change

To become a *talga* meant the loss of royal privilege. It is easy to understand the interconnections sketched above by interpreting figure 1 which shows the directions of possible change of 'identity'.

The AB arrow describes the marginalization of a royal into an autochthon or blacksmith while AC indicates his choice to engage freely in trading activities, thus becoming a *yarga* (trader). The core of social activity is contained at the junction BC (agriculture and trade), and BC is also a zone of transition for marginal groups as they gain access to the realm of power even though the schema denies non-royals an opportunity to join A.[22] Both royals and indigenous (AB) could become blacksmiths (D).

Moos bûudu

Rights and privileges attached to full-fledged 'citizenship' were vested primarily in state membership, and especially in the *Moos bûudu*.[23] In fact, the very possibility of subjecthood was sanctioned by the framework of state membership as a condition of status. The *Moos bûudu* was made of patrilineal descendants of the founding figure of Moogo, namely, Ouedraogo. Without being the actual core unit of government, the *Moos bûudu* set the cultural terms of government as the source of legitimation of material inequality. Its function was fundamentally to define 'the existential core of personhood and social identity' and therefore the 'invisible scaffolding of the sociocultural order' (Comaroff and Comaroff 1991, 131–32). The *Moos bûudu* was therefore 'a category of practice' (Brubaker and Cooper 2000, 62) open to enormous possibilities. At its core, culture was a political design. Identity was equally a performative, a performed representation rather than a purely blood, dynastic and genealogical function.

Essentialized understandings of *mossiness* concealed integration as a defining mechanism at the intersection of social mobility, intermarriage, culture, incorporation and alliances. Identity at the political core was a political project devised to weld together diverse peoples assembled by history, movement and chance. They were bondsmen allied to strongmen, slaves captured in warfare or raids, cultivators, merchants and craftsmen enticed by economic opportunity and prestige—in other words a 'polyglot' population (Scott 2009, 80). One can only grasp the nature of political rule therefore through an engagement of a broader approach to culture, one that encompasses mythology, linguistic usages, ontological and ideological commitments, material culture, rites and rituals, belief and religion, patterns of thought, knowledge and etiquette.

The state's discretionary power was extensive in defining the realm and the conditions of legitimate 'entry into social existence and its attendant citizenship rights'. The state therefore 'continually adjusted the parameters of legal status in relation to its own project, recasting people in a succession of more or less privileged roles inside jural corporateness, while at the same time retaining final rights of arbitration over the boundaries of incorporation and expulsion' (McCaskie 1995, 90).

The Mossi had a peculiar sense of *cultural literacy*. The transfer of cultural knowledge was co-extensive to the institutional void and cultural illiteracy that had to be established in support of knowledge production. Consequently, 'conditional shifts in jural identity—provided by state action or by quarrels between office holders, the flow of political events or by circumstance, chance or even accident—constantly drew people into the state's orbit of attention, and mired them again and again in its embrace' (McCaskie 1995, 94–95). Formally, Mossi identity was to be defined on the basis of the possession of the *Naam*. In reality, the *Naam* was mutable. A degree of ambiguity underpinned the continuity of the *Naam* model despite the changing nature of transmission mechanisms.

The four groups that comprised the Mossi population were formal subjects of the state (*nakombsé, nayiridemba, tasobnamba*), *relative* subjects (indigenous groups), *peripheral* subjects (strangers, traders) and inhabitants who had limited or no relation to the formal state (blacksmiths, *silmiise* pastoralists and *silmimoose*) outside the provision of certain services.[24] Depending on their lineal distance to the ruling *naaba*, a small portion of *nakombsé* had *de jure* access to the *Naam* while the bulk of them were excluded from political competition.

Inversely, a large portion of captives and slaves had *de facto* access to the *Naam*. This differentiated access to the *Naam* had real impact on the distribution of economic resources as well as the repartition of ritual functions. The *Baloum* and *Togo Nanamse*, two of the four chiefs who headed the different branches of the royal residence (*Toogse, Balôngo, Werâsẽ* and *Bîngo* or *Rasam*), looked after royal regalia; they controlled people's access to the *naaba* and thus had tremendous leverage in swinging the fortunes of people, including local chiefs and royal princes.[25] The foreign populations were of Mande, Hausa, Songhai or Asante origin. Some were attached to state administrations as craftsmen, traders, warriors or armorers; there were also Muslim advisors at various chiefs' courts (Skalnik 1978, 479; Levtzion 1968).

The Ethics of Othering: Identity and Centralization

The Mossi achieved a great feat in crafting the *Naam* as a revolutionary idea. Not that it was not. The *Naam* introduced a notion of the political as something that emerges *ex nihilo* in contexts where there is no prior experience of it. In fact, the *Naam* was to be deployed, and expanded as a new sphere of action that would operate in parallel to other fields of action defined by the skills and the expertise held by different social groups.

The *Naam* was held to be eminently political while everything else ensued from the particular rapport explicitly or potentially mustered from association with it. In the same sense, the elevation of the *Naam* as the highest embodiment of the political was a statement of the value of the latter, as endowed with the greatest normative quality. An implication of this was the exclusion of the so-called non-political from the sphere of politics.

The *Naam* was the product of a formidable myth, a legend woven of one heroine's struggles for emancipation, her determination to fulfil a unique destiny, including the achievement of an impossible love. The Mossi exercised a monopoly on the imaginary of a political project through the narrative of Yennega, a Moaga princess who was stranded in the bush and met a horserider who would give her many male descendants all called *Ouedraogo* (stallion). The various narratives around the story of Yennenga mobilized different categories of knowledge—technical, ritual, ecological—in the conduct of their rule. These were also mobilized in the elaboration of Mossi identity as carrier of special qualities.

According to the Mossi, a strong marker of *mossiness* is a peculiar disposition for political entrepreneurship mediated by a rich context of exchange. A true Moaga does not die (even) after seven days of competition.[26] In examining the conceptualization of *mossiness*, this chapter explores the reproduction of Mossi identity from the double perspective of *intentionality* and *process*.

Mossiness was methodically wrought in the collective belief system. It was never clear that it was something systematically imposed on society rather than ritualized and inculcated in people in ways that fostered in them a sense of loyalty toward the state and the sovereign. To put this in context, the duality *Naam/Kasma* pins the segmentary order (*Kasma*) against the political order (*Naam*), and it displaces the former through the introduction of a political ideology that obscures the successoral order of the segmentary systemic.[27] From then on, *Bîngo*, the order of captives, provides the ideal type of citizenry, entirely devoted to serving the *naaba* and transcending kinship and other forms of loyalty such as ethnicity and belief systems.

The transition to the *Bîngo* model is one of institutional syncretism manifest in the establishment of institutions that cut through the usual cleavages. Here, marginal groups became agents of socialization in the same way that they articulated bureaucratization.

As in the Asante case, consent was achieved not through coercion but through hegemony, whereby the state, as *hermeneus*, managed, manipulated, controlled and disseminated ideas: it turned representations from arguments into statements (McCaskie 1995). Thus, *mossiness* was embodied in state agents, in their conduct, their speech, their etiquette. All this served to exemplify the way of the Moaga. In recruiting members from outside the group of strictly 'royals', the state disseminated *mossiness* in the very dissemination of state ideology through a combination of design and necessity. In the end ideology appeared as something accepted rather than imposed.

Again, ideology was not something constructed in the abstract: it was produced in the everyday interaction of the state with its subjects. For instance the Mossi language *Moore* is said to express, beyond its linguistic functions, a sense of being Mossi, that is the Mossi sense of decorum and conduct. It is therefore the site of realization of Mossi identity through the mastering of a set of habitual practices.[28]

While the simultaneous self-constitution of the *Naam* and the production of non-*Naam* others carved out the conditions of politics, the *Naam* was also construed as a sphere that had the potential to inform every aspect of social experience. The means to achieving such an ambition were to be mobilized in the very making of the Mossi state.

Labour played an important role in this: 'at a significant level, the assimilation of alien labor and the practice of exogamy were techniques of social engineering directed towards promoting cohesive efficiency and the aggrandizement of the group or collectivity' (McCaskie 1995, 75). However, interdependence meant limited government, ritual and political reciprocity, necessary interaction, rule by dint of consensus, fear of ancestral sanction, the possibility of subjects' flight as a form of dissent against the state and so forth.

Except for the Mossi and other ruling estates who managed to construct relatively tight foundational stories with a beginning, a place of birth (typically Mamprugu in northern Ghana) and putative agents, identity for the rest was very much situational and linked to particular ecological conditions, the nature of interactions with neighbouring groups, droughts, conquests, intermarriage, raids and so forth (Schlottner 2000, 49). Once they were gathered through intermarriage, populations of the political core had to be turned into the king's subjects through ritual relations and fictitious kinship. The question of identity is here best framed in emphases—in other words, in a web of interactions whereby certain connections and entanglements require different degrees of articulation at different historical periods. Such was the case for the practice of accumulating captives and the circulation of women.

The state's rhetorical arsenal featured the *Naam* as both founding discourse and as an attempt to transcend its own rhetoricity. The language of power is the language of univocality; it forces semantic hegemony onto social figures understood in figurative and equivocal constraints. The state classified people in discrete identities and opposed relational and equivocal representations to them. The state used representations to articulate consent. McCaskie demonstrates a very painstaking process whereby the Asante state sought to reduce the multiple meanings of representation to a single consensual statement.

> In its attempt to implement hegemony, the state is trying to arrogate [arguments coming out of diverse representations], and forge statements from them; but at the same time dissenting, oppositional or 'counter-cultural' elements are trying either to keep these arguments open, or to interpret and appropriate them for their own collective purposes. Thus, a prime consequence of the states' success in implementing hegemony, or in legitimizing its authority, is a persuasion away from plural argument to consensual statement (1995, 20).

Ideas that derived from the *Naam* lexicon and the sociocultural practices of *Naam* centres travelled far and wide—as attested by the ubiquitous construct *Naam/Tenga* one finds across the Voltaic region and the similarities of royal traditions from Mamprugu in the south across the Ghanaian border, Fada N'gourma in the east to Ouagadougou in the central Mossi belt to Yatenga in the North.

FORMS OF INTEGRATION

Pogsiure, or Deferred Exchange in Women

Pogsiure is a mutually binding system of distribution of women between lineages and between the *naaba* and his retinue. The royal version of this, *napogsiure*, allowed the *naaba* to give young girls—given to him as gifts and residing in the royal compound—as consorts to his servants for the double purpose of retaining their service and for aggrandizing the royal service. The Mossi state was most interventionist in the regulation of rights in people given the implications for its very capacity to create its own version of order. The king's liberality in the distribution of women was therefore politically strategic. The worth of the objects of exchange (here women) was not determined by the 'market' of supply and demand.

The frame that determined the circulation, accumulation and redistribution of women was very much sociological.[29] It was subject to alliances, political contingency and the pressure on chiefs to mobilize their following as social capital. Yet because *pogsiure* was different from the type of exchange—for instance of sisters across alliance groups—the woman-value as object of exchange was a mutating, changeable sign that acquired an abstract character. This very much worked in favour of the centralization project: the essence of the exercise resided not in the 'quality' of the women exchanged but in the process of accumulation of transferable assets. The deferred exchange of women thus participated in a series of procedures that reinforced the axiomatic character of power and made conceivable a symbolic order whose historicity was at best rhetorical.[30]

OF SLAVES, CAPTIVES AND SYSTEMS OF SERVITUDE

The *Naam* is an approach to social integration in addition to being a modality of power. When emigrant Mossi first set foot in Moogo, they projected a vision of the *Naam* as a meaning-generating core that defined individuals and groups according to their distance from the centre. The relentless attempt to build a 'political community' suggests a pressing dilemma. The state was to bundle populations at the core for 'the drive to acquire relatives, adherents, dependents, retainers and subjects and to keep them attached to oneself as a kind of social and political capital has often been remarked upon as characteristic of African political processes' (Kopytoff 1989, 40).

Captives and bondsmen made up the majority of state subjects. They were citizens under duress and had in that sense a grievance against the accumulative drive—in people as resources that underpinned the state's propensity for wars and raiding. Among various societies in nineteenth-century Upper Guinea, over half of the population was enslaved or in a dependency relationship. As state bearers sought to aggrandize the attractiveness of political capitals, strangers and captives were ritually integrated through the extension of matrimonial ties.[31]

Kinship tropes—the idea for instance that first-comer groups were cousins to Mossi and the use of metonymy to express family relations between different social categories—imbued state institutions with historicity and morality. They provided Mossi rulers with idioms and metaphors for conceptualizing *Naam/Tenga* relations.

In this context, the role of slavery, coercion and delayed exchange was central to the material basis as well as justification of state involvement in

social engineering. Mossi society is fundamentally integrative, if not assimilationist: 'L'etat des esclaves est l'aboutissement d'une succession d'avatars
qui contribuent à en faire des individus sans liens, ni de parenté, ni d'affinité'
(Meillassoux 1986, 105). This is where the state becomes most competent and
effective in ascribing an identity, providing a status (royalty through alliance)
and the social wherewithal (wives and land) for their integration. The slave/
captive's sole means of integration is membership and jural corporateness
(assimilation; McCaskie 1995, 89).

Captives were an ingathering of diverse groups. They were at once Plato's
auxiliaries (doing the dirty work of the state) and the state's most loyal
members. Officeholders in particular were keen to accumulate the greatest
number of captives. The imperative to strategize to retain subjects in order
to give meaning to political rule translated into a proliferation of titles and
the possibility for bondsmen and dependents, captives, slaves, followers,
retainers and hangers-on to attain prominent political positions.

The very possibility of promoting distinct categories of subjects was
explored in new imaginations of fictitious family models and community.
In all this, kingly dependency on subject attachment increased the capital of
freedom of the latter. In a way, political community and political power were
the work of the subjects rather than rulers themselves (Kopytoff 1989, 62).

From the discussion above, it is fair to say that social territoriality in this
context was not so much a territoriality without territory than it was a frame
of mobility. Sociality and mutuality allowed the ritualized integration of non-
kin and the reintegration of those excised from the moral society. Such sociality ultimately extended, complemented, complexified and problematized
kinship. Until the pressure to accumulate slaves became a continuing requirement of state building and centralization on the basis of 'productive communities' toward the end of the eighteenth century, the Mossi states commanded
little coercive violence.

A common mistake in much writing about slavery in precolonial Africa
is to speak of slaves in terms of the wealth and property of kings—rather
than wealth in land. In reality, the gathering of slaves, captives, bondsmen
and a range of other dependents was the means for kings and princes, hence
states, to secure and accumulate further resources. Surplus to be gained from
agricultural production was important but not considerable; there was, however, the possibility of levying tribute via trade and other transactions. This
particular duty required human resources, hence the common practice among
chiefs of accumulating groups of dependents.

Paraphernalia provided cultural markers (in dress, etiquette, social
manners, language, etc.), the symbolic expression of birthright difference that
demarcated Mossi royals from other social groups. In contrast, as we've seen,
gurunsi (indigenous inhabitant) was shorthand for the uncivilized, uncouth

and backward. There was an element of fixed, static and crucially essentialist understanding of identity and cultural differences which was at odds with a history of intense interactions among groups. Identity was also linked to, and expressive of, particular socio-ecologies: agricultural practices, soil tilling, smithing and so forth. It was also forged, and it could shift, through inter-marriage. The umbrella framework, the *Wende/Tenga* union, consecrated a ritualized integration of non-state groups in the Mossi state, or the ritualized union of two discrete groups depending on how one wants to envisage these strategies. I further discuss this point in chapter 5.

CONCLUSION

Central to the process of state formation, of late political centralization, was the constant circulation of the *Naam* from the core to the periphery and back to the core. Political direction was thus imparted, from the very beginning, to the migratory movement of populations around the Volta Basin from the middle of the sixteenth century. While the precolonial state has been conceptualized on the basis of material from societies across Africa, the con-quest theory, cultural subjugation and subsequent social stratification theories give an oversimplified account of the precolonial state and leave untreated the crucial role played by migration, memories and self-perceptions in shaping state and society, and therefore they do not allow a deeper exploration of alternative theories of the state.

The recent revalorization of *statelessness* as an escape from the stifling and constraining forces of centralized polities offers alternative accounts to a rigid but still lingering historical dichotomy (state versus pre-state). James Scott uses, for instance, public and hidden transcripts in gauging apparent and more subtle ways in which people and communities resist power in Southeast Asia.

In Scott's account of statelessness from the perspective of stateless people, state-making appears as a form of 'internal colonialism'. Internal colonialism is affected through absorption, integration, assimilation, displacing of elim-ination in the process of globalization of state history and a concomitant ana-chronistic reading combined with reified conceptions of political rule. Some of these points were discussed in chapter 3.

Internally, the middle and end of the nineteenth century was a period of uncertainty with a devastating famine falling on Moogo, particularly in the north (the Zogoré Famine); and beginning in 1877, in the aftermath of Naaba Yemde's death, a series of convulsions shook the aristocracy as it fought a fierce *bataille-rangée* over rules of succession. In fact, a succession of short-lived terms triggered protests as members of collateral branches of royal dynasties called into question the legitimacy of prevailing rules while a portion of the dissenters strove for a discontinuity in these rules. Members of the younger generations split into two rigid camps of classificatory brothers.

On the one hand, the 'sons of Tuguri', descendants of Naaba Tuguri (1822–1834), competed with the 'sons of Saaga', descendants of the young brothers of Naaba Saaga (1787–1803). When Naaba Baogo, elder son of Naaba Yemde (1850–1877), was crowned Yatenga Naaba in 1885 as the head of the 'sons of Saaga' branch, he had to contend with a fierce revolt of the 'sons of Tuguri' led by Bagara, son of Naaba Tuguri. With the help of the Fulani and their firearms, the Tuguri branch defeated Naaba Baogo at the battle of Tiou. However, Yatenga's independence was to come to an end with Naaba Baogo's successor as Naaba Bulli signed a protectorate treaty with the French in 1895. As the French sought to 'pacify' Mossi dynasties by supporting their favourite candidates and by attempting to eliminate political struggles altogether, they undermined an essential principle of the Mossi political system that sanctioned and encouraged competition, or 'war', for the *Naam* as something fundamentally good.

Lonsdale once contended that 'all societies, even those without coercive political institutions, are founded on complementary oppositions or moral rifts' (1986, 137). The moral rift in Moogo was the assumption of the superior quality of the *Naam* on one hand and the presumption of an absence of working moral determinations in pre-Moaga society on the other. What propelled Mossi migrants was the capacity for imagination of opportunities that lay in the 'frontier', whether this was real or constructed. The territorial limits of Mossi polities were in this respect irrelevant to their adventure-framework. Moreover, the fact that indigenous populations 'accepted' the rule of strangers needs to be contextualized within a socioeconomic field whereby doing politics was a 'craft' on par with blacksmithing and land-tilling. Engrained was the idea, from then on, that the political was a privileged field to be entered by those outside it.

The argument throughout this chapter has been that Moogo was very much built upon such rhetoric. Ultimately though, responses to the centralized state project, whether ritual or otherwise, stressed the 'unnaturalness' of the state form. In this regard, the rise of the Mossi state as extolled in nineteenth-century historiography responds to a two-fold narrative imperative as (1) a modernizing imperative to enact or deploy the capacity for violence as a source of legitimacy, and as (2) a narrative imperative to represent violence as potentiality. The diversity of previous forms of governance became flattened in the monolith idiom of violence.

There is an important aspect to the discussion above to do with the notion of violence as foundational, even necessary, to political rule. As a foundational trait of colonial government, violence became the criterion for centralizing policies around the time of encounter. Colonial regimes sought 'valid'

African interlocutors among those capable of using violence as the dominant currency of political power.[32] From then on for the colonial administration, African statehood was to be broadly framed by the existence of an intermediary class capable of mediating *colonial government.*

Colonial policies slowed pre-existing migration trends but did not stem them. Colonial interventions interfered with ongoing processes and configurations; they consolidated boundaries where these were perceptible and created new ones where they did not exist. They solidified group identities where these were more or less explicitly formulated and established new groups by amalgamating neighbouring groups. They institutionalized roles and ranks and promoted remunerated chiefly figures to carry out colonial will and policy.

Ultimately, the consolidation of centralized and extractive rule under colonialism diverted the trajectories of pre-existing structures (small-scale/ regional, city-state/federation, state/stateless) into centralized states complete with formal boundaries. Accounts that extol the virtues of nineteenth-century centralization across Africa therefore ignore the fact that it was largely imposed, rather than internally generated, by specific ecological contexts.

Mossi political thought and practice was deeply defined by a singular imperative to realize the *Naam*. This imperative carved the conceptual and ideological context in and through which the state would engage society and the production of social order. At the core of the historical endeavour was the pursuit of an ideal—ever receding—but ever bearing upon social conduct, ascribed and aspired identity and ultimately the contours of social experience for both *Naam* aspirers and those held under its sway. Crucially, the pursuit of this ideal 'circumscribed vital parameters of contact between state and social order. It was in the arena of fundamental norms and values that the state engaged the social order in the structuration of consent and coercion' (McCaskie 1995, 75). The state operated on a distinct agendum that was at once the purpose and limits of its structuration of historical-political possibilities. Conceptually, the division between 'zone of political rule' (the *Naam*) and 'zone of ritual rule' (*Tenga*) is therefore both a useful and tricky device.

NOTES

1. I use Wilks's and McCaskie's perspectives on the construction of Asante identity as a foil. Whereas Wilks reads the expansion of Asanteness as a bureaucratization process, McCaskie explains the consolidation of the Asanti state through the dissemination of state-ideology.

2. See among others Izard (1985) and Fage (1964). While I draw very heavily on Izard's work and I have also been the recipient of his generous insights and advice,

I wish to take a slightly different analytical orientation. The issue is not so much the available material, for Izard collected an impressive amount of information on all aspects of Mossi social life. The problem is in the reading of history and social forms at particular points of time. As one of the most prominent figures in Mossi historiography at a time when ideas about precolonial, centralized African kingdoms were in fashion, and as a student of Levi-Strauss trained in the structuralist tradition, Izard was very much inclined to impose a relatively rigid reading on Mossi history even though he had a great awareness of the implications of Mossi-centred accounts of non-Mossi history.

3. See Hammond (1966, 158) and Izard (1970, 217–73) for a survey of the Mossi petty states.

4. Interview with Ila Ouedraogo, Ouahigouya, April 16, 2010.

5. Scott makes reference to Walter Benjamin (1968, 255–56).

6. The *tom* is made from the ashes of a millet stem finely sieved. The new chief use his hands to put some of it on his forehead while kneeling in a way that marks symbolic allegiance to the naaba and the *nesômba* (dignitaries) for an ordinary chief and to the *nesômba* in the case of the Mogho Naaba or Yatenga Naaba.

7. Michel Izard describes Nakombsé royals as 'brigands de grand chemin [qui] n'ont [jamais] douté de la légitimité du pilage: le roi a besoin de captifs et de boeufs, eux-mêmes, ces nakombgandaogo, ces "types qui se foutent de tout" ont besoin de femmes (on ne leur en donne pas) et de nourriture (ils ne cultivent pas)' (1985, 552). *Pogsiure* thus participates in the production and reproduction of relations of power and therefore in the emancipation/autonomization of the sphere of power through 'matrimonial self-sufficiency'. Delayed exchange practices thus cancel, so to speak, the statutory distance between royals and captives and strangers integrated in the service of the *naaba* (Adler 1989, 391).

8. The chief of Windigi for instance was a captive from the early centralization period in the eighteenth century.

9. These localities all became *chefs-lieux de canton* during the colonial period.

10. The idea of 'class' is here rather unhelpful in the absence of class-consciousness and any explicit attempt by the state, at least during the formative period, to bring about a 'class society'. The issue of the use of 'class' as a fitting description of socio-professional categories in precolonial Africa has been much debated. Arhin (1983, 3–4) for instance suggests the use of 'status group' in the case of Asante whose stratification system can be conceived in terms of 'ranks' rather than 'classes'.

11. Captives of *silmiiga* or *fulbe* origin were tasked with tending the royal cattle. Different forms of labour service were required from captives and other dependent categories, especially by local chiefs. Minor office holders collected the mainstay that maintained the *naaba*, and his retinue and servants. Gifts and tribute thus furnished the sinews of the state while the state's incapacity to project effective authority outside the core afforded degrees of autonomy to local chieftaincies.

12. In the Hausa city-states (and elsewhere), blacksmith dwellings and towns surrounded royal residences and agglomerations. Blacksmiths made the tools that armed and defended the polity.

13. Interview with M. Ouedraogo, Ouahigouya, 16 April 2010.

14. The very succession of *nanamse*, in a continuous process and hardly disrupted by the death of an incumbent—the interregnum of the *napoko* (deceased king's first daughter) is combined with the expulsion of the *kurita* (the king's scapegoat) to mark institutional continuity and at the same time the 'cleansing' of state institutions after a previous administration; see chapter 5—points to the way in which one of the fundamental contradictions of sovereignty (i.e., same institution, different rulers) is resolved.

15. Frederick Cooper points to works by Adu Boahen and other first-generation, postcolonial African historians engaged in a project of re-valorization of an often ignored (and belittled) African past. For Cooper, these works often 'fail[ed] to address the contradictions stemming from specific social structures within Africa' (1994, 1521).

16. A distinction is made between land/space as the territorial basis of political power and land/space as 'Earth' in an abstract and ritual sense.

17. The *siimde* takes place between the two greeting cycles by royal servants and war-chiefs; see Izard (1985, 64).

18. Amadou Hampâté Bâ (1994, 57) discussed the importance of the principle and the provision of the right of use by autochthons to migrant groups throughout West Africa.

19. The pastoral qualities of power inscribed unilinear relationalities for subjects and rulers and an alternative reading to authoritarian rule as a singular frame.

20. 'Fallen *nakombsé*' could become *talsé*, blacksmiths or earthpriests in a mutation that was less a marginalization than an autochthonization process that transformed the pursuit of the *Naam* to a devotion to the *tengsobondo* (ritual control over *Tenga*) and a reference of ancestrality (migration) to that of territoriality (sedentarity); see Izard (1976, 73).

21. Interview with Noufou Ouedraogo, Ouagadougou, 6 December 2009.

22. Adapted from Izard (1976, 79).

23. The *Moos bûudu* is made of members of patrilineal descendants of a given agnatic group—in this instance the descendants of Ouedraogo, the founding ruler. It is bigger than the *saka* (made of descendants of an agnatic core).

24. *Silmiise* were nomadic herders and *silmimoose* were herders-cultivators (offspring of a *mossi/silmiise* union). They merely lived in Mossi society and were not taken into account in the state's definition of 'citizen' and 'subject'.

25. Interview with the Balum Naaba, Ouagadougou, 16 March 2006; interview with La'arllé Naaba Tigré, Ouagadougou, 18 March 2006.

26. Interview with Mamadou Ouedraogo, Ouahigouya, April 2010; interview with Noufou Ouedraogo, Ouagadougou, 6 December 2009.

27. One can be led to see in segmentarity the single most important element in the transmission of political office. In reality, segmentarity comes into play in the politics of the corporate kin group, at the level of local authority and in religious matters whereby reference to the *Naam* is not an issue. In a sense, the introduction of ideology in political practice creates an antagonistic as well as a negating element in the contradistinction between the *Naam* and *Kasma* (segmentary order), that is to say, political versus lineal authority. The ideology of the *Naam* is articulated around the possibility

for ideological shift, hence the scope for manipulation of the terms of transmission. The predictability of segmentary succession is contrasted with the opacity of the political order geared toward a greater society project that encompasses the exercise of political authority in the strict sense.

28. What the Mossi commonly refer to as *buum* (convention). Interview with Kamsogho (or Kamsoro) Naaba, Ouagadougou, 30 November 2009.

29. *Siure* is a mutually binding, juridic practice that relates to the chiefly right over the first daughter of a woman given in marriage (by the chief or king), who is then incorporated into the chief's 'reserve'. For a detailed treatment of the *pogsiure*, see Skinner (1960, 20–23; 1964, 23, 115); De Beauminy (1925, 33); Tiendrebeogo (1963, 21); Izard (1985, 510–28); and Boutillier, Quesnel, and Vaugel (1977).

30. Adler (1989, 373, 377). Adler's study of the Mundang of Chad and Dampierre's work on the Nzakara, the Bandia kingdom of the Upper-Ubangui, both provide useful comparative insights.

31. 'Come and pay tribute' is the name of a royal capital city (Ouahigouya) that tells the formidable tale of a hub of civilization, power and culture that attracted numerous prospective subjects. Like other Mossi capitals, its most widely remembered kings are those that subdued the largest population and displayed the greatest power (Meillassoux 1986, 101). The analogy between the outsider with a child is here useful. At birth, the child is a *san* (stranger) who has no name and so is yet to be purified, cut from the unknown world he comes from and only then integrated in his new society. Names of children changed at different stages of development and incorporation/inclusion into the society of humans. In so far as human beings were primarily envisaged 'in terms of reciprocal *relations* rather than as opposed entities, existing prior to or outside any set of relations, whether these are conceived of as classes or as mobile individuals or as both at once,' the point and terms of entry, and the conditions of exclusion from the sociological universe were important. At any rate, the condition of 'outsider' becomes crucial to the making of identity. The stranger's position involves both 'being outside' a society as well as 'confronting it' (Cheyfitz 1997: 54–55). The outsider is at once an ambiguous individual situated on the margin of (recognized as) 'normal' life-cycle events such as birth and at the periphery of the host society.

32. Gramscian scholars have for a long time discussed colonial hegemony at the junction of consent and collaboration; see John L. Comaroff (1998); Fanon (1967); and Femia (1981). However, a recent reading by a neo-Gramscian makes apparent the fact that not only the colonial encounter, but also the mechanisms of collaboration, were more often than not underlined by violence; see Randolph Persaud (2016).

Chapter 5

Rituals as Political References

INTRODUCTION

There existed within the Mossi state structures functional attributes that represented patterns of coexistence and interaction between power and belief. Unless one understands how rituals are used in the attempt at conciliation of two seemingly discrete spheres of social authority, the formulation of the possibility of sovereignty as something that is contingent and transferable makes little sense. This chapter uses the enthronement ritual of *ringu* to contextualize and conceptualize belief as central to state formation and political legitimacy in Moogo.

Both in the literature and Mossi-centred accounts, the realm of politics (*Naam*) and the realm of rituals (*Tenga*) are presented as distinct spheres of social action that rarely overlap. However, this chapter's argument is that in the very act of conciliation *and* legitimation of state power through the royal installation ritual, the state appropriates the political authority, hence power, that has always been part of the functions of the guardians of *Tenga*.

While ideology can be seen as a tension to be negotiated between indigenousness and otherness, rituals expressed the Mossi theory of kingship as well as its changing character over time. This theory can only be fully made sense of in its articulations in and of social life, and therefore in the context of institutional formation as product of power struggles. During the *ringu*, a king is 'made' and kingship established. The *ringu* exposes the limits of political competition in the attainment of royal *respect*. The latter has to be earned through this ritual enterprise through which the king symbolically 'appropriates' legitimacy, both as territoriality and sacrality.

Belief then becomes a crucial lens through which to apprehend the Mossi state for a more accurate reading of the dynamics of its formation and the negotiated cohabitation between autochthonous and migrant communities. This chapter is about the ritual enactment of cultural literacy. But ritual here is conceptualized at the intersection of normativity and individual and collective subscription to cultural practice. Among the neighbouring Kasena for instance, both *the prescribed* and *the proscribed* have the same term (*culu*), and the apparent contradiction given to the notion of ritual collapses as one thinks about it as 'practice' for one observes an obligation or fails to do so as a voluntary act regardless of whether one has 'belief'.[1]

In the oral traditions of the Voltaic region, the birth of the state is described as the outcome of an *original encounter* of the *Naam*—an imported concept introduced to the region by Mossi migrants hailing from 'somewhere east'—with *Tenga*, indigenously conceptualized. The encounter created a dichotomic opposition, violent at places, but which was over time transformed into a 'dual unity' consolidated by an ideology wrought in a specific political thinking and system, what I term the *Naam model*.

The *Naam* is the fundament of the state architecture, the overarching historical and conceptual phenomenon that defines social identity according to people's distance from it. The *Naam* also regulates inter-group relationships on the basis of groups' *de jure* or *de facto* access to it, which in turn is a function of office devolution. The existence of the state—and the articulation of state power—is thus essentially based on that of the *Naam*, not on territory or 'ethnicity' or other criteria typically associated with the state. Mossi rulers invoked the superiority of the *Naam* as both a technology and ideology of power in order to subdue first-comer groups across the Voltaic region to their rule, either through violent or negotiated incorporation, alliances, erasures, co-optations and annexations.

The understanding of belief is a prerequisite to the study of state and society in Moogo. Belief is inseparable from almost all aspects of its social and political life.[2] It is the 'lens' that brings into focus the conditions and changing circumstances of state presence outside the realm of political power strictly speaking. It is the ultimate fulcrum of the state's legitimation process.

Mossi religious practices are a bricolage, a syncretic system that welds indigenous and imported rituals into a new transcendent order that sublimates the contradictions of a belief system that has all the trappings of a hierarchical power structure. In the absence of an explicit theological body in precolonial Moogo, the Mossi state was a willing *hermeneus*, an interpreter of faith and an active regulator of religious affairs; its role as religious 'regulator' was two-pronged.

First, the state attempted to carve what it viewed as appropriate niches for different orders within a recognizable sociopolitical network. Second, the state's ideological structuration shaped belief and moulded ideas of the afterlife in its own image. The state 'occupied', so to speak, the space left vacant by a withdrawn god. Mossi belief reveals a set of human anxieties in grappling with 'meaning' and 'becoming' in the *now*, 'of felt limitations to existence, and of the brittleness in the edifice of human moral order' (McCaskie 1995, 105). However, in its concrete manifestations and practices, it is mostly concerned with the explanation and prediction of space-time occurrences, namely, the legitimation of a political rule of self-made 'state-crafters'.

In the literature on religious practices in 'traditional' Africa, a combination of mistranslations, anachronisms and erroneous applications of proficient knowledge of monotheistic religions to different belief systems has led to dehistoricized accounts of belief as organizing principle and as distinct social category. Religion tends to be presented, in anthropological research, as a source of functionalist instrumentality meant to merely sacralize political rule.[3]

The 'secular turn' of late colonial historiography was as much an effect of feedback processes as a misreading of 'religion' in social action. For even as power was ritually transferred to chiefs, the ritual bond between politics and religion was never broken. However, kings and political rulers were recognized practical capacities to mobilize material resources for the preservation of livelihood and the protection of subjects against external threat. When rulers could no longer bring the rain, they were expected to muster the means to assuage the effects of droughts, famines and other natural disasters. Even when historians of the 'secularized' state sought to isolate it from social action, 'religion was not dogma or tribal trait however; it was history, a description of past relationships between peoples and spirits that held ongoing implications for the identities of the living' (Gordon 2012, 28). Specifically in the Mossi configurations I describe below, practices of belief point to a conception of law as pastoral compact.

In apprehending the place of belief in and its impact on processes of state formation in Moogo, it is important to explore the following questions. If religion is part and parcel of historical experience, how does it inform the state-building process and, by extension, the social project from a state's perspective? In particular, how does the *ringu* fit into the state's enaction of belief in the constitutive transfer of authority from indigenous forms?

This chapter is organized around three sections that explore the implications of the withdrawal of the high god, the transaction of a Mossi political history through the performance of the enthronement journey and the transformation of the historical references of the Mossi state through a divine kingship framework.

The *ringu*, or voyage of enthronement, essentially transacts the constitutive subjection of political power to the procedures of *Tenga* to seal the peculiar transformation of a 'son of the earth' into a warrior. For it is at this junction that a state was born, dated, according to Mossi sources, around the end of the sixteenth century.[4] As such, it is central to the understanding of the nature of the relations between power and belief. I argue that the *ringu* activates the necessary ritual resources of political legitimacy while appropriating political action and agency from the putative representatives of first-comer groups through sacrificial violence and ritual reordering. The chapter thus shows how social integration, along with the consolidation of state legitimacy and state apparatus, was a function of ritual, blood and political alliances within a historically diverse society. It also shows how the state negotiated territoriality, ethnicity and social differentiation in its attempts to consolidate and stabilize state institutions through the elaboration of new rules.

WITHDRAWAL OF THE HIGH GOD AS A PROCESS OF SOCIALIZATION OF BELIEF

The origin of the state was a mythical moment recounted with variations but essentially around the same constitutive elements of *indigenousness—alienness*. The Mossi state as a sociological reality, however, was formed through a painstaking process, with doses of violence and an elevated level of commitment to transformations.

Belief and deference to a high god, or sky god, are a religious particularity the Mossi share with many West and Central African societies. The West African high god is a *deus otiosus*, in other words, a god withdrawn from worldly concerns. An exalted spirit, he is not the object of unmediated forms of worship; he is instead imagined and narrated in mythological structures. As the creator of all things material, the one that organized and reordered a chaotic world, he is yet strangely distant from its creations. This distance creates a contradiction in human approaches to the divinity as an intimate presence conceivable in every element of his enduring creation. Divine withdrawal, therefore, elicits a pressing need for explanation and representation of the absolute and its embodiments.

However, the withdrawal is only partial as the work of creation is never totally complete. Lesser divinities need a hand in dealing with situations of extreme exigency. They 'humanize' the high god in familiar forms, thus bearing characteristics, emotions and imperfections with which human beings are able to identify. I wish to argue that the withdrawal of the high god, at least in the Mossi context, triggers a politically useful *socialization process*, first operated through the representation of the sun as a 'fecundator' but more so through the attribution of sacred qualities to elements and places of social interaction more receptive to the demands of human existence.

This particular framework is one of historical and religious symbiosis. Two things follow from this. First, the transfer of sacral attributes from high to lower deities is a prerequisite to social action as an expression of religious allegiance. Lower deities in turn define the direction of social action, thus creating a dynamic relation with religious consumers who infuse divinities with specific meanings. Second, the notion of sacred places as bargaining sites endows human interactions with the divine with consequential qualities. One way to understand these dynamics is that the domain of power is an open circle subject to multiple interpretations and the injection of novel ideas and ideals. Equally, representations of a withdrawn high god denote anxieties about the sustainability of precarious cultural forms.

In fact, the lack of an explicit and extensive representation of the high god points to existential anxieties not fully addressed in relation to the existence and/or availability of immediate succour in times of distress. In the Mossi experience, however, though removed in a hierarchical sense, *Wende* (the Mossi high god) is brought back into the realm of the concrete through its association with *Tenga*, the earth divinity. Belief in Moogo, however, cannot be properly understood without replacing in context the dynamics of categorical distinctions of state and society in what they contribute in defining the parameters and scope of religious practice.

Belief is part of the historical experience and it is at the heart of the epistemological and ideological fundaments of the Mossi state. It places the individual, society and the state at historical junctions mediated by a set of precepts constructed according to a changing understanding of the mutual workings of nature on culture.

In Moogo, religious syncretism articulates a valuable association of political power and production. Historically, the socialization process of the high god bears the strong imprint of determined and determining human agency. It was assumed by a category of conquerors, *nakombsé*, who presumably imposed the idea of the *Naam* on autochthonous populations. Before the arrival of the Mossi, *Tenga* was most probably the superior divinity of the indigenous groups. The sacred association of the earth divinity (*Tenga*) with the god of migrant Mossi (*Wende*) gives birth to *Wennam*, eminent symbol of a peaceful resolution of the encounter between Mossi conquerors and their future subjects. *Wennam* is an original construct that provides a cognitive solution to a fundamental social question that is the working cohabitation of groups with divergent structures, lifestyles and belief systems.

In the arid land of Moogo, fatalism and pessimism toward the action of divinities has a particular poignancy to it. Man's 'disposition for suffering is repeated like a mantra, it is skin-wrapped to the psyche of ordinary Mossi and to considerable degrees rouses the Moaga's pluck in the face of difficulties' (Ilboudo 1966, 53–55). However, to reduce religion to an ethics of existence would be an ahistorical representation of Mossi belief.

Belief in these circumstances is not the privatized, modern, Christian one that tends to stress 'the priority of belief as a state of mind rather than as constituting activity in the world' (Asad 1993, 47). In discarding the possibility of belief as 'a corpus of practical knowledge', therefore, the accumulation of knowledge that culminates in belief, this modern understanding of belief is but a mere 'religious perspective' for belief is certainly not to be seen as a distinct mode of consciousness (Asad 1993, 47, 48). Asad's view arguably goes against a phenomenological approach that views religious symbols as *sui generis* and productive of an independent religious sphere, the idea that a religious world is a distinct experience unaffected by common-sense experience and vice versa.

The personification of lesser deities is for instance premised on the belief that they become endowed with the capacity to question and tamper with the work of the high god. The latter leaves to the 'spirits' the latitude to change his creations in ways that may be harmful to human beings. The earthpriests are, by vocation, the designated agents of the spirits' will. The translation into 'earthpriest' is a cultural import which is unsatisfactory and misleading on many accounts, not least because of the social place, the role and the expectations attached to the function. The earthpriests were the receptacle and the willing mouthpieces of the spirits. Their posture merely displayed the inflections of a changing nature. They articulated in that sense the constant undulations of nature into culture and vice versa.

Contrary to *Wennam*, *Tenga* is the object of an active and intense worship, agrarian in character. In periods before, during and after harvest, Mossi offer prayers and sacrifices for abundance and fertility. The most solemn of these is the *tinsé*, celebrated when the rainy season draws close.[5] It re-enacts a founding story that informs both Mossi and indigenous self-understandings. Like the *Wennam-Tenga* union, it becomes a ritualistic expression of a peculiar philosophical approach to social organization.[6] Earthpriests ensure that rituals are conducted according to 'tradition' so as to keep the social body away from natural calamities as a potential outcome of the wrath of disgruntled ancestors (Ilboudo 1966, 65–66).[7]

PROPOSITION OF POWER AND PRINCIPLES

The syncretic couple (*wen-nam*) is a rather original conception among Voltaic groups. It points to the symbol of fertility, both human and agricultural, given contrasting attributes. It constitutes the central ideological unity of Mossi belief. In effect, the pursuit of a collective identity became 'imbued with a normative transcendental meaning' by virtue of this divine marriage (Eisenstadt, Abitbol, and Chazan 1988, 183).

The syncretism that emerges out of such a union consequently displays a dual nature that suggests that gods are theoretical entities, and rituals and religious practices are intended to apply theory to the control of the world. Rituals are thus made of the same stuff as human social relationships: they are an extension of social relationships, and gods are subjects who apply meaning to social encounters. In this model, man's encounter with god is conceptualized as the ultimate and archetypical social relationship (Horton 1971, 96–97).

There existed, within the Mossi state structure, functional attributes that represented patterns of co-existence and interaction between power and belief. Unless one understands how rituals are used in the attempt at conciliation of two seemingly discrete spheres of social authority, the formulation of the possibility of sovereignty as something that is contingent and transferable makes little sense. The three categories constitute the *naa yiir demba* (people of the chief's house) housed in the *zade*; they form the *moose* body, in other words, the royal service strictly speaking (*togo*, *balum* and *weranga nanamse*). By virtue of their affiliation with the royal service, these dignitaries are chiefs in the institutional sense although they do not control territorial entities.

As first royal servants, the *naa yiir demba* ensure the proper administration of the *naaba*'s public and private life. They supervise the organization of ritual events and the customary duties of the *naaba*. They facilitate access of ordinary citizens to the person of the *naaba*. The *nesômba* mediate every audience and visit to the *naaba*, thus exercising effective administrative control over territorial chiefs, courtiers and a very large portion of the general population. This then becomes an important point in the state's strategy to invest the area of belief through administrative arrangements. In the preservation of the continuity of the royal institution, this particular duty may go against the will of members of the royal lineage in instances where the latter is perceived to be undermining royal action and continuity (Izard 1995, 410–11).

The term *togo* is semantically linked to the idea of oral transmission or the transmission of the 'verb'. The *togo naaba* is the king's mediator with 'people of the earth' who supervise rituals (mediation of social equilibrium) and the use of land (social welfare).[8] Thus, if many local traditions explain the institution of the *Naam* as idea-system, as a violent process, state discourse explains it as something that is 'negotiated' through the power of the verb. The word is thus a founding principle of power and a means to perpetuate it. It seals the alliance between 'power' and the 'earth', and it is the binding tenet of political practice.

The archetypical image of the verb 'penetrating' the earth is re-enacted in agricultural practices and ritual celebrations whereby culture introduces the 'verb of ancestors' into the earth (nature) and therefore life into a static entity and culture into an otherwise uncultivated and untamed space. The humanization of man and the socialization of space are intensely articulated through the symbolism of the humanizing spiritual agent.

The alliance between indigenous/conquerors and power/production/earth creates a symbolic family relationship between the two whereby the 'people of the earth' are, as it were, the maternal parents of the 'people of power'. State intervention in the realm of belief is thus inaugurated through the establishment of symbolic blood ties which re-enact the mythical encounter of earth and power, a first inhabitant and a wandering warrior—hence the acknowledgement of this sacred link lends credence to state authority. The chief priest was the prominent figure of ritual ceremonies and was officially given ritual precedence and authority over the *naaba*.

THE DUAL PRINCIPLE AS MODEL: *RINGU,*
OR HISTORY TRANSACTED

A *naaba*-elect does not become a full-fledged ruler before accomplishing the installation rite which makes him *rima* (sovereign), neither will he be buried in the pantheon of the *rima*, the village of Somnyaa. If the complex sociopolitical structure makes it difficult to envisage the nature of the state's peculiar relationship with belief, the *ringu* ritual provides elements of the historical underpinnings of an ambiguous, strained cohabitation of political power and an indigenous belief system. In a representational cycle, the burial ceremony was the prologue of enthronement for a new *naaba*.

The *ringu* therefore re-enacts the conceptual link between power and belief. It is the ideological bridge between antagonizing yet complementary forces, earth (belief) and power (state), between a hierarchized system and relative autonomy. Like other loosely structured installation rites, the *ringu* seeks to formulate and express a Mossi theory of kingship as well as its changing character over time. The *naaba* acquires sovereignty and hence the means to rule independently literally from the hands of earthpriests through a confirmation ritual that 'frees' him from the constraints of control by the earthpriests.

The rite's afferent symbols and coded language cannot therefore be seen as invested in sacrifices performed for a particular god; they are rather 'performed as empowering acts that transformed a prince into a king.'[9] In doing so, the installation rite embodies an ontological commitment to sovereignty as *trial*. Ritual is both structured event and an action that requires interpreting (Asad 1993, 127). But rituals should not be seen merely as symbols and therefore the restricted process of communication central for instance to British anthropology. The way meaning is discoursed between actors and audience is historically defined. The Mossi *ringu* can rightly be seen, as Asad would suggest, as a process of 'forming and reforming moral dispositions' (1993, 130).

The *naaba* in particular is made to remember, in his body and mind, virtues of humility and attention through the ordeals he is put through. The Mossi say that the *naaba* 'eats kingship' when he becomes a sovereign *rima*. The sovereign is the *na-rita* (one who eats power; Ray 1991, 175). *Ri* means 'to eat'; it is the radical for *ringu* and *rima*. In the context of the installation rite, the act of eating[10] is understood to mean 'to appropriate the substance of'; it articulates in that sense a profound expressive shift in ritual practice. The test for any king is whether he has what it takes to chew his bite.

One has to view the *ringu* as a legitimizing process without which a *naaba* has no real control over the territorial basis of his rule. The installation ritual is tremendously important in the transaction of power for without ritual there is no possibility for conciliation. In fact, past the moment of confrontation and violence that marks the encounter between migrants and autochthons, the challenge becomes conciliation as the place where justice and legitimacy originate.

Through the *ringu*, the new *naaba* familiarizes himself with the territory over which he expects to exert his authority (*ringu* literally meaning *royaume*, or 'kingdom'), both literally and metaphorically. The *ringu* becomes, in this process, the fulcrum of the state's legitimation process. It transposes the state, so to speak, onto the ritual sphere. The *naaba* traces the symbolic contours of his future kingdom in what is a closed course for the *naaba* departs from his *natenga* (royal residence) and comes back to it at the end via a west-to-east journey.[11]

The first phase of the ritual enthronement features the would-be king in an imploring posture, severely rebuffed for 'begging kingship' and eagerly seeking the approval of the autochthonous priests (De Heusch 1997, 221–22). He is scorned whenever he is seen to be coaxing a priest. His friendly attempts to bond with people are met with contempt. People pay attention to him only when he formally pledges 'allegiance' to the moral authority of the various earthpriests encountered in his journey. He prostrates himself before the senior priest and submits to his ritual authority, a strong statement of symbolic hierarchy which also points to a balance of power sought, and carefully orchestrated, by the state itself through an intricate system of performances: 'thus an equilibrium, a counterweight, was established and continually strived for at the very heart of the [state's] conception of power' (Glele 1974, 100).

From the state's viewpoint, to be seen as flexible and acquiescent to the ritual requirements of first-comers in exchange for recognition and legitimacy was as important as being seen as a peaceful figure that negotiated rather than imposed his rule.

A culmination in the installment ceremony is reached when the *naaba* is ritually 'captured' by the inhabitants of Tangazugu, one of the main stops of the enthronement expedition. His journey comes to a dramatic conclusion. He is made to dismount his stallion, the quintessential symbol of the constitutive essence of political power. In exchange he receives a donkey, symbol of the gritty and lowly life of ordinary peasants.

A series of rituals, from the royal residence to Gursi, leads to the effective enthronement of the would-be-king as a *sovereign*. During this journey, the *naaba* is treated like a 'pile of filth' and is the object of all sorts of exactions and disdain (Scubla 2005, 43) for every stop along the installation journey is marked by intense drama. The *ringu* stops were pointed references to significant moments and passages in Mossi history and founding myths. The public humiliation of a future king was the condition set by earthpriests for willingness to relinquish some of their power. The *naaba* in turn had to take humiliation, taunts, insults and all sorts of abuse in stride stoically and with apparent humility. For humiliation was the price to pay for ritual freedom: 'The *naaba* is required to make sacrifices, of animals, chickens. … [If] the population of Peela or Sisamba or another stop of the journey do not like the sacrifices, they would not let him go. He got told off.'[12]

The state's discourse of absolute power in fact greatly contrasts with stories of sequestration and debasing treatment that characterize enthronement rituals. It is not that the chief has to go through public disgrace to better rise as an all-powerful ruler. Everything in the symbolisms of *ringu* denotes an entrenched ambivalence toward power: the *Naam* is at once a foreign substance introduced by migrant-rulers and an occult power transferred to the chief by the earthpriest who either created it or received it from ancestors.

The location of power is eminently liminal, and this is not exclusive to the Voltaic societies. Indigenous traditions, in fact, 'underscore the stressful character of [political] work, revealing the limits of domination … by putting the contingencies of [kingly] domination on display' (Schoenbrun 2013, 655). The triumphant return to the royal compound is in stark contrast to the state of submissiveness of a hesitant and *bare* king at the mercy of the goodwill of the 'people of the earth' (Izard 1985, 150), those very ones he had looked down upon for lacking in culture and political institutions.

At the end of the enthronement voyage, the *naaba* is struck by a form of temporary sterility. The re-enactment of a fundamental trope on the themes of 'death' and 'renewal' speaks to the requirement of both institutional transition and generational transfer. Upon the *naaba*'s death, a collective lamentation rises:

Bounsare Kime! [The fire has extinguished!]
Mogho sama me! [The country has gone mad!][13]

Kingship as a referential institutional frame is momentarily suspended. It has to be symbolically reinstated by the new king, hence the *ringu*, as a way of addressing pervasive uncertainty through the reassertion of the necessity of the state. The end of the investiture reveals the dual fundament of the Mossi monarchy as enacted by a symbolic 'alliance' formed by the king and his stallion.

On one hand there is the *Naam*, the founding principle of authoritative rule associated with the royal lineage;[14] on the other hand *panga* (force, violence), the predatory force conferred onto the *naaba*, points to the emergence of the Mossi state as a centralized power structure with access to different forms of coercion (De Heusch 1997, 220; Izard 1973, 206). *Panga* gives the state carte blanche: it frees it from the constraints of tradition, precedence and morality. The orchestration of state rebirth has transformative ambitions that transcend the moment of legitimation. It is here that the state crafts its own history.

The same enthronement ritual that makes a king sacred also releases the forces of coercion that will later allow the state to 'grab' things and recognition rather than seek them out first from settler societies. If the *ringu* is an instance of the state seeking to gain legitimacy, from then on the tendency is for state power to legitimate itself. The state equally relies on coercive arguments in order to reorganize the basis of moral authority within royal lineages and overwrite the primacy of constitutive ethics of morality that govern conduct. As the saying goes, 'When *panga* is on the trail, *büum* (etiquette, moral conduct) runs away into the bush' (Izard 1979, 350). The holders of *panga* were equally dismissive toward *rog-n-miki*, the body of rules and the source of legal authority that normally governed social conduct. According to Bazémo, *rog-n-miki* is 'that force that perpetuates the past [and] … enacts history' (1993, 199–200). As such, any 'deviation from it was therefore a reason for decline, disorder and anxiety' (Niang 2012, 67).

In precolonial Yatenga, the *ringu* took place in Gursi-Tangazugu although a different *naaba* could express a preference for one particular place (e.g., his father's royal residence) over another. The *ringu* is a highly complex process and a long procedure sprinkled with symbolism and ethical references. It is for the *naaba* a quest for a path, a search for an identity, the tentative formulation of an ideology, a quest for meaning and an itinerary. During the *ringu*, the *naaba*'s wandering suggests a quest for legitimacy but also an attempt to construct historical memory. He enacts a past-present trajectory of past administrations by summoning past configurations in the present.

But the *ringu* is also a process of re-memorization of the constitutive encounter of 'power' and 'earth', intent and adjustment. It is a symbolic voyage into the past for a *naaba* wishing to engage the future according to the principles of encounter. It is a renewal of that founding agreement that is also an emblematic re-enactment of the birth of history: the state inscribes migration narratives on the very land/landscape that welcomed wandering migrants and in the process transforms them into history.

The *ringu* is thus to be read as a restoration of the original alliance, that between a *Mossi* heritage and a *nyonyonse* (first inhabitants) heritage. It expresses a need to reassert in both Moaga and *nyonyonse* conscience, that state power derived from an ancient power it supplanted by re-appropriating its essence.[15] This is what Izard has to say about this historical reactualization performed through the *ringu*:

> Le *ringu* réactualise, intègre et dépasse. L'histoire naît ici: dans la nécessité, pour tout pouvoir, de rappeler qu'il est issu d'un pouvoir antérieur qu'il a supplanté en s'en appropriant la substance, c'est à dire en le reconnaissant dans le moment même de sa négation [The *ringu* re-enacts, integrates and transcends. History begins here: in the necessity, for any power, to acknowledge that it is derived from an anterior power it has supplanted by appropriating its substance, in other words in acknowledging it in its very negation] (1985, 151).

While the Mossi narrative was vocal and verbally articulated, representations of social action and social reality among *Tenga* holders involved non-verbal, non-narratives modes of memory and of rendering. These gave different meanings to sites of encounter, exchange and recollection. 'Ritual' thus becomes merely a generic term that imperfectly renders the content and intent of a series of actions, symbols and enactments whose deployment reveals that many locales, particularly sites of recollection, are generative of social meaning.

There have been attempts to articulate an African philosophy of rule through a reading of the politics of rituals. Two trends are particularly striking. First, a rather simplistic reading of rites and rituals consists of reducing them to mere folkloric performances when in reality there is an ethic of togetherness behind ritual performance. Second, the liberal turn in twentieth-century Africanist social anthropology strove to turn African 'belief systems' into proper and respectable 'religions' with a historicity of their own alongside the formal religions of Islam and Christianity (MacGaffey 2013, 4).

For Mossi, Gurunsi, Dagara and other Voltaic groups, however, there are no two separate categories of 'religion' and 'culture', neither is there a first-order common dimension of belief and a second-order hidden or occult form of belief only experienced by a select few. When one does manage to abstract the profusion of expressions of belief and their performed categories to a hierarchy of order, what is revealed is the fact that belief is at once metaphor, sign, code, language, symbol and knowledge. Its expression and enactment are not just declarative or illustrative but a crucial normative mechanism of social life. But we need to go beyond stating this fact.

If we take our cue from Stephen Turner (1994), we need to focus beyond ritualized objects and symbols and ritualized encounters for how they enhance the capacity of participants. This enhancing is not perceptible through simply focusing on objects of ritual and ritualized situations. The contribution and role of beliefs to elaborations of selfhood, society and social rule support the view that despite the often cryptic nature of its codes and symbols—which is partly a consequence of an overly intellectualist reading of religious expressions—belief is eminently historical. As McCaskie contends, 'belief is construed historically in terms of the force of its *ideas* in lived experience' (1995, 103).

Furthermore, the *ringu* was the quintessential example of a ritual as a 'time of reckoning' during which the apparent contradiction between the stable, moral, institutional order and the shifting incumbency determined by agnatic procedures, the overlaying sociocultural Mossi order over an indigenous marginalized order, the rigid hierarchy of centralization and the loose processes of social incorporation were all ritually resolved 'in an elaborate cultural statement about the nature of the system in place'. As a result, 'a fluctuating and ambiguous everyday reality was ritually objectivized in an ostensibly stable order' (Jean Comaroff 1985, 67).

The idea of the divine kingship in Moogo (see below) has to be apprehended within the constitutive framework of the hierarchical division and correspondences between an 'earth order' (that was never formalized) and the power nomenclature. If at the village level, the *tenga naaba* (village chief) is the counterpart of the *tengsoba* (earthpriest), the *naaba* becomes his own counterpart at the summit of the ritual order and power pyramid in the absence of a first earthpriest. In his body is enshrined a dual representation.

By becoming *rima*, the sovereign becomes a sacred person isolated by his very sacrality (Izard 1985, 153). In this has to be seen a complementary relationship between the ritual symbolism expressed in the *ringu* and the historical and ritual traditions preserved by autochthonous groups (Ray 1991, 99). Earth shrines were clearly productive mills of creative power that were considerably depleted by Mossi rulers' hunger for power. If the *ringu* validates the disarticulation of the political from the ritual order, it equally disarticulates the *tenga naaba*'s political role from his ritual role.

Furthermore, the last night of the *ringu* reveals a particular aspect of the ethics of the divine kingship. The *naaba* spends the night with his *rimpoko* (wife of childbearing age) but is prohibited from making her pregnant. Symbolic sterility in fact befalls both the sovereign and his figurative double, his horse. Enthroned along with the *naaba*, the royal stallion is sacrificed as a ritual substitute, precisely in the very place where the coronation took place: for power has to die, in the physical demise of the horse, for it to be resuscitated (De Heusch 1997, 213–32; Izard 1990, 84).

In the Mamprusi enthronement ritual, the king is 'dragged like a slave' (Rattray 1932, 557) to his palace and forced to sit on a stone. His enskinment (enthronement) is then presided over by the *sagadugunaba*, the senior earthpriest. The defining terms of the rituals are humiliation, debasement and tensions 'that imbue him with the essential power of kingship and seem to embody the contradiction between human transience and the perdurance of kingship and the state' (MacGaffey 2013, 117). Humiliation, sequestration and similarly degrading mistreatment serve to remind the king of the origin of his power, without which he is nothing. For example, he is made to eat forbidden meats.

Throughout the rite, it is stressed to him and to everybody else that 'the people of the earth' *own* the king and kingship. Like the Mossi chief, from an arrogant, aggressive prince he is turned into a passive figure: he becomes the embodiment of the 'living source' and its derivations across Mamprugu.[16] In Mamprusi foundational stories, an immigrant-ruler was invited by earthpriests to be a rainmaker—in particular Gambarana (chief of Gambaga), who officiates during key rituals such as enskinment-funeral rites.

As in Moogo, the *pwanaaba* (female-chief) also plays a key role in the transition to a new king. At various stages, different earthpriests intervene in the elaboration of kingship and the making of power, thus countering, in this manner, the tendency for rulers to obstruct the emancipatory potential of their earthpriests' moral control over political rule. It is as if the proper orchestration of the transfer of the *Naam* was crucial to the very substance of life beyond a need for continuity. Migrant-rulers claimed to detain the *Naam*. In reality, however, the *Naam* had to be 'translated' for kingship. In Mamprugu, the *nayiri* (king) does not 'bring' the *Naam*; the latter is rather conceived as a metaphysical force that 'catches the king'.

In the enskinment ritual, the *tarana*, senior among the king's titled elders, announces the name of the new king and dresses him in his kingly attire (gown and bonnet; Drucker-Brown 1975, 45–48). An important point needs to be made at this junction. One can read here an ontology of interdependence that posits mutually causative action between human beings, ancestral spirits, natural and supernatural elements, material objects and subjects. Interdependence is enacted and reinscribed in the transfer of the 'living source'; there is interdependence between the *nayiri* and the elders, between elders and the *tindanas*, ultimately between the *nayiri* and his Mamprusi subjects as mediated by their putative representatives (MacGaffey 2013, 117).

The implications of interdependence are twofold. First, a notion of statehood in this context necessarily has to be reviewed if our concern is about legitimate authority, public morality and social norms. Second, the dichotomy produced different forms of cohabitation and different conceptions of social structures. In Dagbon and in Moogo, some earthpriests cooperated in cadence with political rulers while others were independent. In Mamprugu, earthpriests operated in parallel with chiefs in a relatively loose structure. Among the Dagara and the Tallensi, the roles of chief and earthpriest could be amalgamated in the same figures. In none of these examples is the distinction between kingship and belief so rigid as to validate the existence of two distinct spheres of life.

Thus as symbol and as mode of communication, the work of ritual was linked to social transformation. Social transformation was the result, as observed elsewhere, of the active interaction between the symbolic and the material worlds (Jean Comaroff 1985, 78). A close examination of the ritual system reveals a fundamental insight, which is that historical practice, beyond a linear account of 'facts', needs to be sought, and it is more fully captured when one engages critically with ritual action. Change is at once a symbolic and material process. The role of ritual essentially is to act upon the phenomenal world through the most effective manner.

The use of the most mundane objects in ritual work was only the apparent side of a transformation effort that infused those objects with symbolizing capacity through the invocation of words whose power and resonance was known only to those thoroughly initiated. The transformative capacity of rituals was harnessed by the sequential dislocation of social categories which were built into the representation (staging/enacting) of tensions inherent in a *rampant* hierarchical system. The terms of this *new* culture were to be constantly renegotiated, as *tengbiisi* and *nakombsé* engaged in roles outside their traditional remit and as people with 'no history or culture' were ritually made members of the state and thus socialized to the mores of *Mossi culture*. In that sense, belief served to crystallize the conditions for the construction of a new identity, that of the Moaga, for the making of the state was also a protracted contest of capturing minds and consciousness.

The impact on how people respond to social norms and interdicts is manifest in the fear of immediate punishment (e.g., being struck by lightning if one commits perjury). Rituals are precisely theatricalized moments that enact human anxieties in a particularly poignant and potent manner. They lend concrete form to fear and hope, the two ends within which oscillate individual emotions (Netting 1972, 233).

The effectiveness of rituals as language and social measure in securing moral compliance translates to fear of ancestral or supernatural sanction. Moments of integration, consultation and decision-making, ritual knowledge and technology of control, harness the power of keepers and direct the use of ritual knowledge as a recognized resource put to specific uses and ends. In addition, there is a system of fines, sanctions, propitiation, purification and restoration that creates frequent opportunities for the mobilization of resources. Specifically, cleansing, purification and in short restoration enhances ritual potency by enlarging the arena of potential political action and the political influence of those involved (McIntosh 1999).

It appears in all this that the essence of royal power is ritual function for the reality of sovereign state necessarily lies in the rehearsal of power and the performance of historicity. In Moogo, the *naaba* does not go to war, the war chief, *samand naaba*, stands in for him. On the other hand, a new *naaba*'s young son is sent to live in a remote village and is never to see the *naaba* again face to face. The son becomes a *kurita* conceived as the negative double of the king, and he represents, with the war chief, the king's ritual scapegoat, the former during the *naaba*'s term in office and the latter for the duration of his life (Izard 1995, 416; De Heusch 1997, 221).[17]

Goody aptly pointed to the ritual opposition which existed, in precolonial Sudanic pluralism, between the horse and the Earth, the one pointing to bearers of force and the other to cult shrines as well as agricultural activities. He drew attention to the fact that while this division marks a clear separation between the concentration of power (state) and the social entities over which it was to be exercised, power was not regularly exercised within the same realm, and state practice was therefore disconnected from economic production (1971, 57–72 in Lonsdale 1986, 170).

A similar principle is performed, through the *ringu*, between political power and socioeconomic production in a broad sense. Where political institutions are no more important than economic ones, the *naaba*'s role is not to rule per se but *to reign*, to be the willing scapegoat of a community of purpose. He performs key aspects of a Mossi theory of state. Variations in ritual over time, therefore, have to be seen as reflecting the changing character of this theory (Walzer 1974, esp. intro. and 124; Evans-Pritchard 1948, 200).

SACRED KINGSHIP: THE POLITICAL *IN* THE RITUAL

Divine Reference and Historical Initiative

Fraser's concept of sacred kingship is relevant to our understanding of *Wende* as an absentee divinity in the Mossi belief system on one hand and in gaining insight into the sacred dimension of the *naaba* on the other (Feeley-Harnik 1985). The *naaba*'s morning appearance inspires the expression 'The sun's shining'. The sun is a positive association to the *naaba*, and his sacred quality infuses the heavens in a transcendental ascension. This exclamation has historical roots in the wandering days of Mossi-Dagomba conquerors. It is said that there is a basic intuition of belief in the impressive and immovable nature of the sky. The sun equally elicits a sense of religious reality; it is the divine sphere and the fundament of aspects of human experience imprecisely captured by the mind. In the same sense that the sun dissipated fear and anxiety for Mossi-Dagomba migrants in their expansionist endeavour northward from Dagomba and Mamprusi, the Mossi describe the appearance of the *naaba* as a moment of great awe: his appearance inspires a sense of protection and guidance to the kingdom. The cult of the sun is however not a religion for a given class—the Mossi aristocracy—but an attempt at abstraction of political authority.

The *naaba* in the Mossi political tradition thus impersonates the divine; he is a sun god in political outfit and therefore the vital centre around which sociopolitical life is made sense of. The sun symbolizes a theoretical transfer of power, and therefore transcendence, through dynastic and lineage-based principles. The *naaba* is a dynastic starting-point and a reference in mapping the route of power transmission according to the common-ancestor model. But divine reference does not grant absolute sovereignty. The *naaba*'s power is a composite one made of components lodged in different offices.[18]

Divine kingship was also a framework formulated at the expense of the king's person as it aimed to preserve the divine character of kingship—not the king per se—and continuity of the model (Evans-Pritchard 1948, 211). Rituals were required to represent the enduring character of office beyond the life of any particular incumbent. Many observers of early eighteenth-century politics within the *Naam* political culture reported on the uniquely competitive, intense, if not violent nature of periods of interregna. What they failed to understand, however, was the unique value attached to the struggle for (conquering) the *Naam*. Individual candidates were backed by different factions that invested tremendous resources, their group reputation and future, for the outcome of the nomination could jeopardize the chances of a particular group's candidates ever competing again for office.

Common to both Moogo and the Dagbamba states was the tradition that consisted in all factions vowing allegiance to the chosen candidate after having furiously competed for the *Naam*. All of this points to misgivings many observers have had with regard to 'succession disputes': the latter were in reality an important aspect of *naam* politics (Drucker-Brown 1975, 131). Nomination decisions could be challenged—as in the case of the nomination of a new Mamprusi *na* in 1864 as widely reported by drum-chroniclers. Such a 'rebellion', in this case an armed struggle between Yamusa and Gani factions, was to ensure that the new *na* could rule without fear of trouble from former rivals.

Religious references in Moogo cannot be made sense of outside the context of particular histories. Existential anxiety pits man against the experience of transcendental power at particular historical times. The response to sacred beings is therefore a function as well of a consequence of the sociopolitical structure that bears the enduring print of the religious dimension and upholds its principles in its working structures.

The idea of a divine presence has to be, for wandering immigrants, that which sanctions their historical-political 'mission'. Charles Long contends that 'the modalities through which the sacred is mediated to us are products of history, but we must ask whether the reality to which we respond through the various modalities is also just a symbolization of historical conditions.'[19]

Another framework is needed, however, to characterize the encounter of a migrant invested with a mission to rule and an autochthonous prone to accommodating such a mission. In that sense, belief has to be apprehended in the rationalization of legitimacy in state power in the state's attempt to control space and time through ritual manipulation. Both endeavours bespeak the state's desire to exercise 'material and symbolic command of the polity *tout court*' (Comaroff and Comaroff 1991, 147).

Belief is a founding principle of the Mossi state in so far as it informs a practice of political power, and it is at the heart of state formation and expansion both in time and space. Archaeological and historical sources reveal the remnants of ancient beliefs in sun and earth cults (Simporé 2004). These are configurations that lend to interpretations that point to *nomadism* and *sedentarization* as an explanation and/or a consequence of such beliefs.

Social stratification in Moogo would then be a reflection of contrasting tendencies. Earthpriests in Moogo are uniquely found among the indigenous *nyonyonse*; they are devoted to agricultural production and to the protection of the sacrality of the land through sacrifices, rituals and the supervision of delimited territorial boundaries that mark the physical frontier between the social, the sacred and untamed spaces. Earthpriests have privileged access to the province of natural forces although the scope of their visibility is unknown.

In all this, belief in the Mossi experience was not a private affair entirely left to individual initiative. In fact, belief was never an isolated individual attempt at spiritual reckoning. It was neither a matter of communitarian ethics nor an individual aspiration to ethics. If belief was not epiphenomenal to power, it was the self-arrogation of the state. When earthpriesthood is the emphasis of analysis, belief tends to be described as something epiphenomenal to the reality of power but there is a strong element of the latter in it.

Power on the other hand was not entirely devoid of a religious dimension for the latter suffused every recess of political action. In fact, it would be correct to say that political action was very much embedded in religious belief. The lack of an interrogative dialogue with the divine meant that the afterlife was a world constructed in tentative and temporary terms in the sense that different administrations could introduce novelties in the practice of belief. It was, in the ordinary mind, a vacated area where imagination was limited and where state projection could essentially thrive.

Given the above, the *ringu* and similar rituals were not just important in constructing a space of interaction of orders with overlapping and at times antagonistic values, aims and interties but in ensuring strength, 'thickness', for state legitimacy. A badly enthroned king was one who failed to perform the installation rite. Such was the case of Naaba Kango (1757–1787), remembered in oral tradition as powerful and feared, yet most effective among Yatenga kings for being unorthodox and rebellious toward 'tradition'. Kango was overthrown by disgruntled contenders to the throne led by Naaba Wogbo as soon as he was elected in 1754. He went into exile in Kong and Segu and enlisted the support of the Kulibali for a successful comeback. Upon his return to Yatenga, he built a spectacular palace in Malian architectural style and decreed that only the 'political society'—in other words, his entourage, the military, foreign captives integrated in the royal order, people of the kingly household and others involved in state activities—were allowed in. He also established a new capital, Waiguyu (Ouahigouya), literally 'Come and submit to my rule'[20] that eloquently spoke of his aversion to seeking ritual sanction. As one informant put it, 'We say here that the power is in Ouahigouya.'[21]

Belief and Historical Experience: The State as Hermeneus

This leads me to the historical dimension of religious experience. Theory in itself, in its attempt to elucidate the world on the basis of its observable and hidden layers of meaning, is an incomplete tool in apprehending the state's endeavour to apply theory to social space and its attempts to use belief for ideological ends. Religious practice in its various forms as text, idea, belief, ritual, symbolic language and social experience is best made sense of when apprehended within and in relation to historical experience at the individual, societal and state level. If 'religion was also a crucial motivating factor that affected the office within the context of the political history of the kingdom' (Bay 1995, 3), its mobilization in the confirmation of a *naaba*-elect provided counterpoints to a unilateral discourse of the triumph of culture, knowledge and political dexterity. The role of ritual in this process cannot be underestimated for it makes explicit, albeit temporarily, what is otherwise merely a belief, which is that the king's power is subject to public control.

The harvest ritual for instance offers an opportunity for reading aspects of the historical enactment of social order as new edicts are proclaimed, freedom of speech is reasserted in the grilling session to which the king is subjected and defiance and contempt inform popular interrogation of political leadership and social engagement.[22] The ceremony is at once a first-fruits sacrament, a military celebration, a historical enactment of the state and a glorification of the legitimacy of the *Naam*. It is also meant to be 'an economic institution of unique proportions,' the centre of the redistributive state (Polanyi 1966, 33 in Bay 1995, 4).

There is a clear ordering as to the way the first mouthful is to be taken: the king follows the ancestors (spirits), and then come close kinsmen and so forth. The order of precedence in the consumption of the products of the soil responds to the priority of filiation to a far-off ancestor (Oubri and Ouedraogo, founding ancestors of Moogo). The festival is therefore a historical enactment of the constitution of state and society: dependency and subjection, interdependency and vulnerably are simultaneously dramatized. The ceremony re-establishes national unity while celebrating the political, social and economic precedence of state power and its bearers. It is the occasion that gathers the entire nation, alive and dead, in a communion of purpose: the spirits of the ancestors and forefathers foregather with their descendants in a physical and metaphorical sense.

In practical terms, the ceremony marks the sloughing off of the old year and its host of ills, misfortunes and unfulfilled expectations as well as the passage from an old to a new year, old crops to new crops. It also marks the symbolic (re)emergence of the king after a long retreat. As Max Gluckmann points out with regard to the *umkosi* (first-fruits ceremony) among the Zulu, 'from the earth and seed, fertilized with medicines, protected by the ancestors, have come the crops, filled with a power inherent in themselves and derived from spirits. The long and arduous round of hoe-culture is almost over, dearth is ended, and plenty is to begin' (1938, 34). The ceremony is also seen as exercising a form of control by balancing tendencies for thriftlessness with an attitude of moderation because of the taboo on early eating. Bonds of kingship and lineage, of peaceful neighbourliness and renewed allegiance, accompany the festivities, and these unique moments are revelled in years later as any significant rite of passage.

The absence of a corpus of dogmas is emphasized in the Mossi religious structure and contrasted to a system of communal obligations that outlines the ethical structure of human activity. Mossi religion is denied ontological depth; *Wennam*, the Mossi god, is conceptualized in parsimonious terms as if to emphasize the absence of an intimate sense of his presence in the human mind (Ilboudo 1966, 54–55). If colonial and postcolonial treatments reduce a multiplicity of divinities to incoherence and a free-for-all disorganization, it remains that the traditional system sustained a regularity no less valid than the clarity and orderliness conceded to modern monotheistic faiths. In the literature of traditional African belief systems, a statement like the following is not unusual: 'In this web of belief every strand depends upon every other strand,

and a [believer] cannot get out of its meshes because it is the only world he knows. The web is not an extended structure in which he is enclosed. It is the texture of his thought and he cannot think that his thought is wrong' (Evans-Pritchard 1940, 194). But such characterizations suffer from an excessive certainty that individuals who subscribe to ancestral belief can never have the capacity to think outside a state of permanent 'possession'. They therefore have limited impact in explaining ritualized forms of invocation in moments of violent collapse. In a system of belief that seeks to apply theory to the control of the world through rituals, divinities are also theoretical entities subject to the instability of history.

Moreover, the above framework can be juxtaposed with a more explicit historical reality that pits belief against state design and against its control of individual agency. *Wennam* can be better understood as personifying an exercise in religious bricolage, in other words, an objectified 'Mossi religion' elevated as state religion. Belief and other forms of subjective experience are conceptualized at two levels, namely, as an independent social framework of its own and as a framework enmeshed in the trammels of historical revolution, social transformation, migration and state building.

This characteristic is in no way unique to the Mossi. Horton for instance discusses the ways in which cosmological beliefs, as a product (dependent variable) of a given social situation, 'go on to acquire an institutional framework which transforms them into independent variables with their own power to bring about ideological and social change' (1971, 95). One has to bear in mind that the degree of integration between religion and social (infra)structure may be an outcome of state design—at least in its attempt to populate people's imaginaries with particular themes.

In Moogo, state attempts to thwart the development of a corporate ritual order akin to a 'clergy' are well documented. The diffuse authority of earthpriests—their perceived knowledge of hidden reality and possession of keys to decode the language of gods—was a threat to state power. State reformulation of the principles of belief very much discouraged the interpretation of visions by the earthpriests even when commissioned by individuals. A consolidated priesthood would therefore never thrive in this context.

Priests and diviners on the other hand evolved in a specific political economy of divination, what McCaskie calls a 'pluralist political economy of belief' (1995, 123), whereby individuals in the pursuit of answers to or a remedy for their anxiety could take their queries from diviner to diviner and from priest to priest until they were satisfied with the answer provided. The secular influence of spirits was limited by this very structure. The priest, in mediating the pervasive nature and manifestations of spirits, was involved in a field of uncertain realization whereby interpretation of an event was only one priest's version that needed to be met by the active confidence of the individual applicant.

The state's attempt to discourage the consolidation of an explicit hierarchy of priesthood was meant to pre-empt collective action and any sign of unity of purpose among religious practitioners. This was most apparent in instances of conflict over interpretation between legal and religious perspectives—more generally speaking, in matters requiring either religious or legal adjudication. Here the state's ideological project lay in attempts to define the possibilities and conditions of belief. The state's approach to belief could therefore be viewed as a desire to act at the very roots of the religious experience. The absence of an explicit exegesis or structured theological body in Moogo meant that the state could play the role of hermeneus (McCaskie 1995, 123–24). This consisted in subsuming belief in the historical reading and recording process:

> There were clear openings here that the state filled by forging a purposefully authoritative reading of … historical experience. In this ideological structuration, belief was annexed and absorbed into the state's promulgation of the historical record (McCaskie 1995, 126–27).

McCaskie shows how, in the Asante case, the state successfully subsumed the epistemological distinctions between knowledge and belief in various ways, and this was made possible by the state's perception of history and by extension culture as 'a matrix of highly self-conscious acts of insertion' (1995, 126). In this schema, the state monopolized the reading of knowledge and belief, authored the historical experience of society and peoples and grounded its hermeneutical understanding in existing contradictions. In doing so, it attributed historical competence to ritual moments while incorporating the latter in the historical record.

The Mossi state also attempted to monopolize the discourse on belief, and to a certain extent with mitigated success. The reformulation and re-exposition of fundamental actions of revelation in the course of rereading or reviewing the historical process came up against histories of origin and foundational myths firmly engrained among pre-Moaga communities.

From the state's perspective, to violate prescribed rules and codes was to transgress at the same time (1) the supernatural order and (2) the socio-political configuration. In other words, to question the state narratives, therefore the ordained conditions, constituted a subversive act against the established social and political orders. The two elements, supernatural and mediated/integrated social order, were both governed by the state. The difference therefore between violation of belief and civil disobedience could be rather flimsy.

The state put forward an idea of the land of ancestors and spirits as exactly mirroring that of the visible world. The implications for social hierarchy were no less important than those of the political system. The royal lineage drew legitimacy for political rule in the invisible world in the same way that it did in the visible one. The system of beliefs was also to be viewed in the way it conditioned negotiations within the state and determined collective attitudes toward public decisions.

A newly enthroned *naaba* had to make allegiance to the earthpriest, the master of land and guardian of the sacred places of ancestors and the divinities. However, considering the pervasive nature of the *Naam*, it is difficult to explain the easy acceptance of earthpriests of the rule of the royal class.

State intervention in the realm of belief could take the form of the promotion of, or favouritism toward, specific priests while denigration campaigns could be secretly initiated to discredit the expertise of priests not particularly acquiescent to the *naaba*'s ways. Equally, priests (and divinities!) could be played against each other in order to alter power dynamics. These strategies reflected changing ideas on the nature of power among competing political factions.

CONCLUSION

Revisiting the *ringu* as reconstruction, enactment and transformation of historical encounter in the context of the formulation and transfer of political legitimacy affords new insights into the intellectual history of the precolonial African state. Belief in Moogo proceeds from a fundamental social bipartition that distinguishes on the one hand the 'people of power' associated with the state/power/war and the 'people of the earth' associated with belief/rituals/ agriculture—a model somewhat widespread among West African societies. This dual pattern is a ubiquitous feature as well as an important grid of reading of state ideology on the one hand and state and society relations on the other.

The sacrality of state institutions in Moogo points to the ritual function as the underlying principle of the political function of royalty—in de Heusch's words, 'the symbolic complex surrounding sacred kingship is the kernel of the state' (1997). The Mossi model posited a balance of power between two alternative sources of ideological construct whereby priests, diviners and a host of figures claiming an ancestral link to the land mediated communication with ancestors and spirits through rituals and provided moral legitimation to social experience.

On the other hand, in the absence of an explicit theological body, the state provides an image of the afterlife as a reflection of the sociopolitical hierarchy devised by the ruling class. This was made possible by the difference in hier-archical structure between kingship/state and the ritual order of earthpriests, which forbade a pyramidal development of the latter. As a result, the *naaba* as king was also the first-chief-first-priest of the state; he was endowed with the sacred quality of a living god.

The functions of gods may thus very well have been manipulated by pol-itical incumbents. These manipulations may reflect ideological turns and changing conceptions of the nature of power and rulership. They materialized in the creation of new offices, the confirmation of new rituals or the pro-scription of old ones. However, state intervention in the area of belief was not always straightforward; it was often a by-product of internecine struggles among royal contenders, and it was equally perceptible in the distribution of offices and the attribution of political functions (the *togo naaba*—the king's mediator—for instance, transacted the 'familial' alliance between the royal dynasty and 'people of the earth'); in the establishment of villages of captives and disaffected royals; in the remains of a military organization devoted to the expansion of the polity; in an effective taxation and gift-giving system organ-izing its collection, accumulation and redistribution; and in the consolidation of alliances through the institutionalized exchange of women.[23]

It remains that the issue of the symbolic equivalence between kingship and its religious counterpart only partly addresses the morality of sovereign vio-lence. Both are manifestations of a sovereignty that sublimates conflict. That said, in the reality of political practice, the problem of ideology has to do with rule; it has to do with the ruler's dilemma in preserving deference for what is essentially a contested phenomenon, and it therefore is about the negotiation of acceptance of a certain view of power.

One has to see, in the sublimation of social conflict, the work of appro-priation that takes away, from the ritual realm, both political capacity and agency. The legitimation process through the *ringu* rituals ultimately has limited determinacy. Mossi rulers have to review the terms of their alliance with the putative representatives of first-comer groups and the basis of their legitimacy through various other controlled endeavours—for instance during the first-fruits rites, the *tinsé*, the *tom yugri*, the *zom-bika*[24] and so on. The crafting of a formal Mossi history was contingent upon this framework for rewritings, reconstructions and revisions.

NOTES

1. See Liberski-Bagnoud (2002, 70); she cites Émile Benveniste who speaks of 'observance' as 'a notion of practice and not of faith' (1969, 267).

2. Broadly conceived to include religion, mystical imaginations and activities and similar variations.

3. See for instance Audrey Richards on the Bemba (1939, 359 in Gordon 2012, 28).

4. For an extensive review of issues of chronology and the history of Mossi states, see Izard (1976, 1980, 1985, 1992); Binger (1892); Kawada (2002); and Skinner (1964).

5. Tradition places the origin of the *Tinsé* with Naba Oubri, the founder of Wogodogo, the most central of the Mossi states. It was then celebrated in commemoration of the funerals of Oubri's mother.

6. *Tinsé* celebrations require a protocol meticulously followed at the different territorial levels that each organize a festival of its own. Thus every chief of province, village or household decides on a date of his choice after the Mogho *naaba* has accomplished certain rites and, following the Mogho *naaba*, offers sacrifices to the ancestors, to *Tenga* and *Tenkuaga* through the mediation of *Tempelem*, the ancestors' land. The *Tinsé* is a solemn cult celebrated before the break of the first rains of the year in the honour of *Tenga* the earth deity (fertility and abundance). It dates to the reign of Naaba Oubri when it was then a commemoration of the funerals of his mother, a strong reference to the family ties referred to previously.

7. Interview with Mamouny Sawadogo, Somnyaga, 17 April 2010.

8. Interview with Mamouny Sawadogo, Somnyaga, 17 April 2010.

9. See Benjamin Ray's (1991) depiction of the Kabaka's installation ritual.

10. Interview with Ila Ouedraogo, Ouahigouya, 10 April 2010.

11. The *ringu* denotes a common conception among Voltaic societies of qualitatively differentiated spatial orientation whereby 'everything that comes into this world is supposed to emerge from the east and to disintegrate or dissipate in the west'.

12. Interview with Naaba Kiba, Ouahigouya, 12 April 2009.

13. Joseph Ki-Zerbo contends that because the *naaba* preserved law and order, the kingdom ceased to exist upon his death; personal communication, May 2006.

14. In Izard's words, 'The *naam* is purely moaga'. Moaga also refers to the way of life and the philosophy of the Mossi.

15. This alliance is periodically renewed during the annual harvest festival.

16. On Mamprugu enskinment rituals, see Susan Drucker-Brown (1992, 77–85).

17. The Samand Naaba is the first archer who exposes the upper part of his body to the enemy's arrows, and he kills himself in case of defeat. The symbolism of the negative-double is even stronger in the belief that the donkey ridden by the Samand Naaba has a symbolic value opposite to that of the horse. Interview with Abdoulaye Sawadogo, Somniaga, 17 April 2010.

18. Fortes and Evans-Pritchard (1940, 11) contend that this feature makes African monarchies prone to civil war: if divine kingship ensured unity during the king's life, it could not prevent unrest during interregna which were particularly unstable.

19. See Charles Long (1964, 338) for a review of theories of divine kingship since Frazer.

20. It is said that the greeting, which consists of prostrating oneself before the *naaba* and covering oneself with *tom* (dust), comes from this injunction; see Niang (2011).

21. Interview with Mamadou Ouedraogo, 16 April 2010.

22. As among the Zulu, this sacrament, the *umkosi omncane* (also known as the *ukunyatela unyaka*, the stepping into the new-year) instituted a new season; see Gluckmann (1938, 25). The celebration implied, says Lugg, 'the casting off of the old year with all its ills, and the ushering in of a new season with hope and anticipation for better things' (Lugg 1929, 357).

23. *Pogsiure* was a system of delayed exchange of women (see chapter 4). *Siure* is a mutually binding, juridic term referring to the chiefly right over the first daughter of a woman given in marriage, who is then incorporated into the chief's 'reserve'.

24. A rite performed to sanction thirty years of reign of a *naaba*. It is a form of symbolic re-investiture.

Chapter 6

The State in Transition

A Recapitulation

Colonialism is not satisfied merely with hiding a people in its grip ... By a kind of perverted logic, it turns to the past of the oppressed people and distorts, disfigures, and destroys it. This work of devaluing precolonial history takes on a dialectic significance today.

—Frantz Fanon

OF SOVEREIGNTY AND STATENESS

A point made in this book is that the principle of government as articulated in postcolonial Africa lacks axiological consistency. On the one hand, it is the case that pre-existing forms have been disintegrated; their relics, their representations and their reinterpretations, however, are made to confront prevalent practices. 'People' on the other hand, often absent in our deliberations on the nature of government, are enjoined to extrude their agency to the realm of exacting traditions. But imaginaries are a place held live and teeming, a place that escapes social engineering and defies the order that prevails. It is the place where subjective consciousness draws its energyforce in a context whereby electoral democracy cannot provide the idiom that enacts the constitution that links individuals, groups and institutions in a coherent project. In this regard in fact, democracy fails to provide a political language of appropriation to enter a 'habitus' which cannot be equated to *tradition* (Bourdieu 1984).

One of the main propositions of this book has been that the state in African contexts (whether precolonial, colonial or postcolonial) was always a transient phenomenon—then and now—carried by the temerity of individuals with ideas and invested with the exigency to enlighten. It was deployed by people of great intent to break open the barriers to more fortune. It was also embraced by men of vision, confident in the power of nationalist unity to liberate and empower. Then and now, it was and remains an idea, an abstract, an ideal, always receding for it was never meant to become fully realized. We know what became of the 'realized' state: it is profoundly violent and it is inherently predatory.

Despite scepticism toward the state form, it is clear by now that what is being presented here is less a critique of a regime (colonial) or a model (nation-state) and more of forms of violence that deny people the means of, and the capacity for, self-constitution. In doing this, I'm certainly not suggesting that we reject the state as an organizing framework but that we keep it *open* as a possibility of governance.

Reflections offered in this book thus far can be read as a build-up toward a discussion of the conditions of the postcolonial state and of postcolonial sovereignty; that is to say, the foundation of legitimate authority that brings state and society together and does not merely subject the latter to the will of the former. This book is not meant to provide solutions but rather to revitalize a critique of accepted canons on political forms and therefore to attend to a critical discussion on basic ideas that inform the study of political formations. It is meant neither to turn the stream back to its ancient course nor to imagine a present that does not exist. Instead, it calls into question the relevance of presumed frameworks such as sovereignty once we dismantle the state-sovereignty tandem and show the multiple configurations of *politics* and governance in context and without being hindered by a priori concepts.

As far as state formation is concerned, at least in the example provided in this book, the ideological imperative proves to have been more important than the economic, social and territorial imperatives. Chapter 4 has shown that despite the effort of the promoters of the *Naam*, the Mossi state never had the material resources of its ambitions.

Chapter 5 in turns shows how state rule was always hedged by procedures of legitimation and an imperative of accountability. Yet the history of state formation in Moogo and state-society relations reveal that the *Naam* could acquire a number of new attributes and could change in meaning, orientation and practice according to sociopolitical circumstances and the vagaries of the integration of disparate groups. A reinterpretation of the *Naam*'s influence on aspects of Mossi politics, society and cultural practice allows us to apprehend its continuing influence on contemporary state and social processes in Burkina Faso specifically and in Africa in general.

The nominal identity of the sovereign state as anthropological standard allows little room for thinking without it. Dipesh Chakrabarty has argued that 'what European imperialism and third-world nationalism have achieved together [is the] universalization of the nation-state as the most desirable form of political community' (1992, 19). It seems unnecessary to belabour the point that the notion of unified sovereignty is but an illusion, not just in Africa but elsewhere too given an ontological foundation on a rather static view of power and social formation.

In conventional political science, state and sovereignty have typically been aligned alongside each other in a manner that has amalgamated the two into a single concept. There have, however, been many societies and communities that predate the capture of sovereignty first by the prince and subsequently by the 'the people'. Without such constitutive amalgamation, the notion of 'popular sovereignty' or 'national sovereignty' sounds like an incantatory formula. Sovereignty is fundamentally an inert frame that marginalizes the possibility of a meaningful political field. What my discussion of the Kasena and the Kusasi shows, for instance, is that one can build societies on a 'democratic' basis through adaptation and flexibility and without necessary reference to a requirement of sovereignty.

In contrast to an idea of the necessity of 'conflict' and constant negotiation as conditions for peace, dissension and transgression (chapter 4), the rigidification of traditional codes in the colonial era has undermined and limited that possibility. It instituted instead transactional logics. The resources of the modern state have become limited to a constant and dangerous licentiousness, that is, the absence of a national imagination which does not erase identities but rather nurtures them to participate in plural communities. In this regard, the choice should never have been either nationalism or ethnonationalism, or the perversion of the resources of the logic of ethnic engagement/disengagement cogently described by Peter Ekeh (1975).

In this concluding chapter's first three sections, I reflect successively on the role of the colonial encounter in consolidating centralization and statehood, on the use of cultural bricolage in dislocated postcolonial contexts, and on Thomas Sankara's revolutionary liberation project that sought to eliminate domestic symbols of legitimacy by conveniently labelling them backward, regressive and counterrevolutionary. In the fourth section, I examine the reasons for a postcolonial experience of the state as dislocation, that is, a process of divergence between state and constituent social units. Specifically, I show how political practice drifted from previous historical experience while the state ceased to make sense as an organic institutional arrangement that reflected broad signifying referents. This then leads to a discussion articulated around three propositions on the condition of the postcolonial African state and its postcolonial subjects. Neither capable of constituting themselves as fully fledged citizens under the postcolonial constitutional regime shaped by European juridical tradition and political experience nor able to engage in political experimentation through a deployment of referential possibilities, postcolonial African agents are continuously caught, the chapter argues, in aborted revolutions that leave little institutional memory to build upon.

CENTRALIZATION AND CONSOLIDATION: THE COLONIAL ENCOUNTER

Toward the end of the nineteenth century, Europeans interfered intensely in African processes to affect state and social structures. Centralized states (a) rose that owed their legitimacy to external, colonial support, often relying on the latter to suppress internal dissent. The Mossi example shows how a precolonial leadership became increasingly decried and delegitimized as Mossi chiefs were empowered as sole political rulers only answerable to the colonial authority and essentially unaccountable to the governed. How did these strategies affect postcolonial constitutional orders? I have skipped the colonial period because there has already been a considerable amount of work done on the topic, and my intent was never to offer a linear, chrono-logical account.[1] However, the significance of the colonial encounter as a politico-cultural phenomenon is yet to be fully deconstructed. In fact, the symbolic exclusions and the deficit of recognition of leading political agents owes a great deal to the colonial disruption and subsequent socioeconomic troubles. In a postcolonial context governed by the tandem state/capitalism[2] that produces a variety of exclusions, particularly the possibility of access to a 'cultural self' and therefore to dignity, control over the terms of culture has come to equate a control over politics.

An attempt to get to grips with the African past also requires that one engages more usefully the contours of the historical present of the post-colonial state because the functions, the operations and the instrumentalities of the African state that have preoccupied many scholars have been reduced to a question of power, a preoccupation with its location, its instrumentalization and its distribution. This has led implicitly to the idea that there is no possible order without the sovereign (Moses and the divine order), no law without the sovereign, no security without order and no security, therefore, for people and goods. Even James Scott and others for whom the structural position of the state has to be constantly challenged nonetheless seem to be stuck in a language of *government*. However, the state is not government (only); *being ungoverned* does not either mean experiencing an absence of government.

Scholars of the failed-state school may have been right on perhaps one element, which is that there is no African state to speak of as authentic—in the *sense of an organic institutional arrangement that reflects recognizable signifying referents*. If the problem of the African state is, however, to be posed in terms of legitimacy and representativeness of currents, imaginaries, aspirations and mental worlds, one can see the conflicting effects of integration policies in a 'democratic' system and citizen-based logic that seeks to erase particularistic asperities. Postcolonial democracy is a dubious project, invoking moments of transition as continuous demonstrations of an infallible collective will.

From the above, state failure is not only the manifestation of the state's inability to exert hegemony over those governed; it is also a form of (dis) articulation of language and polity. A thesis of this book has been that the coherence of politics in past formations hinged upon a close connection between the reality and the representation of political reality and the making of social subjectivities; in other words, that both social thought and political action were informed by common, and not distinct, signs and frames of meaning. This point has in fact been made in relation to the (in)congruence between state institutions and political culture—for instance in Naomi Chazan's study of Ghana, which also supports the idea that postcolonial failure was the '[result] of the inability of specific regimes to give concrete normative and institutional meaning to those values which do exist in [African] societ(ies)' (1978, 29). Some states were therefore overdeveloped apparatuses that exercised dominion without real hegemony (Alavi 1972, 61, 60). For the postcolonial state, forms of customary rule and 'traditional' practices become at once the parameters that inform the normativities that enable different trajectories for the state and its internal other.

Once the violence inbuilt in the nation-state has been identified, the potential for violence contained in other political formations should not be obscured. In the examples provided in this book, the state never 'governed' alone—that is, if government is to be conceived as a complex set of actions and practices designed to organize and stabilize diversity, anxiety and disorder. The state instead acquired a quality of stateness thanks to the legitimation of key processes by 'non-state' actors. The production and the regulation of *public goods* (morality, social order) was a collective endeavour except perhaps for the production of coercion. In the case of precolonial Burkina Faso, this endeavour was framed by specific cultural parameters designed to preserve a Mossi hegemony.

The Mossi state was caught between the centralized control vested in the *Naam* framework and the requirements for co-government, so to speak, between the *Naam* prerogatives whereby the *Naam* holders attempted to present the latter as subject, that is 'to contrive [the reality under the *Naam*] as coherent and closed, uniform and universalistic order' (Comaroff and Comaroff 1991, 17) and opposing mechanisms of social contestation as erratic objections.

I have tried to locate my argument between the extremes poles of *state* and *statelessness* for an antagonistic dichotomy between the two is synchronic.

In so far as disciplinary perspectives go, the discussion here has moved across social and political history, political theory, anthropology and many things in between. What the Kasena example for instance shows is that many decentralized societies have ontological commitments, social and moral outlooks that are articulated in rich oral, visual, ritual and ceremonial forms and with which we need to engage (Connell 2007, xii).

In decentralized societies, the relationship between man and the gods required little mediation. The sanction of the gods for transgression could be embodied in the generation of new normative constraints. The absence of centralized authority makes sense in a context of democratic access to the path of propitiation, redemption and restoration—not, however, in the mundane manner in which we tend to understand 'democratization'.

The relative reticence and apparent detachment of *Tenga* communities toward and from things political rendered them susceptible to exclusion and marginalization from decision-making and the elaboration of public order. A consequence in postcolonial Burkina Faso has been an ongoing debate about the political culture of formerly centralized versus formerly decentralized societies and the relative marginalization of members of acephalous societies in present-day Burkina Faso.

THE POST-INDEPENDENCE STATE: GOVERNANCE AND CULTURAL BRICOLAGE

The book has essayed a commentary on the nature of precolonial rule and political authority. It has shown that strategies of coping with the natural and social environment were writ in complex social relations; *government* associated with statehood was never a necessity to this endeavour. Neither was the state the only condition for collective imagination nor the only generator of values.

Political ideologies such as the *Naam* claimed to mediate the forces of nature and the exalted heights of enlightenment by dint of the chief's power: 'to believe in the chief was to cultivate in hope' (Richards 1939 in Lonsdale 1986, 146). But belief was also the site where the chief's accountability most starkly played out: kings with infertile and ineffective power could be deposed, expelled or killed. The problem with the devolution of power in independent Africa now is that it was instigated by a minority of agents some of whom were animated by specific interests that undermined the welfare and broader aspirations of the majority of Africans.

In the post-independence era, if rituals have disappeared from state practice, their spirit has remained under different guises: not only do people feel the need to identify with these rituals, the very memory of these rituals—and what they were meant to achieve for people—are reconstructed with extended references to the symbolic, the ethical, the permissible, the legitimate and so forth. For instance, the notion of secularism can in no way be confused with the French variant of *laicité*; deliberations on secular politics in African contexts do not respond to the same imperatives because legitimacy of belief forms is established on the premise that the living have obligations toward both the living and the dead.

Given the above, it is no surprise that individuals engage in bricolage and innovative social action even if the signs and symbols of bricolage are in no way in the logic of what pre-existed—people being no longer initiated in these signs and symbols and therefore not conversant with their meaning. This is case of the Kasena, Kusasi and Tallensi in contemporary Burkina Faso and Ghana who use 'culture' to protest against the state. Political scientists have, however, been reluctant to engage culture even while power has always been deeply 'implicated in culture, consciousness, and representation' (Comaroff and Comaroff 1991, 17).

Culture, therefore, becomes a context, a framework, a motive and a political refuge. For one thing, bricolage points to the fact that popular imaginaries could not be contained in generic political arrangements that do not quite resonate with basic popular aspirations. As Berman further explains, 'culture—in the form of concepts, values, and notions of history, communal and individual identities, and modes of discourse, both indigenous and foreign—is the idiom of action and the context of motive and objective' (2004, 23). But it was precisely this idiom that postcolonial revolutionary politics thought to eliminate as the next section shows.

THOMAS SANKARA AND THE CONCEPTUALIZATION OF AFRICAN REVOLUTIONARY MODERNITY

Liberal scholarship in the post-1960s sought to support the nationalist project in conferring legitimacy to the African institutional past within a logic of sameness—in other words, to inscribe nascent African nationalism in the familiar expanse of European history and therefore to lend the African trajectory a familiar rationalist and interest-based logic through conceptual and historical analogies.[3] There was a danger, into which many fell in fact, which consisted of isolating 'virtuous' traits similar to those of 'progressive' European rules and procedures so that one could claim that Africans too had an experience of democratic governance. For instance, the role of the *suo sob* (ritual officer) as counter-power to that of the *tengan sob* (community leader) among the Dagara has often been used as an illustrative example of a 'democratized' governance model in the African past. Obviously, such an exercise was both futile and counterproductive for it tended to decontext-ualize the operational effects of these structures.

The majority of Burkinabe intellectuals who sought to contribute to the elaboration of a usable past had a decidedly Mossi-centred approach.[4] There were many reasons for this. First, Mossi and non-Mossi alike saw a revalorizing dimension in the establishment, by academics endowed with the authority of scientific research and methodological 'objectivity', of a glorious past in which 'Moaga authority' was a metaphor for legitimate leadership. Mossi politicians were therefore inclined to believe that it was their natural right to lead: past competency versus openings in democracy for 'citizenship'.

Evidence of a chiefly past thus became a politically important resource as chiefly groups sought to reclaim political competency, and the conceivability therefore that formerly 'stateless' and captive peoples could become their administrative superiors was anathema. Equally, non-Mossi resented the his-torical prominence of Mossi and more so in a system in which their predica-ment was multi-layered.

The majority of postcolonial leaders attempted to discredit traditional lead-ership. Customary chiefs responded differently to their marginalization; some withdrew, others confronted the new dispensation through adaptation and innovation. In Burkina Faso, the Mogho naaba (Naaba Saga II, 1942–1957) took the risky initiative of creating his own political party, Union pour la défense des intérêts de la Haute-Volta (UDIHV), thus competing with the largest anti-colonial movement in West Africa, namely Rassemblement démocratique africain (RDA; Skinner 1964, 180). In this and similar endeavours, however, some practices were selectively chosen as representa-tive of precolonial experience and their underlying axioms of political mor-ality extensively perverted in parochial interests.

Unsurprisingly, the naaba's party had the support of the colonial authority but was fiercely opposed by intellectuals from the anti-colonial movement. Even more radical was Naaba Kougri's (1957–1982) desperate attempt to overthrow the first government of independent Burkina Faso under Maurice Yameogo. But the chiefs' collaboration with colonial authority had led to irreparable damage, and they no longer commanded high levels of respect and trust as before.

If both the colonial project of modernization and postcolonial imperative of decolonization amounted to interventions with dislocating effects, their strat-egies, purposes and legitimacies were certainly different. The postcolonial constitutional program of Thomas Sankara (1983–1987) is an illustration of how the postcolonial African state formation became a series of requirements that Africans should overcome their 'primordial' attachment to kith and kin and locality and spiritual beliefs and commit to the modernizing ambition of the nation-state. This demand was accompanied by a witch-hunt of chiefs as conspicuous avatars of 'primordialism'. A similar purge took place in Ghana under the revolutionary leader Kwame Nkrumah who went robustly after traditional chieftaincy (Woronoff 1972, 247–48).

Sankara's advocacy of a narrowly conceived African originality led to the alienation and the ostracizing of a range of domestic symbols of legitimacy. His professed African-centred policies targeted customary rule as an inconvenient symbol of cultural archaism, historical backwardness and reactionary politics. Sankara embarked upon a 'modernization' project spearheaded by his National Council of Revolution. In an effort to rid the new Burkina Faso of a Mossi 'feudalist' system, he saw to it that chiefs no longer received a salary or any form of subsidy from the state. In his public pronouncements, Sankara never missed an opportunity to attack the chiefs. He set up committees for the Defense of the Revolution all over the country in villages, cities and provinces. These were popular fora that were supposed to do the groundwork and put the revolution in practice. However, despite an ambitious programmatic framework, Sankara never quite managed to reach rural populations without the mediation of the very chiefs he was intent on marginalizing (Savonnet-Guyot 1985, 20, 43).

Sankara sought to enlist the help of earthpriests while sidelining the customary political chiefs in a drive to promote rural projects but he was largely unsuccessful. His rural education campaign was a relative disaster. Sankara's reluctance to engage pre-existing structures of governance meant that the revolution was carried out in spurts and never really led to the kind of deep-going and transformative effort that obtained elsewhere in Europe and Latin America. There was, however, a broader context to Sankara's revolutionary drive; he saw it as his mission to turn around a country that had been used as a reserve for forced labour and seen by colonial authorities as little worthy of investment in infrastructure and economic development. These were, therefore, compelling social and economic conditions that could only be changed through radical intervention (Harsch 2013, 360).

The very idea of forced labour is strongly associated with slavery and the oppressive head-tax system under colonial rule. Both postcolonial forms of taxation and the colonial head-tax/hut-tax are disarticulated from a notion of community building: they are predatory mechanisms of economic exploitation whereas in precolonial settings, taxation could constitute a form of currency that endowed meaning to a notion of community.

In Africa as elsewhere, escape from the exploitative grip of the state with its constraining taxation model took the form of forced migration, exile and flight. The point here is that in the centralized state, taxation is devoid of meaning in the sense in which it used to be understood. Where, for instance, rituals establish reading grids and correspondence/equivalence systems, the possibility of such a reading is completely absent from the taxation system in centralized states.

Sankara's 'democratic and popular revolution' was underpinned by the Marxist approach outlined in his famous programmatic speech of 1983 (Political Orientation Speech; Prairie 2007). The Marxist rhetoric was effectively mobilized in presenting the 'objective conditions' of Burkina Faso at the time of the revolution: that of 'a backward, agricultural country where the power of *tradition* and ideology emanating from a *feudal-type* social organization weights very heavily on popular masses' (Prairie 2007, 40 in Harsch 2013, 363; emphasis added).

Amidst frozen aid and withdrawal of Western support, Sankara imposed budgetary austerity on the state and civil servants and put the country on a path to self-reliance through temperate governance and extensive investment in social programs and infrastructure. At a United Nations speech in October 1984, he suggested to the great powers, and with a touch of irony, that his small country had the desire 'to venture new paths in order to be more prosperous and to cease being the backwater of a satiated West'.

Sankara focused in particular on modernizing agriculture and on supporting farmers with financial and technical aid. In all this, Sankara genuinely sought to redynamize social and communal solidarity through collective mobilization. The *groupements naam* (collective working groups inspired by the tradition of the *Naam*) were particularly involved in support of his program (Harsch 2013, 365).

In seeking to discard previously recognized symbols of legitimacy, Sankara and his allies, however, put various constraints on the revolution. These were presented as necessary measures for (un)certain ends. Sankara's high-handed treatment of customary chiefs denoted an acute struggle that was to pervade national politics and an unstable path to sovereign democracy. This struggle opposed two currents: a top-down, transcendent type of sovereignty adopted by both the political and 'traditional leadership', and a stream of constituent and immanent ambitions consistently muffled in procedural arrangements.

The adoption of European experiments of government in the form of a Westphalian state and constitutionalism were expected to bring about 'progress' enabled by institutional grounding and political maturity. The underlying political-economic logic and architecture, however, created specific forms of exclusion and marginalization rationalized through market instruments. The subsequent weakening of traditional ethics of exchange led to a subversion of afferent values, some of which became invested in the consolidation of specific interests.

Further, the search for African socialist models following the immediate independence period can be seen as a momentary 'deviation'; its transformation into governance models was determined by external demands in the context of a developmentalist agenda. When all failed, thinkers and practitioners alike turned to non-state actors and institutions. The question no longer was alternative institutional models but rather for state and non-state entities to seek to capture power and to control politics and therefore the rents that accrued to power holders and political entrepreneurs (hence patrimonial politics).

As *transactional logic* came to be the dominant mode, the ethics of the state was reduced to this: there is no single text, no single signifier for what the state is or what it stands for outside of elections and token institutions—parliaments are dismissible, constitutions can be changed, institutions can be manipulated or divested from their original purpose and so on. In postcolonial times, the modification of fundamental covenants (constitutions) does not have the same meaning as transgressing rituals that participate in the making of the everyday subjecthood of social actors. And it is rightfully that Lonsdale contends that 'rulers have turned to brigandage for lack of a national past by which to judge and, in judging, bind themselves' (1986, 165).

An objective of this book has been to show that the virtue of stateness for the African state was not always in conformity with the Westphalian state, which, at any rate, cannot be seen as a singular source of ontological validation of statehood.

Instrumentalized in the wholesale adoption of Western norms in postcolonial Africa was the idea that governance was to flow entirely from the state apparatus, being duly imposed upon the governed through new, ritualistic voting that was merely meant to sustain said logic but had little bearing on the subjective evocations of postcolonial 'citizens'. Given this, the reluctance to understand and deliberate on the relevance of the postcolonial state for African contexts, and an equal reluctance to investigate the moralities and the intentionalities that underlined configurations and practices of governance in precolonial societies, is rather jarring. Even more jarring has been the absence of an effort to devise an alternative model of governance for a colonial regime experienced by many ordinary Africans only in the repressive mode. If the idea was to turn Africa into Europe, Fanon suggests that Africans could as well have let Europeans do just that because they would have done it better (Fanon 1961).

Specifically, constitutions were framed in a foreign language and idioms inspired by the European experience in Europe. In fact, it would not be controversial to say that postcolonial constitutions were 'conditional' concessions that ensured colonial continuity, therefore dependency. They consecrated an original divide between state and society. What this orientation does is to obscure the fact that constitutions are not abstract institutions but rather 'the product of social practice' (Nugent 2010). The omission of the African experiential past and moral orders further marginalized their systems of values and the allocation of entitlements, rights and obligations of social hierarchies and solidarities.

Constitutions thus hung over societies but had no bearing on (the repressed organic potential of) society. Constitutions were made to be ethical frameworks that sanctioned relations between governors and governed on the basis of signs, idioms, sensitivities and legal understandings that did not quite allow an effective meaning-making exercise precisely because they were borrowings from foreign cultures and sensibilities. Past moral economies, the realms of exchange and reciprocities, were thus profoundly altered by colonial intrusions and the modernization project; the palimpsestic imprints of these intrusions arguably reside in the instrumentalized use of societies for the benefit of the state and state power, starting with 'indigenous chiefs' (Balandier (2001, 9).

As a matter of example, in Dagara country, the dissociation of the political from the sacred was effected by colonial rule. The *tengan dem* (*chef de village*) and the *tenga sob* (*chef de la terre*) thus came to exercise distinct roles and functions: the village chief was a colonial creation imposed upon localities, and *the chef de terre* withdrew or was made to retreat into increasingly reduced spaces and parameters. Here and there in French West Africa emerged new cults that were refuges from and spaces of resistance to colonial oppression—for instance the Boron cult in the 1930s that spread around Bobo-Dioulasso; and the Dieu de San that spread over a wide geographical expanse and reached the Ivory Coast, the French Soudan and parts of Upper Volta in the 1940s and 1950s (M. Somé 1999, 84–86). In Moogo, *Tenga* came to be elevated as an 'invisible scaffolding of the sociocultural order' and therefore the raw materials that bound together the operations of culture through social and symbolic linkages (Comaroff and Comaroff 1991, 132).

In a most stimulating essay, Harry West argues that the Muedan world in northern Mozambique is endlessly fashioned and refashioned by those who construct interpretative metaphysical visions of it and then offer these constructs for debate and contestation. In contrast, the Mossi, like most formations keen to maintain hegemony, sought to close off this very field of contestation by determining a direction for public debate. Alternative expressions were therefore only possible outside the field of control of the state. In particular, earth chiefs, diviners and other key non-state actors played the role of metaphysical entrepreneurs in asserting new fields of imagination and expression for individuals looking to construct forms of subjectivity outside the state framework. In postcolonial Africa, some of these possibilities have emerged in churches, new modes of contestation initiated by young people and in unconventional discursive forms elaborated by participants animated by common anxieties (West 2001).

Posed here are conjunctural questions about public morality, the constitution of self and intergenerational connections but also, crucially, the fact that there is a remnant of vitality that animates collective subjective consciousness and which finds expression in many innovative ways.

PROBLEMATIZED STATEHOOD: DIVERGENCES AND DISLOCATIONS

The quest for innovative modes points to the depth of divergences and dislocations that are rife in postcolonial African experience. At the least, it is a warning against the all-too-common embrace of epistemological regimes that identify 'the African state' or the state itself for that matter as a discrete, unproblematic category. There was no lack of political consciousness of, understanding of or attention to the historicity of the models of government bequeathed by colonial regimes and that of precolonial structures. There were, however, multiple difficulties in the actualization of such understanding and attention, specifically the deep inadequacy of the postcolonial state with the ethical and moral deliberations that inform individuals' actions. In the early days of the anti-colonial movements, nationalist leaders drew on a common collective stock. They were able to defend a national project in the name of self-government ('We will govern in your name') in a republican form that was everybody's right and inheritance.

The execution of these ideals required essential reforms that were just not possible. In France, for instance, five republics would be required for the actualization of its main ideals. The republic was never to become that collective container that rewarded past struggles. In Africa, the absence of a reimagined state led to contestations of various forms, including an outright rejection of the state as a parasitic thing that had been displaced and subordinated to external exigencies and interests. Escape came under different guises. People escaped from the state in resistance, informality, avoidance, *faire-semblant*, subversion and other means that could free them from state tutelage.[5]

The neopatrimonialist literature and its subset of dustbin theories on one hand and the state-failure literature on the other see the African state in a permanent state of confused informality and/or dysfunction. But if the state is always a transient, transiting institution as I have demonstrated in this book, its dilemma precolonially, under colonization and in postcolonial Africa, remains. I argue that it is a question of naturalizing the state into the structures of African societies and not the other way around. The state, as an external idea and entity, has never really found the proper formula to integrate into these structures outside an opportunistic drive to conquer, exploit and subdue.

In political theory and international relations, there has been a constant need for the state as a figure that acts on the world rather than a view of social and political organizations in terms of bodies that interact and influence each other. The state acts on the social world through language, linguistic rhetoric and metaphorical eloquence. The effects of the *Naam* and *Tenga* were experienced differently in temporal, linguistic and conceptual distance. On the one hand, in so far as *Tenga* was implicated in the maintenance of moral order and social well-being, its healing capacity was framed as a delayed remedial process.

On the other hand, the *Naam* had the power to literalize itself—in other words, to produce immediate effects as possible cure(s). Conceptually, this difference translated into differentiated narratives—of potency, efficiency and relevance as opposed to uncertain potency, untested power and marginality. This sense of immediacy has always fed state fantasies of (omni) potency, supremacy and hence inevitability. For this reason, statehood was constantly imagined as a superior technology and art.

Up until the colonial period, pre-existing forms of political, social and cultural order overlapped and were not always clearly demarcated from each other. *I use the idea of the state in transition thus to mean that the process of convergence between state and constituent social units was never fully achieved and was at best fraught with many tensions if not marked by dislocation.* The latter takes place 'where social practices and historical experiences drift apart' (Lentz 1994, 462). Furthermore, chapter 3 shows how processes of institutional transition also reflect notions of selfhood and subjectivity as a constant work in progress. In other words, the stuff that constitutes people, an ecological milieu, mind, body, memory and anxiety, also informs the ontology of social institutions.

The postcolonial nation-state was meant to erase fundamental antagonisms and build a nation out of disparate aspirations and experiences, and it was to do so under a common state framework. In Burkina Faso, former precolonial minorities, under a Mossi system of rule, found in electoral politics a way to experiment with political participation under new terms. On the one hand, they abandoned the ritual codes and signifiers that had sustained a sense of togetherness and self-government vis-à-vis the state. On the other hand, what ceased to make sense under the system of ritual practices was as much the new political configurations as a capacity to (re)constitute relations that were legible. I am not suggesting that one should try to reinvent past modalities but that the recognition of pragmatic limits should not preclude the possibility of extracting, abstracting and adapting their essential components. And people are already doing this in their own way, but in doing so, they also cause various conflicts.

There are numerous examples of conflicts of 'jurisdiction' in Burkina Faso, of individuals and communities claiming a ritual affiliation that conflicts with their civic affiliation. In Dagara and Birifor, these conflicts are common. In places where the local authorities are somewhat flexible, people are allowed to keep their 'traditional' affiliation so as to be able to relate meaningfully to members of their communities.[6] In places where such flexibility does not exist, the sense of dislocation and intergroup hostility tends to be greater for one fundamental reason: the very terms of the postcolonial problem are not granted.

RECENTRING THE DEBATE: THREE PROPOSITIONS

Discussions of political structure and social change in stateless societies— especially those that seem the most 'remote' to Western modernity or seem to follow their own trajectory of modernity—have taken centre stage in recent (re)evaluations of global history primarily because of the perceived distinctiveness of their political postulates. The importance of practice, of the 'embodied disposition to certain usages' in the elaboration of meaning, of a practice of time and of change cannot be exaggerated (Landau 2009, 446).

In fact, the dynamism of stateless communities and the creative possibilities of 'open polities' (in constantly changing societies) even as they are enmeshed in complex regional relations, in 'vital cultural discourses' and in multiple other processes impresses a historical orientation on community building in its most minute expressions (Comaroff and Comaroff 1991, 126).

A reading, therefore, of authority through 'non-political' spheres of social intervention does two things. First, it allows me to break a common boundary between epistemology and ontology and a related, common distinction between a mighty 'subject' and an infinitely pliable 'object' that is central to Western theory. Knowledge is not always something elaborated, and passed on, to others as a category of practice that mobilizes the subject's mental capabilities. Knowledge does not reside in anyone's head. Instead, it is produced in many forms and under many different guises, and it acquires form and content out of challenges as individuals confront limits, consciously, unconsciously, subliminally.

Second, it allows me to make the point that what is missing in the postcolonial African state is a cultural dimension for it is culturally void. One rightly wonders, How can something as crucial as culture be absent from state-building?[7] The structuring role of lived experience, of culture-specific imaginaries and of the cultural parameters therefore of statehood have been taken out of the equation. However, the nationalization/enactment of modernity through the channels of stakeholder groupings becomes a divisive methodology that is detrimental to community-building. From this and other observations above, I would like to make the three following propositions.

First, colonial intrusion disrupted, instrumentalized, atomized and discredited mediating mechanisms—encompassing values, rites and traditional texts—meant to interpret programmatic frames in their 'inspiring, recommending, prescribing, authorizing, justifying' dimensions (Asad 1993, 140). Under modernization, culture, custom, history and identity became the same thing; the construction of versions of the past and imaginaries of the future therefore rendered, taxing the subsequent realization of subjective consciousness.

As something that denotes both time and history, the temporalization/temporality of modernity meant an overdetermined focus on state-building (i.e., state institutions) at the expense of society-building.[8] African constitutions thus hover over the constituencies whose welfare they protect only in abstraction. As Landau notes, 'Time has long been a tool used to subordinate colonized people' (Landau 2009, 439). Time was used to compel Africans to operate on the time of modernity and the time of the centralized state.

Constitutional ordering and the politico-juridical scaffolding that were to put the African state on the path of certain modernization thus dictated the postcolonial mode. 'In this vision, state formation essentially equalled formation of state institutions, and hardly considered the formation of new kinds of interaction, and new balances of power, between state and civic institutions' (Doornbos 1990, 190).

From this angle, therefore, despite a proliferation of projects of reform and revitalization, whether in various nation-building projects or the pan-African movements during the decolonization era and following independence, the postcolonial state became merely the embodiment of a colonial heritage under successive administrations. In particular, the constitutions inherited from colonial powers instilled acquisitive dispositions in agents responsible for institutional upkeep.

As local chiefs were promoted by colonial authorities, their capacity to mediate ancestral spirits was undermined; they became effectively disempowered (Gordon 2012, 50–68). In fact, their *capacity* to become ancestors was compromised by the fact of the de-legitimation of their authority. Some of these chiefs became instruments of colonialism answerable to the colonizer only and susceptible to dismissal by the latter. They contributed to collecting poll taxes and to recruiting individuals for forced labour regimes.

The consequences of constitutive misgivings crystallized distorted processes. This is to say that the dysfunctions of the postcolonial state took root in historically specific designs to render non-Western political and juridical foundations immature and anti-modern. The postcolonial moment was therefore marked by two major aberrations: a tendency to make the state an avatar of (Western) modernity built on the deliberate erasure of the precolonial past and an implicit recognition of the usefulness of colonial institutional legacy.

Second and integrally related to this, the preoccupation with grounding an African statehood outside any consideration for prevalent understandings of the purposes and intentionalities of governance, local sensibilities toward particular political practices of consent, legitimating of rule and so forth was but cultural suicide. The juridico-political instruments at the disposal of post-colonial rulers were naturally perverted and divested to the service of private interests and personal ambitions in the absence of an ethics of the commons.

Equally, when efforts seem to have been made to historicize community formation, these produced client systems devoid of their precolonial functionalities. Patrimonialist theorists are therefore quick—although not entirely wrong—to point to these as features of African political culture(s) but they miss an important point: if postcolonial political actors have attempted to present patronage-based politics as *African*, they have merely reproduced the forms without their underpinning values.

The uneven nature of available knowledge (and institutional memory) of precolonial polities is not the most vexing issue. More egregious is a strong tendency, in political science and Africanist scholarship, to treat Africa's past as predictably confusing and therefore understandably unstable in its present.[9] Fundamentally, this has to do with skewed archetypes and intellectual assumptions, problematic research approaches to things African, the inadequacy of the tools used and so forth. Many scholars set about reading Africa's past and present experience with the disposition—conscious or otherwise—that they will be dealing with singularly puzzling phenomena.

It is fair to say that evolutionist perspectives in political science did to the state what structural-functionalism did to culture in anthropology as perspectives that tended to deny that both 'state' and 'culture' were frameworks of action and meaning that articulated the interacting dynamics of mutating elements. As such, they could not be static but very dynamic, and they did not follow one single path of development complexification. African cultures went through phases of intense absorption of elements of Western and other cultures as much as phases of innovation, therefore constantly reinventing their foundations and expressions.

A historical and ideological bias with regard to African history on one hand, and toward the history of the state on the other, has produced a scholarship that effectively dis-embeds the state from the very processes that encapsulated it. It has also produced a tendency for an intellectual division of labour whereby state history and high politics are taken in charge by political scientists and political historians while society and culture are investigated by anthropologists and folklore scholars.

If we take for granted Spruyt's contention that the centralized state was more efficient an institution in organizing security and commerce given a mechanism of legitimation that was activated around the sovereign state, what made the nation-state stick in the end? Even if we disregard the fact that Spruyt exaggerates a bit with regard to the legitimation process given that the latter was not without violence, such a process enabled anchoring, recognition and correspondence. For Cooper, the deficit of imagination seems to be a fundamental failure of postcolonial societies.

> Europe learned to imagine the nation from the tensions that emerged within its old empire and passed the imaginative possibility along to its new colonial conquests ... The kind of politics that eventually took over colonial states was this nation-centered one, focused on the European-defined boundaries and institutions, on notions of progress shaped by capitalism and European social thought (1994, 1540).

In the African context, centralization was effected through the constitutive violence of *commandment* which was not a mere transposition of Western sovereignty but rather 'a very specific imaginary of state sovereignty' that created and reproduced the modalities of its own violent logic.[10] In postcolonial Africa, commandment endured alongside new constitutional dispensations that competed to establish the *logical structures* within which its intelligibility was to be grasped (Bartelson 1995). However, when reduced to a question of government, the colonial experience appears as an '*experience sociologique grossiere*', as rightly characterized by George Balandier (2001, 9), because of the manner in which it fundamentally distorts the conditions it reveals.

For Laurentie (1944), distortions resulting from colonial configurations were based on a disproportionate imposition of power justified by racial, civilizational, technological and legal rationalizations and therefore licentious conditions.

To reverse the prevailing trend thus requires a systematic reconstruction of an African specific that is not constrained by a comparative demand. The reaffirmation of African 'indigenous' modes of subjectivity—apparent for instance in the syncretic practices of the new religious orders, whether Pentecostal or Islam-inspired, that have sprouted up across the continent— attests to a quest for spaces productive of *meaning* in the midst of intolerant and complex conditions and to an extent consonant with past forms and experience. However, a secular system is only possible because there are religious orders and a religious dimension to people's attachment to non-state frameworks such as the Sufi orders in West African Sahel.[11]

Third, postcolonial states are built on morally and ethically uncertain grounds. Past moral orders and 'African' practices are often seen as an obstacle to state-building and therefore to the modernization project as well. Concomitantly, the belief that the state would come to be inscribed in the African landscape as necessary and inevitable, as something that would become productive of the desired 'affective and behavioural norms compatible with contemporary state-level politics' (Chazan 1978, 5), subtended such an endeavour. The new legal and institutional strictures perverted the basis, the logic and the conditions of political competition. It was never, however, clear what the postcolonial state was meant to be or what goods and morality it was meant to create or cultivate for African peoples.

In Africa and elsewhere in the postcolonial world, states were meant to serve an ideological function, which was to extend the model of sovereign statehood the world over. Postcolonial states thus became disembodied from historical structures and could therefore not fully become carriers of existing legitimacy (Boone 2003).

By way of an opening therefore, one can imagine a way out of a predicament of dislocation, disintegration, dysfunction, disconnection, the corruption of public life and so on by reviving a sense of the dynamic nature of life/reality as the Kasena did, and still attempt to do, in the manner they engage '[the] cycle of growth, maturity, aging, decay and rebirth … [in integrating] the ludicrous and the serious, paradoxes and consistencies, through inversions and parallelism, so as to make death meaningful … as a reality that is pregnant with life' (Abasi 1995, 473).[12]

Current legal, economic and centralized state strictures limit the possibility of 'regeneration', 'alternation' and 'circulation' in the sense of a capacity to face change and the capacity to overcome the destructive forces of 'social death'. Generations are confined to a repetitive set of gesticulations (voting, gathering, rebelling, dissenting) as they assign subjective meanings to political objects associated with the centralized state and juxtapose them with existing values.

CONCLUSION

To a question I briefly touched upon in the introduction about why the state won over other political forms in the African context, and to a question I proposed as central to my enquiry about the nature of internal forms against which the state was built, the double crisis of legitimacy and accountability that bedevils the postcolonial state provides a critical opening.

The conclusive enforcement of the centralized-state form by colonizers—not because of an inherent superiority vis-à-vis non-state forms but because it fitted the underpinning logical structures of colonial government—led to both the reification and the homogenization of institutional architectures across the continent (Lonsdale 1986, 140). As a result, the many formulations of species of state, statehood and stateness became marginalized.

I have tried to stay away from a common conception of African polities in 'clash points', in ethnonyms or in evolutionary grids (Landau 2009, 440).[13] An important point I have tried to make is that the postcolonial state offered no moral resolution to the dilemma of 'community', social solidarity and legitimate authority. In fact, it opened into a gradual and sustained art of mastery—for Africans—of the terms of being and becoming in imposed political forms for in reality, and in the spirit of continuity of the colonial objective, the essence of the endeavour consisted of capturing the imaginary of a people on the path to alienation.

Political imaginaries linked to the past are, however, dismissed in political practice as 'traditions', and people are not encouraged to imagine alternative frames of reference. The traditional/cultural past has therefore receded into a realm of scattered memories and narratives, vague recollections and shaky visions, but these animate and motivate people in ways that are not properly captured by the modern/traditional dychotomy. Given the impossibility of translating memories of past arrangements into actual practice, past idioms and accounts of constitutional deliberations inevitably get mobilized in instrumentalized 'ethnic' and 'identity' politics.

Our incapacity to read African political forms outside a patrimonial and patronage political model results from a difficulty in engaging past moral economies, the realms of exchange and reciprocities that underpin the constitutional lives of communities. What has also been lost in the intellectual exercise is a capacity to understand the state and governance not just as technostructure but more properly as the manner in which people are made to behave and the manner in which they are able to relate to others and respect each other, a space therefore where people are able to construct a *vivre-ensemble*. What does crony capitalism, for instance, mean? How do we understand it? One needs to look at networks of dependency and how they function. One cannot clearly grasp the logic of these solely through a rent-accumulation framework.[14] One needs to understand these networks in context for the very possibility of the community depends on their constitution. A good grasp of their underlying ideas, their nature and their finality would require engaging different notions of *space* and *time* which are direly missing in prevailing neopatrimonialist views.

The goal of this book has therefore been to offer accounts of different forms of sociality and accounts of community-making in diversity. To avoid confining these accounts to those interested to things 'African', I have tried to engage foundational concepts and arguments of liberal political thought particularly as they relate to discussions of sovereignty, community, sociality and moral constitutions. These accounts of being together or being-in-the-world *tout court* should therefore be taken seriously as useful openings for a more critical political philosophy and history.

I'm not suggesting here that precolonial constitutional and institutional structures were consistently inclusive and progressive, that they were always examples of accountability and virtue for all constituencies (captives, slaves and other social dependents were certainly excluded). Centralization often led to politicization and the marginalization of technician classes (e.g., smiths, artisans and certain categories of commoners). The dissolution of public and specialist commentary on political rule in the process of centralization did contribute to dismantling procedures of accountability in Moogo, for instance, from the middle of the eighteenth century, especially under the rule of Naaba Kango.

Even in the absence of formal jurisprudence and formal codifications, the enactment of constitutional processes as remembered or as imagined in the recollections of historical agents have a strong bearing on their capacity for self-government. My concern, throughout this book, has been to show that we need to look at the intellectual tradition of 'other' peoples if we are to understand the way they relate to each other and the way they relate to things and their environment. At any rate, to view African experience in its 'premade staticness' in the flattened accounts of an African institutional past would be falling into a common objectification of 'culture' and 'tradition'.

NOTES

1. Mamdani (1996), for instance, shows how those rules elevated by colonial authorities as 'traditions' were stripped of important mechanisms of accountability.

2. For Comaroff (1998), this tandem has by and large been insufficiently interrogated by both liberal and Marxist scholars; the state can be seen neither as a mere extension of capital nor as a mere administrator of the common good. Instead, levels of imbrication of state and capital reflect at times conflicting interests but more often the capacity of capital to mould executive and judicial structures of state institutions.

3. See Keith Hart (1985, 257) on the intellectual commitments of West Africanist scholarship and the impulse to explain African social phenomena in a comparative guise.

4. Dynastic records and chronicles indicate that the Mossi were prone to triumphalism and self-idealization.

5. It would not be wrong to assert that there are no true republics in Africa, not even South Africa or Botswana, which are commonly seen as the most accomplished democracies on the continent. Africans hardly identify with the institutions that govern their daily lives. Even the so-called socialist models failed to bring back and integrate past models of mutuality and solidarity that were capable of striking a chord with the lived experiences of Africans.

6. M. Somé (1999, 87–88) examines recurrent conflicts between the villages of Lofing and Mébar, Mébar and Bakandi, Bakandi and Gnibama, Bakandi and Lofing and so forth. Local administrations tried to be 'accommodating' by allowing people to vote.

7. I owe this insight to Baba Buntu; see also d'Arboussier (1949).

8. What Sembène calls 'meta-colonialism'; in other words, the conditions that obtained in postcolonial Africa: an Africa that could no longer go back to what it was but couldn't be itself either (Mowitt 1993).

9. Despite having amassed what seems like rich data on the history of Dagbon, Staniland (1975) comes to this conclusion.

10. On the notion of colonial commandment, see Mbembe (2001, 25).

11. Even for someone like Charles Tilly, the capacity to pillage resources and consolidate one's power could not be enough if the latter were to be sustained. From a Tillian viewpoint, an imperative of complementarity would have required that the colonial and postcolonial states put something in place after they had destroyed previous orders—in other words, subordination but not total subjugation. It is fair to say that neither imperative was implemented in colonial and postcolonial Africa.

12. As Abasi further contends, 'for the Kasena, life finds in death both its measure and its renewal' (1995, 475).

13. The precolonial/colonial/postcolonial division is unfortunate but inevitable. One should strive, however, in adopting such a chronologico-historical division, to avoid a conception of precoloniality as 'nationalism's modernity'; see Lalu (2009, 160).

14. The example of Mossi *pogsiure* shows a possibly different ethics of accumulation in the sense that a chief accumulated for himself but also for others. *Pogsiure* also constituted a form of pacific conquest that underlined this particular accumulative logic.

Appendix: Glossary of Mooré Terms

The transcription of Mooré terms follows the dispositions of the 69/012 / PRES decree of the government of Upper Volta (17 January 1969) as set out by the National Commission on Voltaic Languages. The generic term used is Mossi/Moose (pl.), Mooga or Moaga (sing.). Mooré is the language spoken by the Mossi and Moogo and refers to the territory that comprised all Mossi states. It must be pointed out that the translation provided here is merely an approximate rendering of the meaning of these Mooré words. Many Mooré terms and expressions can only be understood in their context. The reader is referred to Alexandre (1953) for alternative and additional meanings for terms used in the present work.

Balum (from *balemde*, a form of greeting): one of the main dignitaries (high ranking officials) of the *naaba*; chief of Balôngo, he is in charge of the internal matters of the court, and he mediates relations between the *naaba* and the community of Yarse traders

Basga: thanksgiving ritual held after the millet harvest and marking the New Year

Bega: ritual ceremonies annually held to honour *tenga* (lasting five lunar months throughout Moogo and starting around January, right after the *napusûm* ceremonies). Contrary to the *napusûm*, however—held between the naaba and different chieftaincies and royal administrators—*Bega* celebrates the relationship between the naaba and the earthpriests. It is essentially a ritual celebration for thanking *tenga* and for invoking for good harvests.

Benda: drum-chroniclers

Bendre: instrument, drum, half-spherical calabash

Bimbiegu (literally 'a bad thing'): name of the Dagbon *ya naa*, or king

Bîn/Bin (or *Rasam*) Naaba: name given to the head of Bîngo (of captive origin); *Bîn* is used for the Yatenga Naaba's residences (except in Ouahigouya, the main one)

Bingdemba (sing. *bingneda*): residents of Bîngo, royal captives

Bîngo (from *bingi*, to gather, keep in reserve, maintain with care): section of the royal town adjacent to the royal residence and exclusively inhabited by families of captives; heads of Biisigi, Ziya and Sisamba also have the title *bîn naaba*. The *bingdemba* also comprised groups of foreign origin such as the Dogon, San and also Mossi who were reprieved after having been condemned to death.

Bugo (pl. *buguba*): fertility priest; 'sacred' chief of pre-Moaga society, most probably of Kibga (Dogon) origin; his ritual control is over the mystical power in the *bugudo*; oral traditions give the example of *nakombsé* that were possessed by the *bugudo* and gained entry into the ranks of *buguba*, thus becoming autochthons through this ritual transformation.

Bugulana: shrine owner in Dagbon

Buguli: shrine keeper in Dagbon

Burkina: free man; generally distinguished from a *yamba* (captive)

Bûudu/buudu: patrilineal descent group. See **Moos bûudu**.

Fulse (sing. *Fulga*; also *Kurumba*): indigenous to Moogo, they speak Alrumfe and they make up most of the *tengbiisi*

Gângaogo (*gângaago*; in Nakombgangaodo): brigand, a strong man who takes part in political rebellions and illegal raiding and looting; he is sometimes admired for his bravery and impudence.

Kabsgo: drummed (only) or a drummed and oral recitation of royal genealogy of royal dynasties. It literally means 'permission' because the narrator has to request permission (from certain people and objects) to say the name of the ancestors.

Kambose (*kambonsi* in Dagomba; sing. *kanbonga*): heterogeneous group comprising Marka from Bay (the Sourou valley), Bambara from Segu and Djula from Kong; they are associated, in Mamprusi, Dagomba, Nanumba and Moogo with military activities and the use of firearms. In Yatenga, they were mostly armed bodyguards.

Kantome: spirits; beings of the wild

Kibse (sing. *kibga*): refers to Dogons; indigenous, pre-Moaga people part of whom fled to the cliffs of Bandiagara at the time of Mossi conquest

Kîims roogo: sacred house (altar) dedicated to the ancestors

Kiimstênga (*kiimstese*): ancient royal residence; also the 'place of the ancestors'

Kînkirga (pl. *kînkirse*): (bush) spirit

Kombere (pl. *kombemba*): vassal/provincial chief (Ouagadougou); appointed by the naaba, he can nominate local chiefs

Koom filiga (from *koom* [water or millet beer] and *filiga* [to thank]): first harvest celebration to mark the consumption of new millet

Kpandana: senior earthpriest in Mamprugu

Kurita (opposite of *Narita*, also called 'reigning-dead'): negative double of the king; generally a young son of a *naaba*, he is sent away to 'eat death' following a *naaba*'s death and is supposed to never see again the (new) *naaba* during his lifetime. He cannot become himself a *naaba*. The *kurita* is then the living-representative of a dead *naaba*.

Lunsi: state drummers, chroniclers and praise-singers in Dagbon

Mamprugu: founding kingdom of the Mamprugu-Dagomba-Mossi states. *Mamprusi* designated both the territory and the people.

Marãse (sing. *marânga*): traders and artisans said to have come from Songhay and to have established themselves in Yatenga for centuries

Moaga: singular of *Mossi* or *Moosé*, it can also mean 'someone who is uncircumcised', a man from the savannah

Moogo: literally 'bush' or 'savannah'; the territorial basis of the Mossi states system. Moogo comprised, at the end of the nineteenth century, four main states (Ouagadougou, Yatenga, Tenkodogo, Fada N'gourma) and a number of satellite states such as Yako, Mané, Tatênga, Zitênga, Téma, Conquitênga.

Mooré: language spoken by the Mossi; part of the Gur-Voltaic cluster of languages. It is also 'the manner of being' of the Mossi, a code of comportment and self-presentation.

Moos bûudu: composed of patrilineal descendants of a given agnatic group, it is bigger than the *saka* (made of descendants of an agnatic core) and more generally descendants of Ouedraogo. See **Bûudu**.

Moosê: section of the royal compound for royal servants of non-captive origin (Nakombsé and Talsé); conceptually opposed to Bîngo

Mossi (Mosi, Moose, Mole, Moshi): generic name for the descendants of Naaba Ouedraogo and more generally the 'ethnic' group whose members identify themselves as descendants of immigrants and rulers of Moogo

Na: masculine response to a call (Present!) opposite of *t'ma* for women, it is also the invariable response of obedience given to the naaba. The suffix *m*, which denotes power and strength, distinguishes *Na* from *Naam*, which is rather abstract.

Naaba (pl. *nanamse*): chief, king, head, secular office holder, holder of the *Naam* (e.g., Mogho Naaba, Yatenga Naaba, Yako Naaba); normally used for royal chiefs but also extended to non-*naam* holders with specific forms of authority such as *saab-naaba* (chief blacksmith), *fulga naaba* (chief of the Fulse)

Naam (authority, power, might, prerogative of the *nakombsé*): evokes the idea of a power (an aptness, an aptitude) that emanates from the divine and which allows one man to rule another

Naam kugri: the 'stone of power' is a vestige from the time of Naaba Yadega, located in Tangazugu: the newly enthroned naaba is made to sit on the stone under the sun in humility before the *tengbiisi* in order to receive their blessing (agreement)

Naam wûbri (*Wûbri naafo*): altar upon which the *naaba* makes annual sacrifices

Nakombga (pl. *Nakombsé*): descendants of migrants from Mamprusi-Dagomba and elsewhere (Moose, Mossi); in the strict sense, a son of a *nabiiga* (prince) who did not become a *naaba*

Nakombgandaogo. See **Gandaogo**.

Namoos: political 'chiefs' among the Dagara

Napoko: first daughter of a *naaba*, she assumes the interregnum upon her father's death to ensure there is institutional vacancy in between two administrations; also called 'woman-chief'

Napusûm (from *pusûm*, prosternation): annual greeting ceremony; it essentially gathers the three orders of political authority that make up the *Naam* order (*nakombsé, tasobnamba* and *nayiridemba*); the *napusûm* serves to re-enact the alliance between the *Naam* and *Tenga* (although *tengbiisi* take a marginal part in it) and the Mossi's allegiance to their sovereign. *Nakombsé, nesômba* and other dignitaries offer bunches of new ears of millet to the *naaba* during the *napusûm*.

Narita: reigning king; opposite of *kurita*

Nayiridemba (sing. *Nayirineda*): courtiers, royal dignitaries and servants

Nayirii kpaamba: king's ouncilors in Mamprugu

Nayiritese: servant villages

Nesômde (pl. *nesômba*): literally good, trustworthy people, the state dignitaries who comprise the electoral college; they are the *naaba*'s ministers, their number and titles vary according to the state (for instance Ouidi in Ouagadougou is Werânga Naaba in Yatenga) and most of them have authority over territorial divisions

Nesômkurse: literally 'little *nesômba*; low-ranking royal officials/dignitaries, generally under the authority of *nesômba*

Nîniga (*samo*): population indigenous to Moogo

Nyonyonse (*ninissi, ninisse, niniosé, ninisi* or *nioniosse*). See **Yonyoose**.

Ouahigouya: literally 'Come and submit to my rule'; main city of Yatenga, made capital under Naaba Kango (1757–1787). It is said that the greeting, which consists of prostrating oneself before the *naaba* and covering oneself with *tom* (dust), comes from this injunction.

Oubri (Wubri): founder of Wubritênga Ouagadougou, descendant of Ouedraogo

Ouedraogo/Wedraogo (literally 'stallion'): putative ancestor of all Mossi

Panga/Pânga (*pang, pas*; pl. *pasé*): generally translated 'power' but *panga* has more to do with violent manifestations of power, individual and state. It refers to the physical power of state 'enforcers' such as royal servants.

Pangsoba: holder of *panga*

Pogsiure (pogshiure, pogsyre; napogsyure for the royal version): system of delayed exchange of women. *Siure* is a mutually binding juridic term referring to the chiefly right over the first daughter of a woman given in marriage, who is then incorporated into the chief's 'reserve'.

Polo naa: contingent war-chief among the Dagara

Ri: literally 'to eat' in the sense of 'to appropriate the substance of', it is the radical for *ringu* and *rima*

Riallé (Riyaaré or Diiyaaré): Yennenga's husband, thus ancestor of the Mossi

Rîmbio: close relatives of the *naaba*

Rog-n-miki: custom, tradition, 'what one found when one was born'

Rumnamba: a *naaba*'s first wife

Saaba (sing. *Seya*): blacksmiths

Sagadugunaba: senior earthpriest

Saka (pl. *sakse*): settlement of related members, gathered around an agnatic core (*bûudu*), its size is generally smaller than a village. It is very similar to a 'clan'. *Zaka* (pl. *zakse*) on the other hand refers to the 'inner' courtyard of a house (as opposed to *samânde*, the 'outer' courtyard. It is generally rendered as '*quartier*' in French. The *saka* is divided into *yiya* (sing. *Yiri*) which are intermediary kin groups (translated as 'household'). *Saka* is a unit of a *yiri*. *Saka, yiri* and *zaka* all constitute segmentary divisions of the *bûudu* and are headed respectively by a (*bud kasma*) *sak kasma, yir kasma* and *zak kasma*.

Samând naaba: dignitary under the supervision of the *togo naaba*; also adjutant to the *tapsoba*. In wartime, he leads the infantry to the fight riding a donkey. A trench is dug for him and he is buried in it up to the waist. As head of the archers, he commands his men in this position. In case of defeat, he is killed on the spot.

Setba: artisans

Siimde: greeting ritual

Silmîise (sing. *silmîiga*): Peul, Fulani, cattle herder

So ('to hold', 'to possess'): *soba* or master

Soba: master or possessor; e.g., *teng-soba, tapsoba, pângsoba*

Sondre (pl. *sonda*): patronymic, as opposed to *yure*, an individual's given name; more specifically, a classificatory name for an extended agnatic group or socio-economic category—e.g., *Ouedraogo* for Mossi; *Sawadogo* for *tengbiisi*; *Kindo* and *Zalle* for blacksmiths; *Sore* for *yarse*

Suo sob: ritual officer among the Dagara

Talga (pl. *talsé*): commoner, non-royal

Tâpo: war as a social phenomenon and institution. See **Zabre**.

Tâ-soba, *tapsoba* (*wogdogo*) or *tasoba* (Yatenga): commonly translated 'chief warrior' but the tâ-soba was not always a military chief; he could be of captive origin or recruited from the ranks of *nakombsé* who had lost territorial command but were still influential in villages formerly ruled

Tenga/Tênga (*tése*): the earth, land, soil, settled, cultivated or uncultivated land, a territorial expanse, earth cult (Napagha *tenga* as 'wife' of Naaba Wende) or village; *tenga* also refers to the 'earth altar' at which the *tengsoba* makes sacrifices

Tengan sob (also *tindana*): shrine priest and community elder among the Dagara

Tengbiisi (sing. Tengbîiga): sons of the earth or indigenous persons; refers to members of indigenous groups of Moogo

Tengdemba: literally 'people of the earth'; generally opposed to *nakombsé*, holders of political power, and it is closer in meaning to *tengbiisi* (sons of the earth); the term also refers to people indigenous to Moogo

Tengpeelem (literally 'white earth'): bare ground, the area or territory over which an earthpriest has ritual authority; it also refers to the place where ancestors are buried

Tengsoba (pl. *tengsobdamba*): earthpriest, earth custodian, literally 'custodian of the earth'

Tengsobongo (or *têngandẽ*): territory or area under the ritual control of the *tengsoba*

Tinsé: annual festival during which sacrifices are offered to the mother of the first Wubritênga (Ouagadougou) Naaba who was a daughter of an indigenous Nyonyoga

Togo Naaba (from *toogẽ*, 'to say'): the first, in hierarchical order, of the *naaba*'s dignitaries (often mistakenly translated as 'ministers'); spokesperson of the *naaba*, he is the mediator between the *naaba* and earthpriests; chief of Toogẽ

Tom yugri: ritual of allegiance

Tulubere weefo: royal horse put to death when the *naaba* dies, it can only be mounted by the *naaba*. *Tulubere* also designates the horse's forehead ornament.

Ula (province of Yatenga): the chief of Ula is an important military personality

Wedkin Naaba: head groom, adjutant to the Wiidi Naaba

Wedraogo (Ouedraogo): founder of the *Moos bûudu*; ancestor of all Mossi

Wende: ultimate cause of life; identifies the chaotic nature of time and space with no beginning or end. *Wende* and *basga* are temporal indications for Mossi who have a particular perception of time: past and future in the present and as frequently enacted in ceremonies and rituals.

Weogo: the bush; refers to uncultivated or fallow areas outside the village property, what lies beyond a village's permanent fields

Werânga (*wedranga*) Naaba (Widi/Ouidi Naaba in Ouagadougou): one of the four royal dignitaries; chief of Werâsẽ or Wedrâsê; among other functions, he controlled access to the *naaba* and acted as a mediator between the *naaba* and the *nakombsé*

Wogdgo Naaba: represents the *ninisi* and is in charge of installing a new *mogho*

Yamba (pl. *yemsé*): slave, captive; generally opposed to the *burkina* (free man)

yaralentîise (sing. *yaralentîiga*): literally 'Those that are hanged on trees', people accused of having sexual relations with animals (generally a female donkey). The crime of zoophilia in Moogo could be both metaphorical or real and it was a social transgression harshly punished by society. One could 'become' *yaralentîiga* through sexual relations with somebody accused of being *yaralentîiga* or through undifferentiated filiation. In Yatenga, *yaralentîise* were not given proper burial but dumped outside Mossi society in the village of Renea, in the northwest of the kingdom.

Yarse (sing. *yarga*): Sarakole traders and artisans established in Moogo for centuries; they introduced Islam and have contributed to Moogo's economic development

Yiimkemde: literally 'old house'; ancient (abandoned) royal palace occupied by a eunuch with the title *Yiirsoba* (head of household); could also be occupied by a *naaba*'s wife in the royal residences where the *naaba* did not stay

Yonyoose (sing. *yonyooga*): indigenous people of Moogo

Zab yuure (pl. *zab-yuuya*): tentatively translated '*nom de guerre*', it is both a motto (shibboleth-name) and a (self) praise-name which a newly nominated *naaba* chooses for himself. The *zab-yuure* generally reflects the particular circumstances that saw the advent of a new administration; it also expounds the guiding principles and values held by the new *naaba*.

Zabre: squabble, dispute, a more casual version of *tâpo* (war); the Mossi use *zabre* to describe dynastical struggle for the *Naam*. See **Zab yuure**.

Zom-bika: rite performed to sanction thirty years of reign of a *naaba* and a form of symbolic re-investiture

Bibliography

Abasi, Augustine Kututera. 1995. Lua-Lia, the 'Fresh Funeral': Founding a House for the Deceased among the Kasena of North-East Ghana. *Africa* 65 (3): 448–75.

Adams, William Y., Dennis P. Van Gerven, and Richard S. Levy. 1978. The Retreat from Migrationism. *Annual Review of Anthropology* 7:483–532.

Adler, Alfred. 1989. L'Echange différé: Esquisse d'une analyse comparative. In *Singularités les voies d'emergence individuelle*. Paris: Plon.

Agamben, Giorgio. 1995. *Homo Sacer: Sovereign Power and Bare Life*. Stanford, CA: Stanford University Press.

Alavi, Hamza. 1972. The State in Post-colonial Societies—Pakistan and Bangladesh. *New Left Review* 74.

Alexandre, Gustave. 1953. *La langue Möré*. 2 vols. Dakar: Institut Français d'Afrique Noire.

Allman, Jean Marie, and John Parker. 2005. *Tongnaab: The History of a West African God*. Bloomington: Indiana University Press.

Amadou Hampâté Bâ. 1994. *Oui mon commandant! Mémoires II*. Paris: Actes Sud.

Anafu, Moses. 1973. The Impact of Colonial Rule on Tallensi Political Institutions, 1898–1967. *Transactions of the Historical Society of Ghana* 14:17–37.

Arens, William, and Ivan Karp. 1989. *The Creativity of Power*. Bloomington: Indiana University Press.

Arhin, Kwame. 1983. Rank and Class among the Asante and the Fante in the Nineteenth Century. *Africa* 53 (1): 2–22.

Asad, Talal. 1993. *Genealogies of Religion: Discipline and Reasons of Power in Christianity and Islam*. Baltimore, MD: Johns Hopkins University Press.

Asiwaju, Anthony I. 1976. Migrations as Revolt: The Example of the Ivory Coast and the Upper Volta before 1945. *Journal of African History* 17 (4): 577–94.

Bakhtin, Mikhail Mikhaïlovich. 1981. *The Dialogic Imagination: Four Essays*. Austin: University of Texas Press.

Balandier, George. 2001. La situation coloniale: Approche théorique. In *Extraits*, 1–31.

Bartelson, Jens. 1995. *A Genealogy of Sovereignty*. Cambridge: Cambridge University Press.

Bay, Edna G. 1995. Belief, Legitimacy and the Kpojito: An Institutional History of the 'Queen Mother' in Precolonial Dahomey. *Journal of African History* 36 (1): 1–27.

Bayart, Jean Francois. 1993. *The State in Africa: The Politics of the Belly*. London: Longman.

Bayart, Jean Francois, and Stephen Ellis. 2000. Africa in the World: A History of Extraversion. *African Affairs* 99 (395): 217–67.

Bayart, Jean-Francois, Stephen Ellis, and Beatrice Hibou. 1999. *The Criminalization of the State in Africa*. Bloomington: Indiana University Press.

Bazémo, Maurice. 1993. Captivité et pouvoir dans l'ancien royaume de Ouagadougou à la fin du xixe siècle. *Dialogues d'Histoire Ancienne* 19 (1): 191–204.

Bell, Catherine. 1992. *Ritual Theory, Ritual Practice*. Oxford: Oxford University Press.

Benjamin, Walter. 1968. *Illuminations*. New York: Schocken Books.

Benveniste, Émile. 1969. *Le Vocabulaire des institutions indo-européennes, 2. Pouvoir, droit, religion*. Paris: Éditions de Minuit.

Benzing, Brigitta. 1971. *Die geschichte und das herrschaftssystem der Dagomba*. Meisenheim am Glan, Germany: Anton Hain.

Berman, Bruce J. 2004. 'A Palimpsest of Contradictions': Ethnicity, Class, and Politics in Africa. *International Journal of African Historical Studies* 37 (1): 13–31.

Binger, L. C. 1892. *Du Niger au Golfe de Guinee par le pays de Kong et le Mossi, 1887–1889*. Vol. 2. Paris: Hachette.

Boahen, Adu 1961. The Ghana Kola Trade. *Ghana Notes and Queries* 1:8–14.

Boone, Catherine. 2003. *Political Topographies of the African State: Territorial Authority and Institutional Choice*. Cambridge: Cambridge University Press.

Bouda, Barthelemy. 1986. L'exploitation traditionnelle du fer dans la région de Pabré. Université de Ouagadougou.

Bourdieu, Pierre. 1984. *Distinction: A Social Critique of the Judgement of Taste*. London: Routledge.

———. 2014. *On the State: Lectures at the Collège de France, 1989–1992*. Edited by Patrick Champagne, Remi Lenoir, Franck Poupeau, and Marie-Christine Riviere. Translated by David Fernbach. Cambridge: Polity.

Boutillier, Jean Louis, André Quesnel, and Jacques Vaugel. 1977. Systèmes socio-economiques Mossi et migrations. *Cahiers O. R. S. T. O. M.* 15 (4): 361–381.

Breusers, Mark. 1999. The Making of History in Colonial Haute Volta: Border Conflicts between Two Moose Chieftaincies, 1900–1940. *Journal of African History* 40:447–467.

Brubaker, Rogers, and Frederick Cooper. 2000. Beyond 'Identity'. *Theory and Society* 29:1–47.

Butler, Judith. 2010. *Frames of War: When Is Life Grievable?* London: Verso.

Chabal, Patrick. 1992. *Power in Africa: An Essay in Political Interpretation*. Basingstoke, UK: Macmillan.

Chakrabarty, Dipesh. 1992. Postcoloniality and the Artifice of History: Who Speaks for 'Indian' Pasts? *Representations* 37:1–26.

Chazan, Naomi. 1978. Political Culture and Socialization to Politics: A Ghanaian Case. *Review of Politics* 40 (1): 3–31.

Cheyfitz, Eric. 1997. *The Poetics of Imperialism: Translation and Colonization from* The Tempest *to* Tarzan. Philadelphia: University of Pennsylvania Press.

Clapham, Christopher. 1998. Degrees of Statehood. *Review of International Studies* 24:143–157.

Colson, Elizabeth. 1997. Places of Power and Shrines of the Land. *Paideuma* 43:7–57.

Comaroff, Jean. 1985. *Body of Power, Spirit of Resistance: The Culture and History of a South African People*. Chicago: University of Chicago Press.

Comaroff, Jean, and John L. Comaroff. 1991. *Of Revelation and Revolution*. Vol. 1 of *Christianity, Colonialism, and Consciousness in South Africa*. Chicago: University of Chicago Press.

Comaroff, John L. 1998. Reflections on the Colonial State, in South Africa and Elsewhere: Factions, Fragments, Facts and Fictions. *Social Identities* 4 (3): 321–61.

Comaroff, John L., and Jean Comaroff. 2006. *Law and Disorder in the Postcolony*. Chicago: University of Chicago Press.

Connell, Raewyn. 2007. *Southern Theory: The Global Dynamics of Knowledge in Social Science*. Cambridge: Polity.

Cooper, Frederick. 1994. Conflict and Connection: Rethinking Colonial African History. *American Historical Review* 99 (5): 1516–1545.

Cresswell, Tim. 1997. Imagining the Nomad: Mobility and the Postmodern Primitive. In *Space and Social Theory: Interpreting Modernity and Postmodernity*, ed. George Benko and Ulf Strohmayer. Oxford: Blackwell.

Curtin, Philip et al. 1978. *African History: From Earliest Times to Independence*. London: Longman.

Dacher, Michele. 2005. Review of Danouta Liberski-Bagnoud, 'Les dieux du territoire: Penser autrement la généalogie'. *Cahiers d'Etudes Africaines* 177.

D'Arboussier, Gabriel. 1949. Les problèmes de la culture. *Afrique Noire*, numéro spécial de la revue Europe, May–June 1949.

Davis, David C. 1984. Continuity and change in Mamprugu: A study of tradition as ideology. PhD thesis, Northwestern University.

———. 1987. Then the White Man Came with His Whitish Ideas: The British and the Evolution of Traditional Government in Mampurugu. *International Journal of African Historical Studies* 20 (4): 627–46.

De Beauminy. A. 1925. Une féodalité en Afrique Occidentale Française: Les Etats Mossi. *Bulletin de l'Afrique Française-Renseignements Coloniaux* 35 (1): 24–36.

De Heusch, Luc. 1971. *Pourquoi l'épouser? Et autres essais*. Paris: Gallimard.

———. 1997. The Symbolic Mechanisms of Sacred Kingship: Rediscovering Frazer. *Journal of the Royal Anthropological Institute* 32:213–32.

Delafosse, Maurice. 1912. *Le pays, les peuples, les langues*. Vol. 1 of *Haut-Sénégal-Niger (Soudan Français)*. Paris: Larose.

Deleuze, Gilles, and Felix Guattari. 1987. *A Thousand Plateaus: Capitalism and Schizophrenia*. Minneapolis: University of Minnesota Press.

Der, Benedict. n.d. The 'Stateless Peoples' of North-West Ghana: A Reappraisal of the Case of the Dagara of Nandom. Unpublished ms. University of Cape Coast.

Diallo, Boureima. 1996. Et si les Moose venaient d'Egypte. *L'Observateur-Dimanche* 36, 26 July–1 August.

Doornbos, Martin. 1990. The African State in Academic Debate: Retrospect and Prospect. *Journal of Modern African Studies* 28 (2): 79–98.

———. 2002. State Collapse and Fresh Starts: Some Critical Reflections. *Development and Change* 33 (5): 797–815.

Drucker-Brown, Susan. 1975. *Ritual Aspects of the Mamprusi Kingship.* Cambridge: Cambridge University Press.

———. 1981. The Structure of the Mamprusi Kingdom and the Cult of Naam. In *The Study of the State*, ed. Henri Claessen and Peter Skalnik, 115–31. The Hague: Mouton.

———. 1989. Mamprusi Installation Ritual and Centralisation: A Convection Model. *Man* 24 (3): 485–501.

———. 1992. Horse, Dogs, Donkey: The Making of a Mamprusi King. *Man* 27 (1): 71–90.

Duncan-Johnstone, A., and H. Blair. 1932. *Enquiry into the Constitution and Organisation of the Dagbon Kingdom.* Accra: Ghana Publishing.

Duperray, Anne-Marie. 1985. Les Yarse du royaume de Ouagadougou: L'écrit et l'oral. *Cahiers d'Etudes Africaines* 25 (98): 179–212.

Durkheim, Emile. 1976 [1915]. *The Elementary Forms of the Religious Life.* Trans. J. W. Swain. London: Allen & Unwin.

Echenberg, M. J. 1971. Late Nineteenth-Century Military Technology in Upper Volta. *Journal of African History* 12 (2): 241–54.

———. 1975. Paying the Blood Tax: Military Conscription in French West Africa, 1914–1929. *Canadian Journal of African Studies* 9:171–92.

Eckstein, Harry. 1979. On the Science of the States. *Daedadus* 108 (4): 1–20.

Eisenstadt, S. N., Michel Abitbol, and Naomi Chazan. 1988. *The Early State in African Perspective: Culture, Power and Division of Labor.* Leiden: Brill Academic.

Ekeh, Peter. P. 1975. Colonialism and the Two Publics in Africa: A Theoretical Statement. *Comparative Studies in Society and History* 17 (1): 91–112.

Englebert, Pierre. 1997. The Contemporary African State: Neither African nor State. *Third World Quarterly* 18 (4): 767–76.

Evans-Pritchard, E. E. 1940. *The Nuer: A Description of the Modes of Livelihood and Political Institutions of a Nilotic People.* Oxford: Oxford University Press.

———. 1948 [1962]. The Divine Kingship of the Shilluk of the Nilotic Sudan. In *Social Anthropology and Other Essays*, 192–212.

Evariste, Poda N. 1998. The Individual's Freedom of Expression in Dagara Society: Myth or Reality? *Research Review* 14 (2): 84–95.

Fabre, L. T. 1904. Monographie de la Conscription de Débougou. January 1904, Archives Outre Mer Aix-en-Provence, AOF, 16304, 14 Mi 686, 6.

Fage, J. D. 1964. Reflections on the Early History of the Mossi-Dagomba Group of States. In *The Historian in Tropical Africa*, ed. Jan Vansina, R. Mauny, and L. V. Thomas. London: Oxford University Press.

Fage, J. D., and Roland Oliver. 1975. *The Cambridge History of Africa: Volume 4 c. 1600 to c. 1790.* Ed. Richard Gray. Cambridge: Cambridge University Press.

Fage, J. D., and W. Tordoff. 2001. *A History of Africa: The Cambridge History of Africa Vol. 4 1600–1790.* Cambridge: Cambridge University Press.

Fanon, Frantz. 1961. *Les Damnés de la Terre.* Paris: Francois Maspero.

———. 1967. *Black Skin, White Masks.* Trans. C. L. Markmann. New York: Grove Press.

Feeley-Harnik, Gillian. 1985. Issues in Divine Kingship. *Annual Review of Anthropology* 14:273–313.

Femia, Joseph V. 1981. *Gramsci's Political Thought: Hegemony, Consciousness, and the Revolutionary Process.* Oxford: Clarendon Press.

Ferguson, James. 2006. *Global Shadows: Africa in the Neoliberal World Order.* Durham, NC: Duke University Press.

Ferguson, Phyllis. 1973. Islamisation in Dagbon: A Study of the Alfanema of Yendi. PhD diss., University of Cambridge.

Ferguson, Phyllis, and Ivor Wilks. 1970. Chiefs, Constitutions and the British in Northern Ghana. In *West African Chiefs, Their Changing Status under Colonial Rule and Independence,* ed. Michael Crowder and Obaro Ikime, 340–52. Ife, Nigeria: University of Ife Press.

Fiedermutz-Laun, Annemarie. 2005. The House, the Hearth and the Granary— Symbols of Fertility among the West African Kasena. *Medieval History Journal* 8 (1): 247–65.

Fortes, Meyer. 1940. The Political System of the Tallensi of Northern Territories of the Gold Coast. In *African Political Systems,* ed. M. Fortes and E. E. Evans-Pritchard. London: Oxford University Press.

———. 1945. *The Dynamics of Clanship among the Tallensi.* London: Oxford University Press.

———. 1967. Colioque sur las cultures Voitaiques. *Recherches Voitaiques* 8:174.

———. 1970. The Structure of Unilineal Descent Groups. In *Time and Social Structure and Other Essays,* ed. Meyer Fortes. London: Athlone Press.

Fortes, Meyer, and Edward Evans-Pritchard. 1940. *African Political Systems.* London: Oxford University Press.

Frobenius, Leo. 1986 [1912, 1922]. *Histoire et Contes des Mossi.* Wiesbaden, Germany: Franz Steiner.

Gabrilopoulos, Nick et al. 2002. Lineage Organisation of the Tallensi Compound: The Social Logic of Domestic Space in Northern Ghana. *Africa* 72, no. 2.

Ghana National Archives, Accra (GNA). 1905. Report on Tour of Inspection, March to May 1905. ADM 56/1/50.

Glele, Maurice Ahanhanzo. 1974. *Le Danxome.* Paris: Nubia.

Glissant, Edouard. 1990. *Poétique de la Relation.* Paris: Gallimard.

Gluckmann, Max. 1938. Social Aspects of First Fruits Ceremonies among the South-Eastern Bantu. *Journal of the International African Institute* 11 (1): 25–41.

Gomgnimbou, M. 2009. Les chefferies 'sans etats' chez les populations dites 'Gurunsi'. In *Histoire des royaumes et chefferies au Burkina Faso precolonial,* ed. P. C. Hien and M. Gomgnimbou. Ouagadougou, Burkina Faso: DIST (CNRST).

Goody, Jack. 1956. *The Social Organization of the Lowiili.* London: HMSO.

———. 1957. Social Organization and Fields of Social Control among the Lodagaba. *Journal of the Royal Anthropological Institute* 87:75–104.

————. 1971. *Technology, Tradition, and the State in Africa*. Oxford: Oxford University Press.

————. 1978. Oral Tradition and the Reconstruction of the Past in Northern Ghana. In *Fonti Orali-Oral Sources-Sources Orales*, ed. B. Bernardi, C. Poni, and A. Triulzieds, 285–95. Milan, Italy: F. Angeli.

————. 1996. *Succession to High Office*. Cambridge: Department of Archaeology and Anthropology, Papers in Social Anthropology 4.

Gordon, David. M. 2012. *Invisible Agents: Spirits in a Central African History*. Athens: Ohio University Press.

Gray, R., ed. 1975. *The Cambridge History of Africa: Volume 4 1600–1790*. Cambridge: Cambridge University Press.

Grovogui, Siba. 1996. *Sovereigns, Quasi Sovereigns, and Africans: Race and Self-Determination in International Law*. Minneapolis: University of Minnesota Press.

Hammond, Peter B. 1966. *Yatenga: Technology in the Culture of a West African Kingdom*. New York: Free Press.

Haour, Anne. 2013. *Outsiders and Strangers. An Archaeology of Liminality in West Africa*. Oxford: Oxford University Press.

Harms, Robert W. 1987. *Games against Nature: An Eco-Cultural History of the Nunu of Equatorial Africa*. Cambridge: Cambridge University Press.

Harsch, Ernst. 2013. The Legacies of Thomas Sankara: A Revolutionary Experience in Retrospect. *Review of African Political Economy* 40 (137): 358–74.

Hart, Keith 1985. The Social Anthropology of West Africa. *Annual Review of Anthropology* 37 (1): 13–31.

Helman, Gerald B., and Steven R. Ratner. 1993. Saving Failed States. *Foreign Policy* 89:3–20.

Herbst, Jeffrey. 2012. Responding to State Failure in Africa. *International Security* 21 (3): 120–44.

Hill, Jonathan. 2005. Beyond the Other? A Postcolonial Critique of the Failed State Thesis. *African Identities* 3 (2): 139–54.

Horton, Robert. 1971. African Conversion. *Africa* 41 (2): 85–108.

————. 1976. Stateless Societies in the History of West Africa. In *History of West Africa, I*, ed. J. P. A. Ajayi and M. Crowder. Harlow, UK: Longman.

Ilboudo, Pierre C. 1966. *Croyances et pratiques religieuses traditionnelles des Mossi*. Paris: Le Centre national de la recherche scientifique.

Illiasu, A. A. 1971. The Origins of the Mossi-Dagomba States. *Research Review* 72:95–113.

Ingold, Tim. 1993. The Temporality of the Landscape. *World Archaeology* 25 (2): 152–74.

Insoll, Timothy. 2009. Materializing Performance and Ritual: Decoding the Archaeology of Movement in Tallensi Shrines in Northern Ghana. *Mater Religion* 5 (3): 188–310.

Izard, Michel. 1969. *Les Yarse et le commerce dans le Yatenga précolonial, Dixième séminaire international Africain, 'Le développement du commerce et des marches Africains en Afrique Occidentale'*. Ouagadougou, Burkina Faso: Centre Voltaïque de Recherche Scientifique.

———. 1970. *Introduction à l'histoire des royaumes Mossi*. Paris: C. N. R. S.

———. 1973. La lance et les guenilles. *l'Homme* 13:139–49.

———. 1976. Changement d'identité lignagère. *Journal des Africanistes* 46 (1–2): 69–81.

———. 1979. Transgression, transversalité, errance. In *La Fonction Symbolique*, 289–306. Paris: Gallimard.

———. 1980. Les archives orales d'un royaume Africain. *Recherches sur la formation du Yatenga*. Laboratoire d'Anthropologie Sociale.

———. 1985. *Gens du pouvoir, gens de la terre: Les institutions politiques de l'ancien royaume du Yatenga*. London: Cambridge University Press.

———. 1987. Le royaume Mossi du Yatenga. In *Princes et serviteurs du royaume: Cinq etudes de monarchies Africaines*, ed. C. Tardits, 59–106. Paris: Société d'Ethnographie.

———. 1990. De quelques paramètres de la souveraineté. In *Systèmes de pensée en Afrique noire*, ed. Luc De Heusch, 69–92. Paris: Le Centre national de la recherche scientifique.

———. 1992. *L'odyssée du pouvoir: Un royaume Africain, etat, société, destin individuel*. Paris: Editions de la Maison des Sciences de l'Homme.

———. 1995. Une trifonctionnalité Africaine? Représentations de la souveraineté et catégories socio-fonctionnelles dans le Yatenga. *Cahiers des Sciences Humaines* 312:407–25.

Jackson, Michael. 1977. *The Kuranko: Dimensions of Social Reality in a West African Society*. London: Hurst.

Jackson, Robert. H. 1990. *Quasi States: Sovereignty, International Relations and the Third World*. Cambridge: Cambridge University Press.

———. 1992. Juridical Statehood in Sub-Saharan Africa. *Journal of International Affairs* 46:1–16.

———. 2000. *The Global Covenant: Human Conduct in a World of States*. Oxford: Oxford University Press.

Journet-Diallo, Odile. 2007. *Le créances de la terres: Chroniques du pays Jamaat (Joola de Guinée-Bissau)*. Paris: Bibliothèque de l'Ecole des Hautes Etudes.

Kaboré, Gomkoudougou V. 1962. Caractere feodal du système politique Mossi. *Cahiers d'Etudes Africaines* 8:609–23.

Kawada, Junzo. 1979. *Genèse et evolution du système politique des Mosi méridionaux (Haute Volta). Study of Languages & Cultures of Asia & Africa Monograph Series 12*. Tokyo: Asia Africa Gengo Bunka Kenkyûzyo.

———. 2002. *Genèse et dynamique de la royaute: Les Mosi meridionaux (Burkina Faso)*. Paris: L'Harmattan.

Kiethéga, J. B. 1993. La mise en place des peuples du Burkina Faso. In *Découverte Du Burkina, T. 1.*, 9–29. Ouagadougou, Burkina Faso: Sepia.

Kicthéga, J. B. et al. 1994. *Trame historique de l'epopée Moosé*. Ouagadougou, Burkina Faso: Sepia.

Ki-Zerbo, Joseph. 1978. *Histoire de l'Afrique noire d'hier à demain*. Paris: Présence Africaine, EDICEF/UNESCO.

Kleinschmidt, Harald. 2003. *People on the Move: Attitudes toward and Perceptions of Migration in Medieval and Modern Europe*. Westport, CT: Praeger.

Kohler, Jean-Marie. 1971. *Activités agricoles et changements sociaux dans l'ouest-Mossi*. Paris: Office de la Recherche Scientifique et Technique Outre-mer.

Kopytoff, Igor, ed. 1989. *The African Frontier: The Reproduction of Traditional African Societies*. Bloomington: Indiana University Press.

———. 1999. Permutations in Patrimonialism and Populism: The Aghem Chiefdoms of Western Cameroon. In *Beyond Chiefdoms: Pathways to Complexity in Africa*, ed. S. K. McIntosh, 88–96. Cambridge: Cambridge University Press.

Kuba, Richard, and Carola Lentz. 2002. Arrows and Earth Shrines: Towards a History of Dagara Expansion in Southern Burkina Faso. *Journal of African History* 43 (3): 377–406.

Lalu, Premesh. 2009. *Deaths of Hintsa: Postapartheid South Africa and the Shape of Recurring Pasts*. Cape Town: HSRC Press.

Landau, Paul S. 2009. Transformations in Consciousness. In *The Cambridge History of South Africa, Volume 1: From Early Times to 1885*, ed. Carolyn Hamilton, Bernard K. Mbenga, and Robert Ross. Cambridge: Cambridge University Press.

Laurentie, Henri. 1944. Notes sur une philosophie de la politique coloniale Française. In *Numéro Spécial de Renaissances*, 8–15.

Law, Robin. 1980. *The Horse in West African History: The Role of the Horse in the Societies of Pre-colonial West Africa*. Oxford: Oxford University Press.

Lentz, Carola. 1994. A Dagara Rebellion against Dagomba Rule? Contested Stories of Origin in North-Western Ghana. *Journal of African History* 35 (3): 457–92.

Lévi-Strauss, Claude. 1974 [1962]. *The Savage Mind*. London: Weidenfeld & Nicolson.

Levtzion, Nehemia. 1968. *Muslims and Chiefs in West Africa: A Study of Islam in the Middle Volta Basin in the Pre-colonial Period*. Oxford: Clarendon Press.

Liberski, Danouta. 1991. *Les dieux du territoire: Unité et morcellement de l'espace en pays Kasena (Burkina Faso)*. Paris: École Pratique des Hautes Études.

Liberski-Bagnoud, Danouta. 2002. *Les dieux du territoire: Penser autrement la généalogie*. Paris: Le Centre national de la recherche scientifique.

Long, Charles H. 1964. The West African High God: History and Religious Experience. *History of Religions* 32:328–42.

Lonsdale, John. 1986. Political Accountability in African History. In *Political Domination in Africa*, ed. Patrick Chabal. Cambridge: Cambridge University Press.

Lovejoy, Paul E. 1980. *Caravans of Kola: The Hausa Kola Trade 1700–1900*. Zaria, Nigeria: Ahmadu Bello University Press.

Lt. Fabre. 1904. Monographie de la conscription de Diebougou. January 1904, Archives Outre Mer (Aix-en-Provence), AOF, 16304, 14 Mi 686, 6.

Lugg, H. C. 1929. Agricultural Ceremonies in Zululand and Natal. *Bantu Studies* 3 (1): 357–383.

———. 2007. Ritual Territories as Local Heritage? Discourse on Disruptions in Society and Nature in Maane, Burkina Faso. *Africa* 77 (1): 86–103.

Lydon, Ghislaine. 2009. *Trans-Saharan Trails: Islamic Law, Trade Networks and Cross-Cultural Exchange in Nineteenth-Century Western Africa*. Cambridge: Cambridge University Press.

MacGaffey, Wyatt. 2013. *Chiefs, Priests, and Praise-Singers: History, Politics and Land Ownership in Northern Ghana*. London: University of Virginia Press.

Mahama, Ibrahim. 2004. *History and Traditions of Dagbon*. Tamale: Ghana Institute of Linguistics, Literacy and Bible Translation.

Mamdani, Mahmood. 1996. *Citizens and Subjects: Contemporary Africa and the Legacy of Late Colonialism*. Princeton, NJ: Princeton University Press.

Mann, Michael. 1993. *The Rise of Classes and Nation States, 1760–1914*. Vol. 2 of *The Sources of Social Power*. Cambridge: Cambridge University Press.

Marie, Alain et al. 1997. *L'Afrique des individus: Itinéraires citadins dans l'Afrique contemporaine*. Paris: Karthala.

Marshall, J. Y. 1978. Vestiges d'occupation ancienne au Yatenga: Une reconnaissance en pays Kibga. *Cahiers ORSTOM* 154:449–84.

Mather, Charles. 2003. Shrines and the Domestication of Landscape. *Journal of Anthropological Research* 59 (1): 23–45.

———. 2005. Accusations of Genital Theft: A Case from Northern Ghana. *Culture, Medicine and Psychiatry* 29 (1): 33–52.

Mauny, Raymond. 1961. Tableau geographique de l'Ouest-Africain au Moyen Age d'apres les sources ecrites, la tradition et l'archeologie. Dakar, Senegal: Institut Fondamental d'Afrique Noire.

Mbembe, Achille. 2001. *On the Postcolony*. Berkeley: University of California Press.

McCaskie, T. C. 1995. *State and Society in Pre-colonial Asante*. African Studies Series 79. Cambridge: Cambridge University Press.

McIntosh, Susan Keech. 1999. *Beyond Chiefdoms: Pathways to Complexity in Africa*. Cambridge: Cambridge University Press.

McNaughton, Patrick R. 1988. *The Mande Blacksmiths: Knowledge, Power, and Art in West Africa*. Bloomington: Indiana University Press.

Meillassoux, Claude. 1986. *Anthropologie de l'esclavage: Le ventre de fer et d'argent*. Paris: Presses Universitaires de France.

Mendonsa, Eugene. 1979. Economic, Residential and Ritual Fission of Sisala Domestic Groups, Ghana. *Africa* 49 (4): 398–407.

Merleau-Ponty, Maurice. 1962. *The Phenomenology of Perception*. London: Routledge.

Migdal, Joel. S. 1988. *Strong Societies and Weak States: State-Society Relations and State Capabilities in the Third World*. Princeton, NJ: Princeton University Press.

Monson, Jamie. 2000. Memory, Migration and the Authority of History in Southern Tanzania, 1860–1960. *Journal of African History* 41 (3): 347–72.

Morris, Chief Commissioner. 1904. Correspondance to Governor of the Gold Coast, 6 Feb. 1904, PRO, CO 96/417, enclosure 1 in Gold Coast Confidential of 1 Mar. 1904.

Mowitt, John. 1993. Sembene Ousmanes *Xala*: Postcoloniality and Foreign Film Languages. *Camera Obscura* 11 (1 [31]): 71–95.

Mudimbe, V. Y. 1985. African Gnosis Philosophy and the Order of Knowledge: An Introduction. *African Studies Review* 28 (2/3): 149–233.

———. 1988. *The Invention of Africa: Gnosis, Philosophy, and the Order of Knowledge*. Bloomington: Indiana University Press.

———. 1994. *The Idea of Africa*. Bloomington: Indiana University Press.

Murphy, William, and Caroline Bledsoe. 1989. Kinship and Territory in the History of a Kpelle Chiefdom (Liberia). In *The African Frontier: The Reproduction of Traditional African Societies*, ed. Igor Kopytoff. Bloomington: Indiana University Press.

Nacanabo, Noraogo Dominique. 2003. Le Moogo au xixe siècle: Aspect politique et administratif. In *Burkina Faso: Cent ans d'histoire*, ed. Y. G. Madiega and O. Nao. Paris: Karthala.

Nancy, Jean-Luc. 2000. *Being Singular Plural*. Minneapolis: University of Minnesota Press.

———. 2008. *Philosophical Chronicles*. New York: Fordham University Press.

Nash, S. D. 1914. Report on the Navarro District. NAG ADM 56/1/61. Jan.–June 1911.

Nayar, Jayan. 2013. The Politics of Hope and the Other-in-the World: Thinking Exteriority. *Law and Critique* 24 (1): 63–85.

Netting, R. 1972. Sacred Power and Centralization. In *Population Growth: Anthropological Implications*, ed. B. Spooner. Cambridge, MA: MIT Press.

Niang, Amy. 2011. Naam: Ideology as State History. PhD diss., University of Edinburgh.

———. 2012. In the Beginning Was Naam: Political History and the Dis-order of Discourse. In *La terre et le pouvoir: Festschrift for Michel Izard*, ed. Dominique Casajus and Fabio Viti. Paris: Le Centre National de la Recherche Scientifique.

———. 2014. Reviving the Dormant Divine: Rituals as Political Reference in Pre-colonial Moogo. *Journal of Ritual Studies* 28 (1): 77–89.

Nugent, Paul. 2010. States and Social Contracts in Africa. *New Left Review* 63.

Pageard, Robert. 1963. Recherches sur les Nioniosse. *Etudes Voltaïques, Nouvelle Serie, Memoire* 4:5–71. Ouagadougou, Burkina Faso: Institut Fondamental d'Afrique Noire.

———. 1965. Une enquête historique en pays Mossi. *Journal de la Société des Africanistes* 35 (1): 11–66.

Peel, J. D. Y. 1968. *Aladura: A Religious Movement among the Yoruba*. Oxford: Oxford University Press.

Persaud, Randolph B. 2016. Neo-Gramscian Theory and Third World Violence: A Time for Broadening. *Globalizations*. 13 (5): 547–562.

Polanyi, Karl. 1966. *Dahomey and the Slave Trade: An Analysis of an Archaic Economy*. Seattle: University of Washington Press.

Prairie, Michel. 2007. *Thomas Sankara Speaks: The Burkina Faso Revolution, 1983–87*. New York: Pathfinder Press.

Public Record Office, London (PRO), 1910. C096/493, enclosure 3 in Gold Coast No. 41 of 19 Jan. 1910.

Rashid, Ismail. 2000. Escape, Revolt, and Marronage in Eighteenth and Nineteenth Century Sierra Leone Hinterland. *Canadian Journal of African Studies* 34 (3): 656–83.

Rattray, Robert Sutherland. 1932. *The Tribes of the Ashanti Hinterland.* 2 vols. Oxford: Clarendon Press.

Ray, Benjamin. 1991. *Myth, Ritual and Kingship in Buganda.* Oxford: Oxford University Press.

Read, Captain Moutray.Rreport on a tour of inspection through the 'Lobi country' in 1905, GNA, ADM 56/1/50.

———. Report on tour of inspection, March to May 1905, Ghana National Archives, Accra (GNA), ADM 56/1/50.

Richards, Audrey 1939. *Land, Labor, Diet in Northern Rhodesia: An Economic Study of the Bemba Tribe.* Oxford: Oxford University Press.

Roberts, Richard, and Martin Klein. 1989. The Banamba Slave Exodus of 1905 and the Decline of Slavery in the Western Sudan. *Journal of African History* 21 (3): 375–94.

Rotberg, Robert I. 2004. *When States Fail: Causes and Consequences.* Princeton, NJ: Princeton University Press.

Sahlins, Marshall. 1983. Other Times, Other Customs: The Anthropology of History. *American Anthropologist* 85 (3): 517–44.

———. 2008. The Stranger-King or, Elementary Forms of the Politics of Life. *Indonesia and the Malay World* 36 (105): 177–99.

Saltman, Michael. 1987. Feudal Relationships and the Law: A Comparative Inquiry. *Comparative Studies in Society and History* 29 (3): 514–32.

Saul, Mahir. 2007. Méthodes en histoire orale genèse de l'autorité politique au Moogo. *L'Homme* 2 (182): 215–32.

Savonnet-Guyot, Claudette 1985. Le prince et le naaba. *Politique Africaine* 20:29–43.

Schildkrout, Enid. 1978. *People of the Zongo: The Transformation of Ethnic Identities in Ghana.* Cambridge Studies in Social Anthropology 20. Cambridge: Cambridge University Press.

Schlottner, Michael. 2000. We Stay, Others Come and Go: Identity among the Mamprusi in Northern Ghana. In *Ethnicity in Ghana: The Limits of Invention*, ed. Carola Lentz and Paul Nugent. Basingstoke, UK: Palgrave Macmillan.

Schmitt, Carl. 1975 [1932]. *The Concept of the Political.* Chicago: University of Chicago Press.

Schoenbrun, David L. 2006. Conjuring the Modern in Africa: Durability and Rupture in Histories of Public Healing between the Great Lakes of East Africa. *American Historical Review* 111 (5): 1403–39.

———. 2013. A Mask of Calm: Emotion and Founding the Kingdom of Bunyoro in the Sixteenth Century. *Comparative Studies in Society and History* 55 (3): 34–64.

Schoffeleers, Matthew. 1999. *Guardians of the Land.* Lilongwe, Malawi: Kachere.

Scott, James C. 2009. *The Art of Not Being Governed: An Anarchist History of Upland Southeast Asia.* New Haven, CT: Yale University Press.

Scubla, Lucine. 2005. Sacred Kingship, Sacrificial Victim, Surrogate Victim, or Frazer, Hocart, Girard. In *The Character of Kingship*, ed. Declan Quigley. Oxford: Berg.

Sedogo, Vincent. 2010. Projet de création d'un 'Empire Moaaga', Capitale Sabse. Ouagadougou, Burkina Faso.

Sharpe, B. 1986. Ethnography and a Regional System: Mental Maps and the Myth of States and Tribes in North-Central Nigeria. *Critique of Anthropology* 6:NJ33–65.

Simporé, Lassina. 2004. Eléments du patrimoine culturel physique du Riungu de Wogdogo: Approche archéologique et historique. Université de Ouagadougou, Ouagadougou, Burkina Faso.

Skalnik, Peter. 1978. Early States in the Voltaic Basin. In *The Early State*, ed. H. J. M. Claessen and P. Skalnik, 469–94. The Hague: Mouton.

———. 1987. On the Inadequacy of the Concept of the Traditional State. *Journal of Legal Pluralism* 25 (26): 301–25.

Skinner, Elliott P. 1960. The Mossi Pogsioure. *Man* 60:20–23.

———. 1964. *The Mossi of Upper Volta*. Stanford, CA: Stanford University Press.

Smith, M. G. 1956. On Segmentary Lineage Systems. *Journal of the Royal Anthropological Institute* 86 (2): 39–80.

Somé, B. B. 1969. Organisation politico-sociale traditionnelle des Dagara. *Notes et Documents Voltaïques* CVRS 2 (2): 16–41.

Somé, Magloire. 1999. Le sacré et le système politique traditionnel des Dagara du Burkina à l'épreuve de la colonisation. *Revue CAMES* 1:74–89.

Southall, Aida W. 1963. *Alur Society: A Study in Processes and Types of Domination*. Cambridge: W. Heffer.

Spruyt, Hendrik. 1994. *The Sovereign State and Its Competitors: An Analysis of Systems Change*. Princeton, NJ: Princeton University Press.

Stahl, Ann Brower. 2001. *Making History in Banda: Anthropological Visions of Africa's Past*. Cambridge: Cambridge University Press.

Staniland, Martin. 1975. *The Lions of Dagbon: Political Change in Northern Ghana*. Cambridge: Cambridge University Press.

Tait, David. 1955. History and Social Organization. *Transactions of the Historical Society of the Gold Coast and Togoland* 1 (5): 193–210.

———. 1961. *The Konkomba of Northern Ghana*. London: Oxford University Press.

Tamakloe, E. F. 1931. *A Brief History of the Dagbamba People*. Accra, Ghana: Government Printing Office.

Tauxier, Louis. 1912. *Le noir du Soudan: Pays Mossi et Gourounsi, Documents et analyses*. Paris: E. Larose.

Teschke, Benno. 2003. *The Myth of 1648: Class, Geopolitics and the Making of Modern International Relations*. New York: Verso.

Thomas, Nicholas. 1991. *Entangled Objects: Exchange, Material Culture, and Colonialism in the Pacific*. Cambridge, MA: Harvard University Press.

Tiendrebeogo, Y. 1963. Histoire traditionnelle des Mossi de Ouagadougou. *Journal de la Société des Africanistes* 331:7–46.

Tilly, Charles. 1975. *The Formation of National States in Western Europe*. Princeton, NJ: Princeton University Press.

———. 1990. *Coercion, Capital and European States AD 990–1990*. Cambridge: Blackwell.

Turner, Stephen P. 1994. *The Social Theory of Practices: Tradition, Tacit Knowledge, and Presuppositions*. Chicago: University of Chicago Press.

Turner, Terence. 1994. Bodies and Anti-Bodies: Flesh and Fetish in Contemporary Social Theory. In *Embodiment and Experience: The Existential Ground of Culture and Self*, ed. T. J. Csordas. Cambridge: Cambridge University Press.

Vansina, Jan. 2004. *How Societies Are Born: Governance in West Central Africa before 1600*. Charlottesville: University of Virginia Press.

Verdier, Raymond. 1965. Chef de terre et chef de lignage: Contribution à l'étude des ystems de droit foncier Négro-Africains. In *Etudes de Droit Africain et Malgache*, ed. Jean Poirier, 333–59. Paris: Cujas.

Viriasova, Inna. 2013. Life beyond Politics: Toward the Notion of the Unpolitical. PhD diss. Western University, London, Ontario.

Wai, Zubairu. 2012. Neo-patrimonialism and the discourse of state failure in Africa. *Review of African Political Economy* 39 (131): 27–43.

Walker, R. B. J. 1992. *Inside/Outside: International Relations as Political Theory*. Cambridge: Cambridge University Press.

Walzer, M. 1974. *Regicide and Revolution: Speeches at the Trial of Louis XVI*. London: Cambridge University Press.

Werbner, Richard. 1989. *Ritual Passage Sacred Journey: The Process and Organization of Religious Movement*. Washington, DC: Smithsonian Institution Press.

West, Harry. 2001. Sorcery of Construction and Socialist Modernization: Ways of Understanding Power in Postcolonial Mozambique. *American Ethnologist* 28 (1): 119–50.

Westermann, D., and M. A. Bryan. 1952. *Languages of West Africa*. Oxford: Oxford University Press.

Wilks, Ivor. 1975. *Asante in the Nineteenth Century: The Structure and Evolution of a Political Order*. London: Cambridge University Press.

———. 1985. The Mossi and the Akan States, 1400 to 1800. In *History of West Africa*, ed. J. F. Ajayi and M. Crowder, 465–502. Harlow: Longman.

Wilks, Ivor, Nehemia Levtzion, and Bruce M. Haight. 1986. *Chronicles from Gonja: A Tradition of West African Muslim Historiography*. Cambridge: Cambridge University Press.

Williams, Raymond. 1973. *The Country and the City*. New York: Oxford University Press.

Wiredu, Kwasi. 1996. Time and African Thought. In *Time and Temporality in Intercultural Perspective*, ed. D. Tiemersma and H. A. F. Oosterling. Atlanta, GA: Rodopi.

Wolf, Eric. 1982. *Europe and the People without History*. Berkeley: University of California Press.

Woronoff, Jon. 1972. *West African Wager: Houphouet versus Nkrumah*. Metuchen, NJ: Scarecrow Press.

Yelpaala, Kojo. 1983. Circular Arguments and Self-Fulfilling Definitions: 'Statelessness' and the Dagaaba. *History in Africa* 10:349–85.

Zartman, I. William, ed. 1995. *Collapsed States: The Disintegration and Restoration of Legitimate Authority*. London: Lynne Rienner.

Zoanga, J. B. 1978. The Traditional Power of the Mosi Nanamse of Upper Volta. In *The Nomadic Alternative: Modes and Models of Interaction in the African-Asian Deserts and Steppes*, ed. W. Weissleder. The Hague: Mouton.

Index